Magical Dogs 2

Magical Dogs 2

Connecting the Dots,
Connecting the Dogs

Patti Kerr

Along the Way Press
Flemington, New Jersey

MAGICAL DOGS 2: Connecting the Dots, Connecting the Dogs

COPYRIGHT 2018 by Patti Kerr
Along the Way Press
23 New York Avenue
Flemington, NJ 08822

Front and Back Cover Photos: Joseph Frazz
Back Cover Headshot: Sharyn Hankins
Cover Design: James Lebbad (Lebbad Design)
Editor: Raquel Pidal
Interior Design: Sans Serif, Inc.

ISBN: 978-0-9845989-1-5

Disclaimer:
This book and any associated products (including websites, blogs, e-books, promotional products, and other products) are provided for entertainment and informational purposes. The author is not a veterinarian or dog care professional and does not advocate any particular product, item, technique, or position contained herein. Nothing herein should be interpreted as a substitute for professional medical care by a qualified veterinarian or professional. Check with your trusted veterinarian if you have any concerns about your pet or before embarking on or pursuing any treatment protocol. Every effort was made to ensure that all links or contact information provided were correct at the time of writing. The publisher and author cannot be held responsible for any inconvenience or damage caused by any subsequent changes or for the use (or misuse) of information contained or implied herein.

Contents

*Dedicated to Jigga, Brooke's best friend
and one of the original Magical Dogs*

Prologue:
Connecting the Dots

My first dog, Brooke, came into my life when I was in my late forties. When she passed, I had no prior experience to fall back on and was unprepared for the intense emotions and grief that overwhelmed me. What sustained me in those early days and weeks was the outpouring of support and understanding from others who had lost a beloved dog. In cards, letters, phone calls, and emails, they shared stories of dogs that had come into their lives, as if by magic, and changed them.

Their stories started a rumbling deep within me and my world began to shift on its axis. The result was a feeling I call Divine Inspiration. When it hits me, I know I need to follow where it and my heart lead. Suddenly my life headed in a new and unexpected direction, and I wrote my first book about the magic of dogs, *Magical Dogs: Love and Lessons from Our Canine Companions*.

Early in the writing of that book it became very clear that the dogs were in charge. Every time I reached out to someone for an interview, a roadblock appeared. Every time I sat back, waited, and trusted, without fail, I was led in a new, unexpected, and wonderful direction. As if by magic, I was connected to a person, dog, and story I never could have imagined. Over time, it became abundantly clear that I was simply the person the dogs had chosen to tell their stories.

After the release of *Magical Dogs,* people began asking about my "next dog book." While flattered, I hemmed, hawed, and hesitated to answer because I knew it wasn't up to me. When or if I would write another dog book was up to Divine Inspiration and the dogs. Once again, I sat back, trusted, and waited—and on a cold winter day in New Jersey, Divine Inspiration arrived in the form of a dog found lying in a puddle on the side of the road.

That morning, I logged onto Facebook and saw a post in our local

Ladies of Hunterdon County group. The photo showed a dog lying on the edge of the road covered from his neck down by a blanket, his head resting gingerly in someone's lap. The post said the dog had been found lying in a puddle on the side of a road. Since the dog was not wearing a collar or tags, everyone was scrambling to figure out who he belonged to and what had happened.

The instant I saw the photo, my heart began to flutter. There was something about this dog. I found myself completely and totally captivated by him and stayed glued to my computer for updates.

The dog was transported to a local veterinarian by Animal Control. As people continued searching for his owner, Big Dog Rescue Project stepped up to cover the dog's medical expenses. One week later, when no one came forward to claim the dog, a volunteer for the rescue named Kristy posted that she had taken him home to foster. Kristy thanked everyone in the group for their concern and help and posted regular updates and photos of the dog, now known as Zeke.

I was transfixed by every photo and update Kristy shared. Something about Zeke touched me on a deep level so I sent Kristy a message asking if I could meet Zeke. I knew it would be completely understandable and reasonable if she declined my request—I was, after all, a stranger. Within the hour, Kristy wrote back: "Zeke and I would love to meet you! How about Wednesday afternoon at one o'clock?"

I was both excited and nervous. I knew meeting them might possibly lead to wanting to share their story and write another book. The more I thought about it, the more I began to lose my courage. Was I blowing my feelings of compassion for Zeke out of proportion? He was only one dog. Were there other dogs waiting to have their stories told? Were the dogs ready to begin another book? More importantly, was I ready?

I repeatedly picked up the phone to call Kristy and cancel but repeatedly put it back down. Another lesson the dogs had taught me in the journey of writing the first *Magical Dogs* book was the importance of trust. Zeke had shifted something inside me. Believing it was Divine Inspiration, I decided to trust that I was being led in this direction for a reason. I also decided to ask for a sign that meeting Kristy and Zeke was the next step on my journey.

Two days later, on February 13, I began my day by posting several pictures of Brooke. It would have been her fifteenth birthday so I wrote a short tribute to her, calling her my angel. Shutting off my computer, I glanced across the room at Brooke's picture on my nightstand. Next to her photo was *Daily Guidance from Your Angels* by Doreen Virtue, a book I read regularly for inspiration and guidance.

I knew there was a message waiting for me inside the book. I placed the spine of the book on the nightstand and allowed it to fall open on its own. It opened to page 191 and I read: "Take Steps Towards Your Life Purpose . . . You specifically want to know: What should I do next on my life path? The answer is to follow the inner wisdom guiding you to take vital action steps . . . contact a particular person . . ."

Zeke's face flashed before me.

It was my sign that meeting Zeke was the next step on my journey. Whether meeting him would result in writing his story or another book remained to be seen. For now, I simply needed to meet him—and trust.

With Kristy's permission, I brought my dog, Ava, along for the visit. It was an unseasonably warm winter day, and as we pulled into their driveway, Kristy and Zeke were standing together in their front yard. Kristy's arms were wrapped around the back part of Zeke's body to support him. Smiling, she motioned for us to join them.

Kristy was warm and welcoming, and as Ava and Zeke stood nose to nose sniffing one another, we began to chat. At the mention of his name, Zeke let out a low-key hoarse bark. Kristy laughed, explaining that was Zeke's signature "bork." With Kristy supporting Zeke, we all slowly walked toward their house.

Kristy led Zeke over to his oversized dog bed. She helped him lie down and get comfortable then settled down next to him. Planting a kiss on his head, she began to share their story.

I was mesmerized as she shared the details of how she and Zeke were brought together. At one point, I asked if it bothered her that she didn't know exactly where Zeke came from or what his life was like before coming to her home. She sat quietly for several moments and looked over at Zeke before answering.

"It is my personality to try and find out as much as I can about every dog," she began, "including contacting veterinarians in other states to ask if there was any little snippet of information they could tell me about a dog. But with Zeke, it's been different. I have been able to accept not knowing anything about Zeke's life prior to coming here thanks to Faith."

Kristy got up, took a picture from a nearby wall, and handed it to me. It was a stunning photograph of Kristy, her husband, and four dogs sitting together on the beach. Pointing to a golden retriever in the picture, she said, "That's Faith. Like Zeke, she came into our life at a time when I was not quite ready for another dog, but the reality is I don't look for the dogs. Just like Zeke, they look for—and find—me.

"With Faith, I learned that what mattered was the time she spent with us, and that helps me with Zeke. I no longer try to figure out his past but focus on his best last days. He isn't thinking about how he ended up in that puddle. He's probably wondering when I'm going to feed him.

"I met Zeke like this. I don't know what he was before. I don't know if a week before he was found he was running around. I doubt it, but I don't know, so my responsibility to him is to try everything I can, and if it doesn't work that is okay. But what if it does?

"I have to carry him in and out and I can't leave him for any length of time in case he gets up and falls. It's a lot of work but I never feel bothered, mad, or annoyed. It honestly feels like Zeke has always been here. Some people say it is coincidence but I believe Zeke was put where he was—and is with us—for a reason. I was taking a break from rescuing another dog when this incredible, wonderful, purebred Labrador retriever is found less than a mile from my home. I voluntarily put myself in this situation because there was something there I can't explain.

"So many people have come to see Zeke and he absolutely loves kids. Any time he hears a child's voice, his whole demeanor changes. If he could he would run as fast as he could to see them.

"I believe at some point in his life Zeke knew love because I can touch his ears, tail, or paws and it doesn't bother him. He lets me reach into his mouth to give him a pill. We can lay our heads on him and there is never an ounce of fear, anger, or aggression. That brings me back to my belief that at some point in his life he knew love—but I don't sit on my couch at night and wonder like I did with Faith. I'm not angry like I was with Faith. I'm not doing that this time."

Zeke grew restless so Kristy helped him shift his body to get comfortable. "We are going to the vet today. He had a bad night and seems to be getting more restless.

"Our plan with Zeke is the same as with all our dogs: we will not let him suffer. My husband and I agree that there are seven days in a week, and as long as more of those days are good than bad, we will keep on doing whatever we can and enjoy every moment we have with him. If that changes, we will reevaluate. I also believe Zeke will tell me when it's time.

"Whether Zeke is with us two days, two weeks, or two years, it doesn't change how much we love him because it feels like he has always been here. If you are a person who loves animals, you will understand what I am about to say: when Zeke passes, I will grieve for him like I have grieved dogs I had for fifteen years.

"And I will feel blessed. So many people know and love this dog. They know his story, and while it may have started out as 'the dog found in the puddle,' it's now about so much more. Look at his life now: he has a family and he knows love. For that, I feel immensely blessed. I feel like I am doing what I was meant to do for Zeke and that he's right where he is supposed to be."

Kristy continued to pet and kiss Zeke and tell him she loved him. Lying on his side, the lumps on Zeke's body were clearly visible. His breathing seemed normal at times; at other times it appeared labored. More than anything, it was obvious that Zeke was content and at peace in the comfort of his dog bed, blankets, and Kristy's love. He looked at Kristy with absolute adoration and devotion. The love and connection between them was evident. It could be seen in their obvious ease and absolute trust with one another.

As I watched them, a quiet knowing overcame me and I knew I wanted to share their story with the world. It was time to start writing again.

Wanting to give them time to relax together before their appointment with the veterinarian, I knelt down next to Zeke. Petting him, I thanked him for allowing Ava and me to visit. "It was an honor to meet you and your mom, Zeke," I said. Hesitating slightly, I continued, "If it's all right with you and your mom, I'd like to share your story with the world."

Zeke ever so slightly lifted his head and looked into my eyes. His expression told me that he understood and was granting me his permission.

Looking up at Kristy, she smiled, quietly nodding her head in agreement. Ava and Zeke sniffed each other once again as I stood up to hug and thank Kristy. Back home, Ava napped as I began to write.

The next day, Kristy sent me a message: "It was so nice to meet you and Ava yesterday. Thank you for wanting to share Zeke's story. It means so much to me and I'm sure to him. He really is loved by so many."

I continued writing, the words flowing effortlessly. Two days later, Kristy posted the following on her Facebook page:

"All I wanted for you was love and dignity, to feel like you were part of a family. I hope I was able to give that to you. I hope that when we said goodbye today, Zeke, you truly knew how much you mean to me and to all of the people who were lucky enough to meet you.

"It was not by accident that we found each other. It was not what I did for you but what you did for me. Thank you for allowing me to love you. Thank you for teaching me that love has no measure of time and that even the briefest of encounters has the ability to change everything.

"I cannot wait for the day I see you again, boy. Happy, whole, and strong. Thank you for choosing me to spend your #bestlastdays with. If I had to do it again, I would choose you every time."

Shocked, stunned, and not wanting to believe what I was reading, I went to the Big Dog Rescue Project page and read:

"He was found in a puddle by the side of the road on January 10. Held on a stray hold for a family that never came looking for him. Joined Big Dog Rescue Project and started his #bestlastdays. Zeke, which translates to 'God strengthens,' received a whirlwind of support from our community. Everyone fell in love with a sweet old dog who never complained and who was thankful for a pat on the head, a cookie, and a warm bed. His foster family quickly fell in love with him and officially adopted Zeke so when his time on Earth ended yesterday, he was surrounded by his family, not alone in a puddle. Godspeed to the bridge, dear Zeke."

I was heartbroken but knew it paled in comparison to what Kristy was feeling. Several days later, I quietly left a card by her front door along with several newspaper clippings she had loaned me the day of our visit. She knew I would not go forward with their story or the book until and unless she agreed and was ready.

I knew if it were meant to be, Zeke would make it happen, so I waited. Time passed. Then one day, Kristy reached out and said she was ready. She wanted to share Zeke's story and tell me the rest of her story.

From the moment I started writing again, the magic began to unfold. Zeke, Kristy, and their story led me to other dogs, rescues, and people who, in turn, led me to other dogs, rescues, and people in unexpected and magical ways. I was repeatedly reminded to trust and simply allow the magic to unfold. Out of nowhere, a phrase began to play over and over in my mind: "Connect the dots, connect the dogs."

As a young girl, I loved doing connect the dots puzzles. Even though I could typically see the end result before ever putting pen to paper, I loved the simple act of connection.

This time, unlike the puzzles of my childhood, I could not see what the end result would be or where I or the book were headed. As I continued to trust and connect the dots and the dogs, I was taken on an amazing and magical journey. I met small dogs, big dogs, blind dogs, dogs who escaped the horrors of puppy mills, a dog who defied death, and a dog who had gone missing for weeks in the Canadian wilderness. I met people whose lives were completely changed by a dog—and dogs whose lives were completely changed by people.

Over and over, I thought back to what Kristy wrote the day Zeke passed: "It was not by accident that we found each other." The same was true for me and the dogs and stories in this book. None of them are here by accident. The dogs found me, thereby making this a book designed by the hearts and paws of some incredibly magical dogs.

A few things before we begin. It goes without saying that the Prologue and Epilogue are written by me, in my own words. Beyond that, every story is told by a person (or persons) in their own words; it is not my retelling or interpretation of their story.

In addition to the stories you will find Let's Paws sections. Some of the stories and those sections contain difficult or sensitive topics and information. I have consciously chosen to include these—not to upset you, but because dogs cannot advocate for themselves and rely on us to do so for them. That means we need to remain vigilant, aware, and informed. It means we need to pause at times to examine our personal beliefs, behaviors, and choices to see if there are adjustments we need to make. The bottom line is that I am providing this information to ensure the ongoing safety, health, happiness, and welfare of dogs and those who love and care for them.

In the Notes section at the end of the book, you will find links to some of the rescues and organizations mentioned in the book in the event you want to learn more about them.

Make yourself a cup of tea, get comfortable, and let's begin with the story of the dog who melted my heart and the woman whose words "Zeke and I would love to meet you!" were the beginning of a very magical journey with some incredibly magical dogs.

Zeke

Chapter One
KRISTY

The day Kristy said she was ready to tell me the rest of her—and Zeke's—story, I was humbled and honored. I knew she was still grieving Zeke, yet she was willing to forge ahead to share more about her story and her dogs with all of us, starting with a magical little dog named Mr. Pickles.

MY PARENTS DIVORCED WHEN I WAS YOUNG BUT I ALWAYS HAD A wonderful relationship with both of them. Living with my dad afforded me the opportunity to grow up in a multiple-dog household. He often came home with a dog, usually a black Lab mix, that he'd found running around the golf course or at the dump.

Shortly after my twenty-second birthday, I decided it was time to move out on my own. Since dogs had always been a part of my life, I decided it was also time for me to get my own dog—even though I could barely take care of myself.

One morning, after telling my dad I wanted to get a dog, he showed me a newspaper article about three basset hounds. The dogs' owner had passed and the dogs had been turned in to a shelter that was searching for homes for them.

I didn't know anything about basset hounds but that didn't stop my friend and me from driving to the shelter. I walked into the crowded lobby

Kristy and Mr. PIckles
Photo courtesy of Jennifer Quinn

and headed straight to the receptionist to tell her I was there to see the dogs from the newspaper. She smiled politely and said there was already a line of people out the door interested in the dogs because they were purebreds. At the time, I didn't even know what a purebred dog was.

Glancing around, I realized my chance of getting one of the dogs was slim to none, so my friend and I left and stopped at a diner on Route 22. While eating lunch, I glanced out the window and read the sign on the building next door: St. Hubert's Animal Welfare Center.

We quickly finished eating and walked next door. The first dog I saw was a fifteen-pound white Shih Tzu named Smitty. He was the complete opposite of every big black dog I'd ever had in my life but there was something about Smitty so I asked to see him.

As I filled out paperwork, a girl from the shelter went to get him. When she carried Smitty in and put him down, he was so excited. He kept trying to run to me but he couldn't get traction on the linoleum floor. When he finally reached me, I sat down on the floor, Smitty jumped into my lap—and peed on me. I looked up at the girl, laughed, and said, "I'll take him!"

I explained that I needed to get permission from my landlord. The shelter staff told me they were closed for the next two days, so if I was still interested in him, I should come back on Tuesday. I offered to leave a deposit but they refused, explaining that people sometimes see a dog, leave a deposit, then never come back. As a result, the dog misses out on other opportunities to get adopted.

Smitty was well below my landlord's weight restrictions for dogs, so after getting approval, I spent the next two days getting everything together I would need for him: a collar, leash, dog bowls, food, toys—and a new name. Smitty didn't seem to fit and he didn't respond to it. Obvious names, like Snowball and Fluffy, didn't feel right either. Suddenly, out of nowhere, Mr. Pickles popped into my head. I had no idea where it came from but I knew it was his name.

Tuesday morning, I got to St. Hubert's well in advance of the opening time, determined to be the first one through the doors. As I pulled into a parking space, I saw a family with two kids already waiting for the doors to open. My first thought was, "Oh heck no! You are *not* getting my dog!"

I gathered up Pickles's leash and collar, walked straight over to them, and, in the friendliest voice I could muster, said, "Hi, are you adopting a dog today?" Before they had a chance to answer, I said, "I am. The white dog inside? I adopted him." I wasn't taking any chances that they or anyone else would get Mr. Pickles.

On my nightstand, I have a picture of Mr. Pickles and me leaving St. Hubert's that day. As I walked out that day with Mr. Pickles, I had absolutely no idea what to do with a dog. Growing up, I had only fed dogs and scooped poop and didn't know anything about good food or training or the cost of veterinary care.

I also had no idea how walking out the door with Mr. Pickles that day would change me. I had no idea how that moment in time would define who I was (and would be) for the rest of my life. On that day, I started on a journey of love and compassion for animals, rescue, and the underdog—all because of Mr. Pickles.

Pickles immediately wrapped himself around my heart. He was loving and happy and I adored coming home from work to his sweet little face and wagging tail. We settled into a comfortable routine, and other than when I was at work, we went everywhere together.

One weekend, Pickles and I were shopping at the pet store in our town. A local rescue was holding an adoption event, and after introducing both of us to the volunteers from the rescue, I filled out a volunteer application. Before long, I was making posters for car washes, working adoption events, and selling T-shirts for the rescue.

While I was busy helping dogs, my life mainly revolved around my sweet Mr. Pickles. Life was good.

Then one day, I got a call at work from the manager of my apartment complex saying that Mr. Pickles was in his office. As I drove to get him, I replayed that morning over in my mind to figure out how Mr. Pickles could have gotten out. The only logical explanation was that I had accidentally left my door open and he had wandered out. I was shocked when I learned what really happened.

Since air conditioning was expensive, I typically left the windows in my apartment open. That day, Mr. Pickles decided to chew a hole through a screen and crawl out the window. My apartment was on the first floor over a parking garage so, once he crawled out the window, he decided to relax and lie in the sun on the roof of the parking garage.

Construction workers nearby saw him and kept an eye on him. They said after a few hours of relaxing in the sun, Pickles simply got up, walked over to the edge of the roof, and jumped. Thankfully he was fine, but the workers scooped him up and brought him to the office.

After that, I only ever left my windows open a crack, if at all. Years passed without incident. My life seemed whole and complete with Pickles—then it got even better when I met a man named Bill who was also a dog lover. Bill and I started meeting on our lunch break to walk dogs at the Bridgewater Animal Shelter. Initially I think Bill did it as a way to get me to like him, and it worked because we started dating. Bill had a wonderful golden retriever named Hunter who quickly became Pickles's best friend so he was over-the-moon happy.

One night, Bill and I were out to dinner when my phone rang. A woman asked, "Is this Pickles's mom?" When I said it was, she said, "I was driving past your building and saw him up on the roof. I pulled over, climbed up on the roof of my car, and I have him here."

I thanked her and told her we were on our way. She immediately asked how long it would take and, after assuring her we were only a few blocks away, she said, "Oh, good, because the ambulance is here. Don't worry. Pickles is fine but I fell and broke my wrist."

We got Pickles, went home, and closed and locked every window in my apartment. Once again, all was well—until one weekend when I went away with friends.

My mom was going to watch Pickles at her home. She knew all I had gone through with Pickles but I reminded her anyway not to leave any windows open. She told me not to worry and to go have fun.

The second night, my phone rang. "Is this Pickles's mom?"

"Haha, Mom, very funny," I said and hung up. Immediately my phone rang again.

"Is this Pickles's mom?" This time, I said it was and the woman said, "I have your dog."

My mother lived in a bi-level. She'd gone out and left only one window open a crack. It was so high up, she was confident Pickles could never get to it.

In the short time she was out, Pickles apparently jumped from the bed to the headboard to a nearby hutch and from there made his way to the window ledge, where he managed to chew his way out. Thankfully, once again Pickles didn't get hurt and had been found by a Good Samaritan.

Pickles had always been such a happy dog and had never given me any problems. Knowing I needed to figure out what to do and how to keep him safe, I asked the staff at The Hungry Hound, a nearby pet store, if they knew a dog trainer. They immediately gave me the name and number for a man named Kristian.

Kristian explained that something triggered Pickles's behavior that very first time—perhaps something outside the window or a desire to be with me. Regardless of what precipitated it, Pickles had been successful and learned that if he kept at it, he could eventually find a way out. After that, Pickles was never again around open windows.

With that problem resolved, Bill, Hunter, Pickles, and I resumed our life together. When Hunter was seven, he passed from cancer. Bill and I were devastated, as was Pickles. Hunter was Pickles's best friend and he was never the same after Hunter passed. I immediately wanted to get another dog but Bill wasn't ready. Instead, he introduced me to his friends Todd and Colleen who volunteered and fostered dogs for a local rescue.

I checked out the rescue's website and filled out their volunteer application. Bill was thrilled. Actually, his exact words were, "This will be perfect, Kristy. You need a hobby." Bill loved fishing and boating and thought if I got involved with the rescue it would give me a hobby and also fulfill my need to get another dog. It has now become somewhat of an ongoing joke between us because at the end of the month when he sees what I have donated to rescue, he tells me maybe I need a different hobby.

I enjoyed volunteering for the rescue, but it didn't change the fact that I had gotten used to having two dogs and still wanted another dog. A year had passed since losing Hunter but Bill still wasn't ready. Then one night while lying in bed, he said maybe we should consider fostering because it would allow us to have another dog in the house without the long-term commitment.

The next day, Bill came home from work to find a dog sitting in our kitchen. Smiling, I said, "Meet Finley."

Bill looked at me, clearly confused. "And who is Finley?"

"You said we should foster. Finley is our foster."

Bill looked at Finley, then at me, and said, "Kristy, it hasn't even been twelve hours since we had that conversation. I meant we should *talk* about fostering. I didn't mean for you to go out the next day and get a dog."

"Well, Bill, I think he's a golden and he's awfully cute. Besides, it's only temporary so don't worry."

Finley got along great with Pickles, as well as with my nieces and nephews, but he was also shut down a lot. He had been abused and spent a great deal of time in his crate. He also had a severe noise and sound phobia. Trucks, motorcycles, thunder, or even someone dropping something would set him off and he would run for the safety of his crate.

After fostering Finley for three weeks, we learned a family in Bayonne was interested in adopting him. They had a son and another dog and it seemed like a perfect fit, but three weeks later, Finley was returned to the rescue.

The family thought he had separation anxiety and my first thought was that they were crazy and just weren't fully committed to Finley. I was still a novice without any real rescue experience and my first instinct was to blame the people. When I learned the family lived across from a fire station and that Finley went crazy every time the siren went off, it was a huge lesson for me that sometimes a dog is just not the right fit for a situation. I realized that rather than blaming someone, it is important to look at the whole picture.

We brought Finley back to our house and began fostering him again. Applications started pouring in and two wonderful families met him and were interested in adopting him. The night before he was due to go back to the rescue to begin the adoption process, I found myself lying on our bathroom floor crying my eyes out.

Bill gave me some time alone before he came in and sat on the floor next to me. I stopped crying long enough to tell Bill that I knew Finley came back to us for a reason. Bill gently placed his hand on my leg and said, "Actually Kristy, he came back because they lived across from a fire station." I remained steadfast and told Bill I knew Finley came back because he needed me.

A silence settled between us. Bill sat, his hand on my leg, while I continued to sob. Finally, Bill broke the silence, saying that he still wasn't ready for a dog but if I really wanted to keep Finley, we would. That is who Bill is. He always puts my happiness first.

The first six months with Finley were a nightmare. Bill couldn't go near him, and in addition to the noise and sound phobias, we soon discovered Finley really did have separation anxiety. Whenever we left the house, Finley urinated and howled from the time we left to the time we came home.

Once again, we began working with Kristian. Separation anxiety requires extraordinary patience on the part of the person. You move forward in small steps, initially leaving the dog for very short increments of time. Very gradually, you increase the time you are away. Many times it feels as if you're never going to get through it.

Five years later, Finley still has some anxiety but he truly is a good, awesome, and amazing dog. He simply needed an understanding person to bring him back to life, so I stand true to my belief that Finley needed me.

Hunter was Bill's once-in-a-lifetime dog. For me, Hunter established my love for golden retrievers. Anytime a rescued golden came within 100 miles of us, I did whatever I could to help the dog or find it a home. As a result, I was becoming known as the "Golden Girl" at the rescue.

That April, I got a call from the rescue about a six-month-old golden who needed a temporary foster for a few days. I didn't hesitate.

Once again, Bill walked into the house after work to find a puppy sitting in our kitchen. Once again, he looked at the puppy, then at me, and asked, "And who is this?"

Once again, I smiled and said, "Meet our new foster, Marlin."

I stood quietly and watched Bill's face. Dogs were part of the puzzle pieces that made up our life. Finley was a piece, Pickles was a piece, and when Hunter passed, we lost a big important piece of the puzzle. Now, as Bill stood looking at Marlin, it was a gentle reminder of what it was like to have a golden in our home again. Slowly, I saw happiness creeping onto Bill's face.

I was scheduled to be out of town that weekend. As I packed, Bill teasingly said he couldn't believe I was leaving him alone with two dogs and a puppy. I reminded him it was just for the weekend because Marlin was going back on Monday.

All weekend, I checked in to see how they were doing and Bill repeatedly assured me they were doing great. On Sunday night, knowing Marlin was due back at the rescue the following day, I asked Bill if he wanted to keep him. He hesitated, saying that while he loved Marlin, he just wasn't sure.

Monday came, and a few hours before I was scheduled to take Marlin back to the rescue, the doorbell rang. Opening the door, I saw an Amazon Prime box sitting on our front porch. Inside were dog bowls, a dog bed, and a leash. Confused, I called Bill. He answered the phone and the first words out of his mouth were, "I want to keep him."

I laughed and said, "Bill, you had to have ordered everything on Friday or Saturday for it to arrive this morning."

"Well, what did you expect?" he said laughing. "You left me alone with him and we sat on the couch watching football all weekend. Of course I want to keep him!" I could hear the joy in Bill's voice.

In the six months since I started volunteering for the rescue, we had acquired two dogs. We were now up to three dogs—and then Faith came into our lives.

My father, a lifelong type 1 diabetic, had gone into kidney failure. The first week of October, I donated one of my kidneys to him. The doctors warned me the recovery would be a difficult eight weeks. Three weeks after the procedure, I got a call from a rescue about a golden coming up from Georgia. When they asked what I thought, I said I thought it wasn't the right time since I was recovering.

However, my dear friend Allie had seen photos of the dog and wanted her. Allie had four children and this would be their first dog. I wanted to make sure the dog was healthy, or at least had the potential to be healthy so, a few days later, a friend drove me to meet the dog.

It was Halloween weekend. If the dog checked out, the plan was for me to keep her for the weekend so Allie could take her kids trick-or-treating and everyone would meet on Monday.

When I saw Faith get off the transport, my heart broke. She had hardly any fur, she was at least twenty-five pounds underweight, and her breasts were hanging, which meant she had been used to breed puppies. She looked like she was on death's door so I immediately took her to our vet for a blood panel. The next day, the vet called and said he couldn't believe Faith was walking, eating, or wagging her tail because based on her numbers, she probably did not have a lot of time. When I asked him how much time, he said, "Four weeks, if that."

My heart broke—not only for Faith but also for Allie and her family. I didn't want their first experience with a dog to end so quickly. Once again, Bill being the man he is stepped in and said, "Let's adopt her. She's not going anywhere. If she has four weeks, let's give her the best four weeks possible."

We started Faith on a regimen of good food, medication, and love. Once we passed the four-week mark, Faith started spending weekends with Allie's family. Next, we made it past the two-month mark. At three months, Faith's fur started to grow back and she began to put on weight. Slowly, Faith was becoming unrecognizable from the dog who had walked off the transport.

While Faith's blood work never looked great, or even good, it remained stable. The veterinarian was baffled. He repeatedly said there was no explanation for how or why Faith was still alive, happy, and showing no clinical signs of illness. The fact that she was still there, three months later, went against everything he had ever learned, known, or seen. At one appointment, he suggested I take Faith to the University of Pennsylvania because he felt veterinary science could learn a lot from her. I promised we would think about it, but Faith wasn't a science experiment—she was our dog. We didn't want her poked and prodded so we went home and started checking things off of her bucket list.

We had fun, made memories, and got through the whole next year. At Christmas, Faith had her own stocking and we watched her run in the first snow of the season. She slept in our already overcrowded bed. She went to the beach that summer and swam in our pool and in the ocean. She ate a lot of ice cream, rode in our Jeep with the top down, went to doggie daycare, and loved wrestling with our other dogs. She always made sure she was the first one out the door in the morning and the first one back in the door at the end of the day so she could get the best spot on the couch. Family, friends, and strangers who met Faith all said she was different. Bill said when Faith looked at you it was as if she looked into your soul; it was almost as if she could reach in and touch your heart. Faith became the love of our lives and fit in like she'd been there forever.

Kristy and Faith
Photo courtesy of Joseph Frazz

We didn't talk about Faith being sick—which was easy because to us, she was perfection. By the time her one-year adoption day came around, Faith's fur had grown back, her sores had healed, and the shine was back in her eyes. We had a party and celebrated, knowing full well we had beaten the odds and proved the doctors wrong. We showed them that love and care *did* conquer all and we continued our lives as a family with four dogs.

The rescue world is like an underground railroad where somebody sees something online about a golden and they (or someone they know) knows me and my love of goldens, and it makes its way to me. It was through that system that I found out about a very sick golden at a shelter.

As soon as the person sent me the dog's picture, I knew I had to help him and immediately reached out to Mary Jo. I had met Mary Jo through volunteering and doing rescue work, and like me, she loved goldens. Even though she had started her own rescue, Big Dog Rescue Project (BDRP), we stayed in touch and often shared opinions and advice on dogs.

We both knew this dog needed a minimum of $5,000 of veterinary care out of the gate—and beyond that was anybody's guess. Neither the rescue I was with or BDRP had the money to cover his veterinary expenses so we reached out to the one place that might be able to help: Delaware Valley Golden Retriever Rescue (DVGRR).

My mother's friend Gina was a former volunteer at DVGRR so she called them. DVGRR said they would take the dog if I got him from the shelter that day.

Mary Jo picked him up and kept him the first night and Bill and I kept him over the weekend. Monday morning, before driving the dog to DVGRR, Bill and I closed on our beach house. That day was a new beginning for Bill and me as well as for this dog. Knowing he still needed a name, I named him Leeward after our beach house on Leeward Avenue.

When Leeward and I arrived at DVGRR, we met Edna, Leeward's foster mother. Gina told me I would love Edna and she was right. I instantly knew Leeward was in good hands.

What I loved about Leeward was that he single-handedly brought four women of different ages from different lives, backgrounds, parts of the country, and rescues together. Leeward was the dog we all came together to save.

With Leeward safe, sound, and getting lots of TLC, I returned home to Pickles. He had begun having hearing and vision problems and at times appeared to be senile. Eventually a specialist determined Pickles had Cushing's disease and also suspected a tumor on his pituitary gland was pressing against the stem of his brain. I asked how fast it would progress and how much time we had, but she said there was no way to know because she didn't have any prior experience to fall back on. Due to the amount of time and energy required to care for a dog in Pickles's condition, most people reach that point and put the dog to sleep. We hadn't reached that point yet.

I drove home in a daze and sat Bill down for a serious conversation. I told him I wasn't getting any younger and both Pickles and my dad were getting older. My dad and Pickles were two of the most important men in my life and I wanted both of them to be at my wedding. I wanted Faith to be in the wedding and we had no idea how much time we had with her. I finally looked at Bill and said, "We've been together for eight years. We need to get married. What are you waiting for?"

The next day, we started planning our wedding, making sure our dogs played an important part in the day and the celebration—then Faith's health took a turn for the worse. On August 11, one month before our wedding, Faith passed.

Faith came to us on hospice care, and while we were blessed to have eighteen months with her, when she passed I was angry. Even though I didn't know all of the details, I knew when her family decided to move, they had tied Faith to a tree, shot her, and drove away leaving her alone to die. She had come from a horrible situation and the probability was that she had had an awful life. When she came to New Jersey, she finally had a family who loved her. She had landed in Utopia and been given a second chance but her body couldn't keep up and there was nothing I could do to save her. How was that fair?

I had stayed in contact with the woman who originally fostered Faith so I sent her a message to tell her I wanted to come down. I wanted to see where Faith came from, I wanted to visit Animal Control, and I wanted to see the place where she had been found. I needed to see and know everything in order to have closure.

A couple of days later, she wrote back and simply said: "Kristy, the day Faith left the state of Georgia, she left all of that behind, and you need to leave it behind, too. Faith would not want you to come here and see that."

Initially I was upset but, over time, I thought about Faith and who she was and I realized the woman was right. Faith would not want me to see any of that because none of that mattered. What mattered were the precious eighteen months we had together.

It helped that our wedding was only one month away because it kept me and my mind busy. The day of our wedding, I missed Faith terribly, but it was a beautiful day and we made sure all of our dogs were a part of the day. Pickles, Finley, and Marlin were there and there was a big picture of Faith.

My father was also there, which had always been my hope and dream. It was over two years since the transplant surgery, and the day of our wedding, my father looked the best he had in years. We all joked that his heart had been fixed, he had a new kidney, and he looked like he was drinking from the fountain of youth. There had always been so many worries in the past about my father's health, but for the first time, he was able to eat what he wanted and was doing fine. Over the holidays, we all got together and talked about my sister's upcoming wedding in February.

Shortly after the holidays, Pickles began having trouble with urinary tract infections. His dementia and senility was progressing and he began circling and sometimes fell over. My father felt it was time to let Pickles go but I was not ready. Pickles and I had been together for over fifteen years and the thought of letting him go was something I could not bear.

Three weeks later, my father hopped in his car, mailed a check to my sister for her wedding, and drove to work. Later that morning, a coworker found him lying on the floor in the break room. When the call came that my father was in the hospital after suffering an apparent heart attack, I was out helping to search for a missing dog. I ran to my car and headed home to pack but, before I got there, my father passed. Bill and I decided he would remain in New Jersey to care for Pickles and I began the long, awful five-hour drive to Virginia for my father's funeral. The following week, my sister got married.

Several weeks later, Edna called and asked if she could bring Leeward to New Jersey for a visit. Leeward had been with Edna for over eighteen months and she wanted to get a picture of Leeward and me under the Leeward Avenue street sign.

Edna came and Leeward and Pickles met for the first time. Edna took pictures of us under the street sign and we all had a wonderful time together. Ten days later, Edna called to tell me Leeward had passed. Three days later, Mr. Pickles passed.

I had only been married six months. It should have been one of the most beautiful, happiest times in my life but instead it turned out to be the most difficult. I had experienced the highest of highs and the lowest of lows. Thank God for my husband, because I do not think I would have made it through those six months without him.

There were days I would be driving to work with tears pouring down my face and I had no idea whether I was grieving for my dad or my dog. Was it wrong and was I bad that the grief for my dad and my dog felt the same?

I remember walking into a deli several weeks after Pickles passed and everyone was laughing, talking, and ordering sandwiches. I stood there feeling like time and my life had stopped. I started seeing a grief counselor but ultimately what finally brought me peace was repeating to myself over and over, hundreds of times a day, that I needed to be thankful for my dad and Pickles and to remember that life goes on.

There are still days—anniversaries, birthdays, adoption days, or if a little Shih Tzu comes into the shop where I work—when I have to close my eyes, take a deep breath, and remember that Pickles took care of me, my dad took care of me, and now my dad is taking care of Pickles. I know they are together and that brings me peace.

Just as I was coming out of one of the worst years of my life—a year when I lost my grandmother, my father, and two of my dogs—I saw a post and photos on Facebook about a yellow Lab who had been found lying in a puddle on the side of the road. The post said the dog was having difficulty getting up or walking so everyone assumed he had wandered away from home and been hit by a car.

After reading where he had been found, I was filled with hope. It was less than a mile from our home. We are a small community where kids ride their bikes, parents push their babies in strollers, and neighbors say hello to one another. I was confident someone would recognize the dog.

People had already begun to post leads about nearby homes and farms where the dog may have lived, but when none of them panned out, I started making calls, including one to Animal Control. I inquired about the dog's condition and whereabouts. Initially, they wouldn't give me a lot of information for security reasons, but after explaining I was with a rescue, they said someone would call me back. A short time later, they called with the name of a local veterinarian who was willing to talk to me.

The veterinarian explained the dog was being held on a standard seven-day stray hold while every attempt was made to locate his owners. When I asked about the dog and his condition, the veterinarian said, "I don't believe this dog was hit by a car. There is no physical trauma to indicate he was hit. I think what we have here is an old dog with arthritis and muscle atrophy and covered in growths."

I was shocked. Having worked in rescue for so many years and seeing the best and worst in human behavior, I immediately thought the worst. I wanted to know everything—what time the dog had been found and who found him.

I was volunteering with Big Dog Rescue Project (BDRP) and had already spoken with Mary Jo. I assured the veterinarian that if the dog was not claimed, BDRP wanted to take him into custody and made arrangements to meet the dog the next day.

The next morning, Mary Jo along with Joe, a photographer who works closely with BDRP, met me in the parking lot of the veterinarian's office. I had only seen the online picture of the dog lying in the road covered by a blanket. I was excited to have the opportunity to see and be with him but when I finally did, I felt both instant relief and overwhelming sadness.

I was relieved that he had made it that far but sad because I knew his old bones never would have carried him to that puddle on that cold winter day. I knew someone had put him there and walked away from him at a time when he needed them the most.

Zeke on the day Kristy met him at the veterinarian's office
Photo courtesy of Joseph Frazz

As soon as he saw me, he eagerly sought affection. I plopped on the floor next to him and he immediately rested his head in my lap. In that moment, I fell completely and totally in love with this sweet old soul.

By law, veterinarians are only required to provide stabilizing care for a stray animal until the owner comes forward and claims them. Knowing the end of the stray hold was still days away, and knowing the dog needed immediate medical attention, BDRP stepped up to the plate. Mary Jo ordered fecal tests and blood work and told the doctor that even if the owners came forward, BDRP would continue to pay for the dog's medical expenses, and if no one came forward, BDRP would take custody of the dog.

In the meantime, people had begun posting fliers everywhere, and as leads poured in, the police visited area homes and farms—all with no luck. When the media found out, an area newspaper started running daily updates about the dog and a New Jersey radio station shared his story. Now known as the "New Jersey dog found in a puddle," he was very quickly becoming a media sensation and there was a tremendous outpouring of support from the community. Everyone was following his story and rooting for him. An online fundraising campaign was started to help cover his medical expenses. Royal Canin, the pet food maker, sent dog food.

When his blood work came back, we all braced ourselves for the worst. Fully expecting it would show cancer, kidney failure, or something equally heartbreaking, we were shocked when it instead came back as typical senior blood work. He had difficulty walking and some large and obvious growths, but other than that, there was nothing glaringly wrong. No fleas, ticks, or parasites. There was obvious neglect in the form of long nails, dirty ears, and severe muscle atrophy but no sign of physical abuse. There was evidence, based on his fur and a red stain under his neck, that the dog had worn a collar. He also had a microchip, although it had never been registered.

Again, my mind went into overdrive. If he had wandered off, based on the type of community we are, why did no one recognize him? Based on his inability to stand or walk any distance, how could he have wandered off? There was no way to know conclusively, but the odds were stacking up that my initial gut feeling that he had been put in that puddle on the side of the road was accurate.

I visited every day and brought him homemade meals. We sat together and I fed him cold cuts from my hand. I used the time to get to know him and inspect his ears, eyes, and entire body. I learned where his lumps and bumps were and tried to gauge their size. I touched his paw pads and gave him belly rubs. Zeke not only wanted human interaction, he craved it. At the time, I didn't realize those days and moments were the start of us building a relationship together.

Wednesday morning, the official end of the seven-day stray hold, I picked him up. Walking out of there together after what felt like the longest seven days of our lives was like coming up for fresh air. Despite needing to be carried after only a few steps across the parking lot, he held his head up high. Once in my car, he actually stood up and looked out the car window as we pulled out of the clinic. He knew he was out of there and he was safe.

He was also filthy. His fur was covered with a heavy awful film and I couldn't even venture a guess as to when he last had a bath so our first stop was at the doggie spa where I work. It felt so good for me and my boss Hilde to clean him. I know it felt wonderful for him, too, because he lay in the tub with such ease. Seeing him so relaxed and comfortable reaffirmed for me that he now felt completely safe.

At our doggie spa, we don't crate the dogs before or after their grooming. Instead, we provide an open, safe, and secure area where they can play and interact with the other dogs under our watchful eye. That gave us our first opportunity to see him interact with other dogs. While he couldn't get up and play, he loved it! He just lay on the floor and took it all in. From there, we went to the BDRP veterinarian for a thorough exam and then to Mary Jo's home where he was going to stay for the next ten days while Bill and I went on a long-delayed and much-needed honeymoon.

Mary Jo and I both knew there was a chance the dog would not make it until I returned home. I'd worked alongside her for so many years so I trusted and respected her and knew whatever she did or decided would be based on what was right for the dog.

Every day I called Mary Jo to check on him. One day she would say he was having a not-so-great day but the next day he would rally. As our vacation drew to a close, I told Mary Jo that as soon as we returned, we were going to bring him home to live with us.

Mary Jo knew what the past year had been like for me and kept asking if I was sure. I was. I didn't even have to think about it. When you work in rescue you come to accept that many times things don't go smoothly, but everything about this went so smoothly that it felt as if the stars had aligned and it was meant to be.

Bill and I started searching for strong male names for the dog. Remembering my grandmother once had a Samoyed named Ezekiel, we looked it up and learned that in Hebrew, Ezekiel means "God strengthens." We decided to name him Zeke, short for Ezekiel.

As soon as we got back, I picked Zeke up. I couldn't wait. Mary Jo and I put a protocol together for him that included pain management, water therapy, acupuncture, and massage. After two weeks, if we didn't see any change or if Zeke got worse, we would sit down and talk about our next step.

When I think back, bringing Zeke home probably seemed like a crazy idea and bad timing. We had moved into our new home two weeks before Christmas. As soon as the holidays were over and before we were unpacked, we brought a new dog home. Who in their right mind does that? I guess the answer is: we do.

We still did not know a lot about Zeke, including how he would be in the house or with our other dogs. Bill and I decided to keep Zeke in the study because there wasn't any furniture in there and it adjoins our family room where we spend a lot of time. Knowing our other dogs had been through a lot along with us, we wanted to keep their lives as stress-free as possible so we didn't want to mingle everyone right away. By eight o'clock that night, it was obvious they were all fine with one another. Zeke was out in the living room with us and part of the family.

Not knowing how much time we had with Zeke, we started a bucket list of things we wanted him to see and experience in the time he was with us. We took him to the beach where he saw the ocean. BDRP got him a wagon so we could take him places. The hashtag for our adventures became #bestlastdays, and every day I wrote about his adventures on Facebook.

On January 30, I wrote: "Today Zeke got to visit this magical place called The Hungry Hound and pick out anything he wanted. He sampled delicious cookies and met new friends. We spent an hour in the yard taking in the cold fresh air and got to meet the neighbors and their dog. They promised him a rotisserie chicken tomorrow. #bestlastdays"

Two days later, we started off with a not-so-great morning, but by noon we had turned a corner. I wrote: "Good days and bad days. Thank you, Arlene and Alison, for coming to visit. Zeke loves visitors and he loves kids. We ventured out to meet the ladies at the animal hospital and Ashley and her sweet little foster dog Vivi. So many people love Zeke and so many people played a part in helping to get him here and have the #bestlastdays—from donations to visits to prayers. Thank you!!!"

The next day, a quieter more relaxing day, I wrote: "Today was a good day for Zeke. While Finley and Marlin were at doggie daycare all day, we had some quality time together and I was able to get some things done around the house. Dina and Lane brought Harlee for a visit tonight and for Zeke it was love at first sight. It is with 100 percent certainty that he had kids in his life at some point. He literally perks up and is so happy when they are around. Every day with him is a gift. We were lucky enough to sneak in a nap together today too!! When you spend the majority of your day snuggling, all is right in the world. #bestlastdays"

The next day, February 3, was another good day. Zeke visited his friends at The Puppy Patch before heading to Aqua Dog Rehabilitation for a massage and acupuncture. That night, we all relaxed together in front of the fireplace as a family.

Three days later, February 6, was an auspicious day in our life together so I made sure to write about it that night: "I'll never know how you came to be the 'dog found in a puddle' but I know you will never be that dog again. And whether you have a few days or a few weeks left, all that really matters is that you will have them here with us. Today we officially adopted Zeke. While that may not matter to some since he is already here with us, it matters to me. If you live and love rescue, you will get it. Thank you to my dear friend Mary Jo at Big Dog Rescue Project for answering my late-night phone call three weeks ago and not hesitating for even one second when I asked, 'Can we save him?' They are all good saves but this one . . . this one is special!!! #bestlastdays"

Several weeks later, Zeke passed here in our home surrounded by his family and friends. He passed knowing what it felt like to be cared for and loved.

There is a saying that "Until one has loved an animal, a part of one's soul remains unawakened." They are some of the truest words ever spoken. Dogs make us better people, and while there are those who think we save them, the truth is they save us. That was true of Zeke, and it has been true of every dog who has ever found their way into our lives.

At this point, the absolute best decision I ever made in my life (other than marrying my husband) was bringing Mr. Pickles home with me that day. Mr. Pickles was my once-in-a-lifetime dog. He was with me through the best and worst years of my life. He was with me through three cars, two apartments, two long-term relationships, and the ensuing heartbreak. He was with me through my twenties and when I moved into my own apartment. For a long time, it was just the two of us, but Pickles was there when I met Bill, when we got married, and when we bought a home. He was with us as multiple dogs came into our lives through rescue, fostering, and adoption. Mr. Pickles was, and will always be, my truest friend.

Bill and I were talking last night about what rescue has done in our lives. In the early days, when it was just Bill, Pickles, Hunter, and me, I could never imagine my life being any better. I was so happy and so in love. We had our dogs, we hiked, and we went to the beach. Everything in my life was right. But you know what? Through the joy and heartache

Family photo: Finley, Bill, Faith, Kristy holding Pickles, and Marlin
Photo courtesy of Jennifer Quinn

of getting dogs and losing dogs, I am still in a place where everything in my life is right.

Right now it's Bill, Finley, Marlin, and me and that feels right. Even though it has been different families at different times, rescue and our dogs have given us a family. No matter what dogs are here or what heartaches we have gone through, I am grateful for it all.

Chapter Two
BIG DOG
RESCUE PROJECT

With so much of Zeke and Kristy's story centering around Big Dog Rescue Project, I reached out to Mary Jo. Doing so began my journey of connecting the dots and the dogs.

Just like when I met Kristy and Zeke, it was an unseasonably warm winter day when I got to Mary Jo's home, and just like Kristy, she was warm and welcoming. As we sat down at her dining room table, we casually chatted about Kristy and Zeke. Mary Jo put a box of tissues on the table between us, smiled, and said, "When Kristy found out we were going to talk today, she said we would probably need these."

Tears happen at almost every interview because they are an outward, visible expression of a person's love for their dog. So yes, there were a few tears shed at Mary Jo's home that day, but there were also a great deal of laughter and joy and many magical moments and stories.

MARY JO

MY DAUGHTER WAS DIAGNOSED WITH AUTISM, WHICH BEGAN years of finding and fighting for programs and services she needed and deserved. It was and still is one of the hardest and most important fights of my life, but it has also taught me the importance of being an advocate.

Knowing it was important for my daughter to be around people, on weekends I provided her various opportunities to interact with people. At stores, I always made sure she handed the money to the cashier so she would look into people's eyes. We always stopped at the pet store to see the animals. One afternoon, a local rescue was there. They said they needed volunteers so I applied. Six months later, I still hadn't heard from them so I called them. That one phone call started it all.

Our first foster was a four-month-old puppy named Tucker. He was

Tucker, Mary Jo's first foster—
and foster failure
Photo courtesy of Joseph Frazz

in our home maybe five minutes when my husband said, "He's a keeper." I reminded him we were only fostering Tucker and that he might already have an application for adoption. He didn't, so straight out of the gate, five minutes into our first foster experience, we became foster failures.

I continued to foster, and as animals started seeping into our lives, I noticed how interacting with them impacted by daughter—and how they made me feel. In a word, it was astounding.

I started a small pet-sitting business. While my daughter was at school, I walked, fed, and took care of other people's animals. Things were going fine until my daughter hit puberty, at which point we went through what was probably one of the worst years of our lives. I turned the business over to a friend so I could concentrate on my daughter and get things stabilized once again.

Once everything calmed down, I began trolling the internet for goldens available for rescue. After finding a beautiful one-eyed golden named Annie, I filled out the rescue's application, checking off that I would take a special needs dog.

I have learned that typically only one or two out of every one hundred applications are willing to take a dog with special needs. Since I have a child with special needs, I wanted to show people that although Annie only had one eye she was still fabulous.

The rescue said Annie already had an application pending, but they had another dog from New Orleans, a seven-month-old golden who was born with only three legs. The breeder surrendered him to be euthanized. I immediately told them I was interested.

One week later, I drove to the airport to pick up Trey Allen. Out of this huge crate came a dog missing his front left leg. He was doing his best to get around, loping rather than walking. Then I realized the leash was holding him back. He couldn't walk on a leash.

When we got home, my husband was lying on my son's bed reading to him. Trey Allen walked in, lay down, and fell asleep next to them. From that point on, Trey Allen slept with our son every night.

Even though he only had three legs, it never bothered him. He was the sweetest dog and a real goodwill ambassador for his breed.

In the midst of all of this, my mother was diagnosed with Alzheimer's and moved in with us. Our household now consisted of my mom with Alzheimer's, my daughter with autism, and a dog with special needs. When we went out for our daily walks, we looked like a little traveling circus.

When Trey Allen was seven, he was diagnosed with cancer. I asked the doctor how long he had and was told he had three months if we did something—and three months if we didn't. It turned out Trey Allen only had two months, and they were the worst two months of my life. I shut down and did nothing but spend time with him until he passed.

Every time I experience a loss like that, I have to take a break. I was helping my mom as much as I could, but I couldn't cure her Alzheimer's. I was helping my daughter, but I couldn't cure her autism. I wanted to do something to honor Trey Allen and the dogs that came before him, and I also wanted to do something to make a difference.

On Facebook, I had crossed paths with a woman in Texas named Lisa. Her mission was to help big dogs since little dogs typically go home from shelters first, leaving big dogs either stuck at the shelter or euthanized. To help the plight of the big dog, Lisa had been pulling dogs from shelters in Texas and moving them to Alicia, a woman in the Seattle area, for fostering and adoption.

One morning, I was following a thread about a golden in Florida named Winston and saw Lisa's name pop up. She had already offered to pull Winston and pay his transport and vet bills if someone could find him a home. Since I was with a rescue, I posted it on our site and on Petfinder to reach a larger population. As a result, we found a home for Winston. I was thrilled and incredibly moved (and impressed) that even though the adoption fee went to the local rescue, Lisa still paid all the expenses for Winston.

Lisa was consistently trying to place ten to fifteen dogs. I knew she and Alicia were doing this as private citizens from the goodness of their hearts (and their wallets), so I reached out to Lisa. I told her I was concerned she would not be able to continue doing this for any length of time. By the end of our conversation, we had decided to set something up on the East Coast just like she was doing with Alicia in the Pacific Northwest.

Lisa would pull a dog and arrange for their transport. Once the dog was in New Jersey, I fostered them while we identified potential adoptive families. There were times I had five dogs in my house waiting to be adopted and thought my neighbors were going to be upset. Instead they were incredibly supportive. As more and more dogs began arriving, I exited from my volunteer work with the local rescue and Big Dog Rescue Project (BDRP) was started. With BDRP, I could finally make a difference and do something to honor Trey Allen and the dogs that came before him.

In the early days of BDRP, it was just me running things here on the East Coast. A year into it, I had an adoption event at Jen's Mutt Hutt Too and brought along a couple of dogs, some T-shirts, and cupcakes. A reporter from the *Daily Record*, a local newspaper, interviewed me. After the story ran I started getting calls from people wanting to volunteer. We now have about ten volunteers, some full time and some part time.

In rescue, when there is a breed you adore, you are led to others who share that love and dedication—and that's how I met Kristy. We shared a common love for goldens. Two years after starting BDRP, Kristy called me about an old golden at Animal Control in a town near me. I immediately hopped in my car.

When I saw the dog, he had lumps everywhere, was missing hair, and seemed pretty sick. Aside from that, he was stunning and honestly one of the most beautiful dogs I had ever seen.

We ultimately took him to Delaware Valley Golden Retriever Rescue (DVGRR), where he was adopted by an amazing woman named Edna. The next time I saw him, his transformation was unbelievable. He truly was the most breathtaking dog I have ever seen.

This was the first dog Kristy and I worked on together. In my position of running a rescue, it is impossible for me to focus on one dog because I need to coordinate everything from transport to foster to adoption for all the dogs coming into our care. Kristy on the other hand is a free agent. She also has a tendency to lock in on one dog and give that dog everything—and that is exactly what happened when she saw Zeke.

The day she found out about Zeke, she called and said, "I just sent you a picture of a dog I would like to support. Let me know what you think."

I took one look at his picture and said, "Absolutely. Let's do this."

Kristy was concerned about the dog's physical and mental condition and was worried he might be languishing. I knew Kristy would do whatever was necessary for this dog, including covering his medical bills, which often happens with those of us involved in rescue work. Since we didn't know the extent of the dog's issues, we set up a page for donations to cover his expenses. That is a common practice for rescues because it not only allows the rescue to provide the animal with the care they need but it also gives people a way to help the animal.

Our goal was to raise $2,000 to defray the cost of his medical bills. Within forty-eight hours, we had over $3,000. There was something about this dog and something about his story. It also says a lot about the people in New Jersey.

I am proud to be from New Jersey. We take a lot of ridicule about our state sometimes and so much of it is not deserved. This was a case in point. When this dog was found in a puddle on the side of the road, the entire state went out of their way to help this old lumpy dog. His story rippled throughout the state, then throughout the country, and finally around the world. People everywhere started reaching out to help Zeke.

While Kristy and her husband went on a long-overdue honeymoon, Zeke stayed at my house. We set him up on a big fluffy bed and he was like a celebrity. People had read about him and wanted to meet him. Every day he had visitors, and every single person who met Zeke fell under his spell and fell in love.

Every time the big yellow school bus pulled up at the end of our driveway, Zeke tried to get up and run to the bus. I realized at some point Zeke probably had kids in his life. He probably had a family and yet they let him go. Those kids and

Mary Jo and Zeke
Photo courtesy of Joseph Frazz

that family weren't going to be there at the end of his life but Zeke never complained. And because he never complained, I never complained. Instead we focused on keeping him totally immersed in love and cookies.

Kristy wanted Zeke to belong to someone so she adopted him. When Zeke passed, he did so in his home surrounded by his family and with people who truly loved him.

Before my husband left on a business trip today, he came in, gave me a kiss, and said, "Keep saving the world, one dog at a time." That's another reason I can do what I do. My husband is so kind and so supportive. I am very lucky to have that.

We currently have a dog here named Sam who was in a shelter ready to be put down. Sam had a severe injury to his right leg and was heartworm positive, but he was so beautiful and forlorn that when one of our volunteers sent me his pictures and asked, "Can we save this one?" I immediately said yes. Since I had experience with tripod dogs, I knew if Sam lost his leg I could care for him. Thankfully it turned out to just be an infection that was healed with antibiotics.

Sam is my heart foster. Sometimes I look at him and think that if our volunteer had not seen him, and if Lisa hadn't pulled him, his life would have had a very different outcome. Instead, Sam was recently adopted, and in three weeks he will be happy with his new family.

You probably saw the note by the front door when you came in that says "Use Garage Door." There are notes tacked up everywhere around the house to remind us that we have different dogs with different needs. For instance, we have a Chow–border collie mix with Addison's disease. The average person would have given him back to the rescue because he has expensive medical needs, but a true rescuer says, "He's mine. We'll figure this out. We're in it, together, to the end." Since he doesn't like other dogs, the notes remind us to be aware as we move around the house since we cannot allow him to interact with other dogs.

Sonic

Sonic is a golden I saw listed on Craigslist. His owner passed and his ex-wife got custody of Sonic. She did not have a backyard and he barked constantly. She knew he deserved a better life so Sonic is here now, too. He is the most intuitive dog I have ever had. If I snap a finger, Sonic turns on a dime. However, he also isn't crazy about other dogs, thus all the signs and notes everywhere.

We converted the entire downstairs of our home into a space for dogs. They have a comfortable space and we have a quiet living space up here. I respect people who say they want a non-shedding dog because I always have a Roomba going. Right now, one of my Roombas needs to be repaired and I am up to my eyeballs in dog hair but it doesn't matter. There is just something about dogs. I love them.

Only about 5 percent of what we do is the actual rescue. The other 95 percent is people skills. A perfect example is the people who wanted to return a ten-month-old puppy to us because he was digging in the yard. We remained neutral and suggested they take the puppy to a trainer or out for a run but they ultimately relinquished the puppy to us. We will get her trained with the skills she needs to become a wonderful dog for someone.

When people ask how many hours a week I volunteer for dogs, I tell them there is no way to put a number on it. I wake up and it's there. I go to sleep and it's there. If I get a call in the middle of the night, it's there. It's probably why there is a high burnout rate in animal volunteer. It never goes away and it can be heartbreaking, but I am constantly humbled by our team and what they do. I have volunteers who help organize and foster and have a wonderful community here that supports me. In my neighborhood alone, I can walk around and see ten BDRP dogs who were going to die in a shelter but are now living large with loving families.

We have an amazing photographer, Joe, who truly captures the beauty of each dog. Jen's Mutt Hut Too and Pet Valu do events for us and help with free baths or grooming for the dogs. Wagmore K-9 Academy assesses dogs and provides discounted training as does Jennifer, an amazing positive reinforcement trainer. The UPS Store in our town makes free copies for us. And the list goes on and on.

Animal rescue takes a village. Consider all the people involved in the rescue and re-homing of just one dog: from the person who pulls the dog to those who transport, foster, and ultimately adopt that one dog. And if the adoption doesn't work out, the dog comes back to the rescue and you start over again trying to find a home. The only way to accomplish this is by having great people, good people skills, and to always do the right thing for the dog.

When you do good things without drama and from your heart, you reap the benefits. That gets me up every morning and keeps me going every day. I have found that a person's religious, political, and personal beliefs don't matter when it comes to dogs. Dogs reach across all boundaries and touch everyone. Everyone wants to support rescue because ultimately it is about supporting the dogs.

There is no amount of money that can equal the feeling you get when a dog who had no future or possibilities suddenly has a family and a home. When you hand a puppy over to a little girl and she cries and cuddles it, or you watch a dog that was on death's door walking away with his new family, there is no price you can put on that. It's not all perfect, but it's pretty close.

LISA

There were two other important pieces to the Big Dog Rescue Project story: Alicia and Lisa who helped found BDRP. Mary Jo helped me connect the dots and I began by calling Lisa in Texas.

ALTHOUGH I'VE LOVED ANIMALS MY ENTIRE LIFE, IT WASN'T until I moved from Arkansas to Texas ten years ago that I got involved with dog rescue. I actually got involved by accident. After getting a Facebook account, I started receiving friend requests from fellow dog lovers, rescuers, and shelters. Before long, I was rescuing dogs on my own and fostering dogs for a rescue group.

My first foster dog in Texas was Bella, a pit bull mix who came from a Canadian rescue. Shortly after she arrived, the rescue in Canada disappeared, leaving me without any way to list Bella on pet rescue sites and no real way to network her for adoption. As a result, Bella was with us for almost two years before being adopted by friends.

Bella was such a smart dog, incredibly spoiled, and easily trainable. While I had never been particularly drawn to pit bulls, through Bella I gained a new empathy for bully breeds, and it breaks my heart they have gained such a negative reputation.

For several years after Bella, I continued fostering and supporting rescues. Many of the shelters I visited in the Dallas–Fort Worth metro area were huge operations, yet over and over, I saw firsthand that they were always full and euthanasia was a daily occurrence.

In Texas, and throughout most of the South, pet overpopulation is an overwhelming problem and the euthanasia rate is extremely high. People are doing their best to help, but the reality is that dogs don't get adopted in Texas as quickly as if they are transported elsewhere.

For me and many Texan dogs, everything changed when I connected with two amazing women through Facebook: Alicia and Mary Jo. Alicia lived in the Pacific Northwest and like me was rescuing independently. Mary Jo lived in New Jersey and volunteered with a rescue there. The three of us connected and started working together.

The demand for Texas dogs in the Pacific Northwest and New Jersey was unbelievable. Dogs were being adopted quickly and going into amazing homes and families. Having outlets in those areas for the Texas dogs continues to be incredible.

As a rescue we try to focus on larger dogs since they are not adopted as quickly as small breeds, but we are dog lovers and take every color, size, and breed.

The dog on the BDRP logo is my dog, Jackson, who we rescued as a puppy while still living in Arkansas. A rescue group had brought puppies to a local PetSmart, and when I walked into the store that day, this ten-week-old adorable little black fuzzball stood there looking up at me with his big puppy eyes. I asked if I could walk around the store with him while I shopped—and ended up leaving with him.

Jackson grew up to be a big, shaggy, lanky Doodle with an extra long tail and a silly, quirky personality. He was the epitome of the goofy, silly, fun qualities of both a poodle and a Lab and people couldn't help but laugh when they were with Jackson.

He would run the length of the house back and forth, then

Jackson, the BDRP logo dog

dash up the stairs, back down the stairs, slide into the bedroom, jump on the bed, and spin around three times before finally plopping down on the bed. Outside, he ran with equal joy and abandon and constantly amused himself by looking up, barking, and chasing the birds flying in the sky over his head. He was a nut and an absolute delight.

Jackson had a special place on the sofa where he sat. If I sat on the chaise opposite the couch instead of next to him, Jackson stared at me until we made eye contact. It was his way of letting me know that he loved me.

Over time, Jackson seemed to get clumsier. Initially we didn't think anything of it. We moved to Texas when Jackson was seven, and six months later, on Mother's Day, we returned home from lunch to find Jackson unconscious. This was the first sign that there was something seriously wrong.

It was determined that Jackson had a grand mal seizure. Two weeks later, he had another one in the middle of the night. A neurologist discovered Jackson had a condition called hydrocephalus, which is a buildup of fluid inside the skull. The accumulated fluid puts pressure on the brain and can cause seizures, blindness, and behavioral changes.

Jackson was placed on phenobarbital to help control the seizures, but it turned out he had myriad other symptoms. Despite consulting with a number of veterinarians and specialists, no one was ever able to isolate the problem and Jackson ultimately became very special needs. I cooked all of his food, then hand-fed him. The only way I could get him

to take his medication was to put it in ice cream, which I also hand-fed to him.

Jackson and I had always shared a strong connection, but when you go through an illness with a dog (or a person), you create a bond you might not have had otherwise. Providing Jackson with the level of care he needed at the end of his life was demanding, time intensive, and all consuming, yet for me, it was a labor of love, a blessing for us both, and ultimately brought us closer than before.

Jackson lived longer than anyone expected, passing when he was twelve. He was

Jackson

my heart dog and absolutely sealed my love for big, scruffy dogs. I am honored that he is on the BDRP logo.

Every dog we rescue has an impact on me, but there are some dogs that really remind me of the importance of what we are doing and make me thankful we were able to get them into a better place. One of those was a dog named Abby.

I had gone to the Fort Worth shelter to pick up a Great Pyrenees that BDRP had tagged for rescue. The shelter was extremely busy, which is typical, but since they knew I was with a rescue, they motioned for me to go ahead and find our dog.

Unsure of his number, I started walking up and down the kennel rows to find him. I passed a cage and saw a dog out of the corner of my eye. Something made me pause, back up, and take a closer look. The kennel card said the dog's name was Abby, she was eight or nine months old, and a possible Doodle mix. More importantly, she reminded me of Jackson.

I spent a few minutes with her, and even in that short time, it was obvious that Abby had a very sweet disposition. Since I was there to pick up another dog, before leaving I told her, "Abby, I promise to keep an eye on you. If you need me, I'll come get you. I promise."

I got the Great Pyrenees, went home, and put Abby out of my mind. After seeing firsthand how sweet and stunningly beautiful she was, I was confident it wouldn't be long before she was adopted.

Shelters post photos of their available dogs on Facebook. Late one night, someone tagged me in one. I was shocked to see it was Abby—and that she was scheduled to be euthanized the next day. I promised Abby if she needed me I would come get her and she definitely needed me. It was almost midnight so I emailed the shelter saying I would come get her the next day. I was waiting when they opened their doors the next morning, and as soon as I got Abby home, I sent her picture to Alicia.

Alicia knew a couple in the Seattle area, Jim and Jim, who mentioned they might be looking for a dog. She immediately told them about Abby, and when they saw her picture, they were instantly smitten. I was smitten with Abby too but at our house she would be one of five dogs. With the Jims, she would be the only dog and showered with the love and attention she deserved.

Abby now lives in Washington State with Jim and Jim. They own a home in the city and another home on one of the islands, and she has an amazing life going on walks every morning in lovely surroundings and going out on their boat. Knowing she ended up in such a special home makes me so happy.

Abby is a special rescue for me because I truly believe it was meant to be. I only spent a few minutes with her so it was fate that I saw her that day and fate that I saw her picture that night. I am so thankful we were able to help Abby have a wonderful life.

There are so many special dogs and so many special stories, but the ones that always touch you most deeply are the ones that come from really sad situations.

There was a county raid on a backyard breeder. The woman was fined for having too many dogs and was forced to surrender some. Among the dogs surrendered were a Great Pyrenees and four puppies who all ended up at a privately run shelter.

This particular shelter is contracted by the county but doesn't have to abide by the same regulations as a city or county shelter. The result is horrible. It is essentially a trailer with no windows, ventilation, or staff. It is always hot and reeks of urine. There is no yard for the dogs. It is my guess that the dogs are let out to use the bathroom and get fresh air maybe once a day—at least I hope that's happening. There is little or no public information about this shelter or the dogs in their care. You have to know someone who knows someone to get the contact information in order to make an appointment to see the dogs. It is a true hellhole.

Initially, I only knew about the puppies. Since I had the number, I called and made an appointment to see them. The man overseeing the shelter is not rescue-friendly, so I fibbed and said I wanted two puppies and my friend wanted the other two.

On the drive there, I did my best to steel my reserve and nerves. I tried to stay focused on the fact that I was going to get the puppies out of there. The man met me outside the building. As we started walking down the row to get the puppies, I saw a Great Pyrenees and asked about him. The man said he had been pulled from the same raid and was the father of the puppies.

After bringing the four puppies home to foster, I couldn't stop thinking about their father. I kept picturing his face and knew what his life was like every single day he lingered in that horrible place. The puppies were quickly adopted, so I went back and got their father out of there.

He had an old man face that reminded me of the actor Walter Matthau so I named him Walter. My initial focus was on getting him healthy since he was so thin. At his vet appointment, Walter tested positive for heartworms, and the treatment was so extensive that I had him for almost nine months.

The months I spent with Walter had a huge impact on me because he was one of those dogs that came from really horrible circumstances—first being used as a breeder, then being trapped at that horrible shelter. Then Walter hit the jackpot. He was adopted by a single dad of twin girls in New Jersey and finally got the happy ending we want for every dog.

A local community magazine in New Jersey did a feature story on Walter and his family. There are no words to explain how rewarding it is to see this beautiful dog finally loved and part of a family.

I am fortunate to have met Alicia and Mary Jo and am grateful for the people I work alongside every day. We are a small but mighty group whose first consideration is and will always be doing whatever is best for the dogs. We take a lot of care and time in choosing the right home

Walter with his family (from left to right) Delphi,
Grace, Mia, and Walter
Photo courtesy of Joe Tarantola

for our dogs because it is important that the home and family be suited to the needs of the particular dog.

We came together through the power of social media to make a positive change and help the dogs in Texas. Together we are doing what we can to make a difference and a spot of good in the world.

ALICIA

Finally, I phoned Alicia, the Pacific Northwest connection to Big Dog Rescue Project. Just like with Mary Jo and Lisa, I was touched by how dogs have impacted her life and all she is doing in turn to pay it forward to impact, help, and change the lives of dogs.

I HAVE A PHOTO OF ME AS A CHILD WITH MY FIRST DOG, POOCHY, who looked like a fluffy American Eskimo dog. She was feisty and occasionally bit me and other people but I loved her anyway.

Back in the '70s, it was commonplace for dogs to live in the backyard, and Poochy was no exception. I constantly wanted to bring her in the house, especially at the end of her life when she started developing tumors and cysts, but my parents refused. Every morning before school, I went out to see her and held my breath wondering if she would still be alive. Eventually, as Poochy got older and weaker, we had to put her down.

After Poochy, my stepfather continued to bring dogs home. Typically they were dogs other people couldn't keep because they were moving or because the dog didn't get along with their children or other dogs. My mother brought home a mixed breed God-only-knows-what dog someone was giving away outside of a department store. I brought home stray cats. So rescuing animals has always been part of my life.

I moved to Seattle in 2004 and acquired enough acreage for my horses and four dogs. In addition to caring for my own animals, I regularly donated to rescues.

Two years later, I met my husband, Scott. He too was an animal lover and we discussed whether there was something more we could do for the dogs beyond just throwing money at the problem. We wondered if perhaps we could bring some of the dogs to the Pacific Northwest and foster them until we could find them a home. We had absolutely no idea how to network to find them homes but we wanted to do something—and that was where it started.

We rescued our first dog in 2010. Fausto was a beautiful one-year-old Rottweiler who had done absolutely nothing wrong yet still ended up at the Fort Worth shelter. A woman sent me his photo along with a message saying: "I know you've been thinking about fostering. How about this guy? It's his last day. He is going to die today."

We pulled him and boarded him in Texas with the intent of bringing him to Seattle as soon as we got him vetted. Before we could get him here, he came down with a severe case of pneumonia. We thought we were going to lose him but he pulled through—after racking up over $4,000 in veterinary bills.

In the midst of his recovery, a writer for a now-defunct newspaper wrote a story about Fausto. The story helped raise funds to cover half of his veterinary bills. We paid the other half.

When Fausto finally arrived in Seattle, we discovered we had rescued the perfect dog. Fausto was incredibly sweet, gentle, and smart. Within ten days, he was adopted by our friend's sister. His name is now Luther and he lives in Arizona with his pug sisters. He is exceedingly loved, lives a life of leisure, and is the absolute light of his family's life.

Our next rescue, Willem, a German shepherd mix puppy, came to us with a terrible case of mange. My nephew's girlfriend saw his photo and fell in love but my nephew's apartment was not pet-friendly.

As soon as Willem got a clean bill of health, we put an "Adopt Me" shirt on him and started taking him everywhere. A local rescue allowed me to do a courtesy listing, but after two months, Willem still did not have any applications or interest—other than my nephew's girlfriend.

Lucky for Willem, my nephew's girlfriend became his wife and they moved into a pet-friendly condo. Willie, as he is now known, lives with them and is the love of their lives. I get to see them all on a regular basis and they have since adopted another dog, a puppy named Lennon, through BDRP.

Having successfully adopted two dogs, Scott and I moved on to our third: Jangles, a Catahoula or Australian shepherd mix who had been dragging his leg at the Fort Worth shelter and was scheduled to be put down. We rescued him and a Texas veterinarian assessed him and amputated his leg. After the surgery, Jangles stayed with a foster mom in Texas to recuperate.

Three days before Jangles was scheduled to arrive in Seattle, our chocolate Lab, Mathilda, started staggering. On Saturday, she was fine; on Sunday, she couldn't walk; on Monday, I put her in the car and headed to the local emergency vet. On the way, Mathilda lapsed into a coma. Sobbing, I carried her into their office. An MRI determined she had a cluster of tumors and a fairly bad brain bleed. They did not think she would recover so the discussion now turned to putting Mathilda down.

In the midst of this, Jangles was scheduled to land at Sea-Tac Airport so my husband stayed with Mathilda while I went to pick up our triad dog.

Initially, I wanted to keep Jangles because he arrived at the same time we put Mathilda down, but he had a lot of energy and wanted a lot of attention. Teddy, as he is now known, was adopted by a lovely couple in Seattle, but something much larger happened as a result of his rescue.

His rescue came about because of two women in Texas I had met: Sherri and Lisa. Sherri was incredibly kind-hearted, loved animals to distraction, and was doing a lot of transport. She introduced me to Lisa who, like me, was donating a lot of money to save dogs, fostering occasionally, and rescuing one dog at a time. Lisa and I partnered on rescuing Jangles and after that we started rescuing other dogs from the Dallas–Fort Worth shelters.

Sherri went to shelters every day to visit dogs, take them for walks, and do a quick temperament analysis. After giving us her take on the dog and what type of home would be good for them, Lisa pulled the dog and paid their vet and boarding bills until I could get them to Seattle and into a new home.

Slowly, Big Dog Rescue Project (BDRP) was coming together. As we set up our Facebook page, Lisa introduced me to Mary Jo. Mary Jo was a work horse, and her location in the Northeast meant she could get more dogs adopted than we could. She quickly became our third party, and two years later we got our 501(c)(3).

BDRP evolved out of a need to get dogs out of overcrowded and desperate situations in the South. We began with four or five shelters and eventually evolved to over a dozen shelters where we regularly get dogs.

Social media can be life-draining, but in our case it has been life-saving since we find most of our dogs on Facebook. Typically someone visiting a shelter takes the dog's photo, writes a description, and shares it on Facebook. One of our volunteers sees it during its round of shares online and we end up pulling the dog. It literally becomes six degrees of separation. That is the wonderful, life-affirming side of social media.

Fortunately, our dogs get adopted quickly and we have great opportunities to put them in pretty perfect situations. We don't allow people looking for a guard, ranch, or outdoor dog to adopt from us—that's not the kind of rescue we are. Our dogs become a member of the family.

We currently have four dogs. Chanel is a chocolate lab–hound mix that Sherri saw at a shelter in Texas shortly after Mathilda passed. We adopted her sight unseen, and she arrived a few months after Jangles was adopted. Riley is a yellow Lab mix that came into BDRP when she was only a puppy. She was adopted when she was four months old, but through no fault of her own, was returned when she was eight months old. She was adopted a second time—only to be returned a few weeks later. At that point, we decided to make Riley our own. JoJo is a collie we found behind a local hardware store when she was only a puppy. We placed ads and tried to find her owners, but when no one ever came forward, we adopted her. Seamus, our black Lab, is a registered therapy dog. Together, he and I visit local memory care facilities and nursing homes.

We consider Chanel, Riley, JoJo, and Seamus to be members of our family and that is true of the majority of people here in the Pacific Northwest. They take dogs to restaurants, wineries, and other dog-friendly places, but that is clearly not the case everywhere.

Many people don't have a concept of how bad it is in other parts of the country where dogs live outside and are clearly not a family's priority. They are not vaccinated, or spayed or neutered. They aren't given heartworm medicine so a high percentage test positive for heartworm. There have been massive distemper outbreaks in parts of the country, a disease that had essentially been wiped out, simply because people did not want to pay the twelve dollars to take their dog to a clinic.

You or I would never dream of taking our dog to a shelter because we were moving, had a baby, or simply didn't have time—but this happens every day. The biggest days for surrendering an animal are around the holidays when people are going away and don't have anyone to watch their dog. Unwilling to pay the fee to board the dog, their solution is to simply surrender it.

What I saw being involved in rescue was eye opening, heartwrenching, and completely outside my way of thinking. How does someone go from loving and caring for an animal to simply discarding them? While I did not know all of the circumstances behind every situation, much of what I saw was devastating, and it began to take a toll on me.

After five years, the stress of rescue began to impact my life negatively. It affected my sleep, quality of life, and ability to just be happy and caused me anxiety. Compassion fatigue hit—and it hit hard.

Compassion fatigue is a very real thing in the rescue world wherein you almost become immune to or unable to handle what you are seeing. With aging parents, ill relatives, and other family issues coming to the forefront, there was a whole lot of life going on and I decided to step back a bit. I still assist with adoptions and home visits, but thankfully we have unbelievably committed and wonderful volunteers who stepped in to take over the actual dog interactions and do what I had been doing for so long.

BDRP was started by three women who were independently saving dogs. We have now grown into a foster-based rescue with committed volunteers. In the last few years, we have found homes for an average of three hundred to five hundred dogs and puppies per year out of Texas.

Recently, the same writer who wrote a story about our very first dog wrote a story about a dog named Wheeler who was in a rural shelter outside of Dallas. Wheeler looked like an oversized Jack Russell terrier. He was two years old and had never been out of the shelter.

Rachel, the girl who house-sits for me, saw the story. She had recently lost her Jack Russell and was drawn to Wheeler. As she told me about him, she looked down and said, "Too bad he is in Texas."

"Rachel." She looked up. "You work for someone who has Texas contacts."

Lisa pulled him from the shelter that day and called to say she had never before seen a dog as shut down as Wheeler. Even at her house, Wheeler kept hiding behind the toilet and would not come out.

The following day, Wheeler arrived in Seattle. When I picked him up at the airport, he was terrified. He was shaking and would not make eye contact, had never been on a leash, and after spending the first two years of his life in a shelter, he had no idea how to be a dog. JoJo, our collie, is a great temperament tester so I put them together, and Wheeler loved JoJo. I let them play, and eventually Wheeler came up and licked my hand. While he was not human oriented, he lit up around the other dogs.

While he is still a little shy, Wheeler now rides in cars and plays with other dogs—and loves Rachel to distraction.

Here is a dog that spent the first two years of his life living in a shelter. He never had a chance to just be a dog but he is now happy and living a wonderful life.

That is the mission of Big Dog Rescue Project.

JoJo, Riley, Seamus, and Chanel
Photo courtesy of Four Foot Photography

Chapter Three

LET'S PAWS: COMPASSION FATIGUE

In the course of doing interviews for this book, several individuals mentioned compassion fatigue and how it impacted them and their lives. I first heard about compassion fatigue while I was working on Magical Dogs: Life and Lessons from Our Canine Companions. *A chapter in that book has information from Dr. Sophia Yin, a well-known and respected authority and trailblazer in the fields of dog training and animal behavior. Permission to include Dr. Yin's wisdom and insights was provided by her estate since Dr. Yin had already passed. Her death was determined to be a suicide. Those closest to her believe she suffered from compassion fatigue.*

The national suicide average for American workers is 1.5 per 1 million, but studies have revealed that animal rescue workers have a suicide rate of 5.3 in 1 million. This rate, shared only by firefighters and police officers, is the highest in America. We need to pay attention to these statistics by shedding some light and awareness on this issue.

We begin with Patricia Smith, the founder of the Compassion Fatigue Awareness Project. A journalist by trade, she learned about compassion fatigue first-hand while working in animal welfare.

COMPASSION FATIGUE AWARENESS PROJECT

COMPASSION FATIGUE IS A COMBINATION OF PHYSICAL, EMOtional, and spiritual depletion associated with the trauma-related work we do for people or animals who are in significant emotional pain or physical distress.

The bottom line is that caring too much can hurt. When caregivers focus on others without practicing self-care, a long list of symptoms can surface. These are all associated with what is now called secondary traumatic stress disorder (STS), another name for compassion fatigue.

It is important to remember that compassion fatigue is not a disease but a specific set of symptoms that reflect the stress placed on the human body, mind, and spirit. Those symptoms include: isolation, persistent physical ailments, sadness, apathy, emotional outbursts, an impulse to rescue anyone in need, substance abuse, hypervigilance, recurring nightmares or flashbacks, and excessive complaining about colleagues, management, and even those they are helping.

Those at risk for compassion fatigue are individuals who are "other-directed", meaning those who care for the needs of others before caring for their own. This pattern leads to depletion; therefore the absolute best thing we can do to alleviate our compassion fatigue is to practice authentic, sustainable, self-care daily. That includes: eating nutritious food; getting restful sleep; exercising on a regular basis; maintaining positive, functional relationships; sustaining a work-life balance; and practicing some form of spirituality, whether through time spent in nature, meditation, prayer, yoga, or whatever embraces and supports peace and wellness.

Healthy caregiving involves an ongoing and steady rhythm of filling up, emptying out, filling up, emptying out. It should be a daily process because without filling ourselves up, we are left with nothing to give others. It also means overcoming feelings of selfishness, self-centeredness, and guilt that often come with caring for ourselves—a pattern that often begins during our formative years. It's mandatory to build a healthy support system as well as strengthen our resiliency skills.

I first learned about compassion fatigue over twenty years ago while working as a training and development manager for a very large shelter in the San Francisco Bay area. I took the Professional Quality of Life self-test and learned I had very high levels of STS. That started me on a personal journey of healing and insights that led to the creation of Healthy Caregiving, LLC, which includes the Compassion Fatigue Awareness Project.

Those working in animal welfare are my favorite caregivers and closest to my heart. The interest in compassion fatigue skyrocketed with the suicide of Dr. Sophia Yin, and that sad situation was a wake-up call to

Patricia's dogs: Sky and Stella

many in the profession. I am often contacted to speak with veterinarians, shelter and rescue workers, wildlife rehabilitators, and a variety of other animal rescue workers. The high level of compassion fatigue I see when speaking with them is heartbreaking.

I am a consultant for the ASPCA in New York and we recently rolled out a nationwide training on compassion fatigue. They are doing extraordinary work to support their staff and leadership and it gives me great hope when I see what can be accomplished when resources are directed toward supporting and educating animal welfare workers.

RESCUER THERAPY

Next I interviewed Dr. Kimberly Johnson, a licensed mental health counselor and the founder of Rescuer Therapy. For over twenty-two years, Dr. Johnson has worked in crisis counseling, psychological first aid, the treatment of severe mental illness, and, more recently, the treatment of compassion fatigue. In addition to being a proud parent of rescued pups, she is a member of various national and local animal responder groups as well as a shelter volunteer.

I BEGAN WORKING WITH COMPASSION FATIGUE BECAUSE OF THIS little guy who is lying next to me snoring right now, Rupert. He is a Cavalier King Charles spaniel who was a puppy mill survivor we got through the National Mill Dog Rescue and a local rescue.

My need to understand more about Rupert's experience led me to hours of online research about puppy mills, and some of what I found was filled with brutal honesty and traumatic photos.

Rupert's first smile

The more I learned, the more I was impacted emotionally, and the more I felt compelled to get involved: first at a local shelter; then with Pet Safe, a local disaster response group; and then with Red Rover, which provides support on many levels when animals and people are in crisis. As I became obsessively involved, I started having strong emotions regarding the plight of the animals, including depressive symptoms, anger, hypersensitivity, and disillusionment.

While trying to understand what I was experiencing, I stumbled across the book *Compassion Fatigue in the Animal Care Community* by Charles Figley and Robert Roop. When I read it, suddenly everything made sense. I began to understand how Rupert's experience, coupled with my experience five months earlier with Hurricane Sandy and the cumulative impact of my years of rescue work, all added up. I saw how real compassion fatigue was and how it impacted me and so many around me.

While compassion fatigue is a term that has been around since the '90s, there has been limited attention paid to the idea of how it impacts workers in the animal care field, and it has taken time for it to become part of our regular dialogue.

Viktor Frankl once said, "What is to give light must endure burning." Those working in the animal field cast a light of caring, empathy, and compassion but the more they invest in those things, the more they are at risk of enduring burning.

Compassion fatigue is a combination of doing good work and the perception of, "The more I do, the better I'll feel." That can often manifest in overworking, because the harsh reality is that there will always be more to do.

For those on the front line of animal welfare and well-being, the emotional and physical impacts of doing good work accumulate and the consequence is an increased risk of experiencing symptoms of compassion fatigue. With animals, we have the added component of our own perception of their vulnerability and experiences along with being confronted by the inhumanity of our fellow humans.

Compassion fatigue can impact those working in the animal care community for a number of reasons, including:

- The massive and overwhelming volume of animals in need;
- The choices they are forced to make, which often mean the difference between life and death;
- Limited resources in the form of financial and/or social support;
- Visible and invisible scars from the trauma experienced by the animals they are helping;
- Lack of understanding or compassion from those around them;
- Fighting to be recognized and respected as the first responders they truly are.

While some of the symptoms are similar to those experienced by people dealing with post-traumatic stress disorder (PTSD), with compassion fatigue the symptoms seem to emerge as stress accumulates and typically come on as a slow burn. They can arise in a person's emotions, behavior, thoughts, cognition, interpersonal relationships, and spiritual or physical well-being.

To diagnose STS, we would look at how a person is dealing with the world. Are they depressed, angry, irritable, or experiencing increased anxiety? Do they have a lowered threshold for frustration? Are they experiencing excessive guilt? Do they feel useless, resentful, hopeless, or helpless? Do they feel isolated or lack enjoyment of life?

Behaviorally, we assess if the person is avoiding discussions about stressful situations, always looking for problems, or avoiding certain work activities. Do they choose to retreat rather than resorting to methods of self-help? Have they begun to return to old self-soothing (and possibly addictive) behavior?

On a cognitive level, does the person have decreased feelings of safety and/or increased feelings of hopelessness? Have they had negative thoughts about themselves? Are they easily distracted or having greater difficulty focusing? Has their world view changed to the point where they believe all people are bad? For example, if they are working in puppy mill rescue, have they begun to generalize and feel that everyone in a certain population is bad even though it is not true?

Their interpersonal relationships may suffer and they may have problems with intimacy and relating with their significant other, family, and friends. They may have increased conflict in relationships, boundaries may become blurred, and they may become bitter.

On a spiritual level, they may feel hopeless and begin questioning the meaning of life.

Physically, there may be gastro-intestinal issues, problems with joint or neck pain, increased fatigue, and changes in eating or sleeping patterns.

Animal workers and rescuers do valuable and heroic work, but they can (and often do) face difficult and extreme situations. In addition to all they do on a daily basis, they may also face the harsh reality of auctions, hoarding situations, and natural disasters or catastrophes—which have the potential of putting the worker into a trauma situation or pushing them beyond their existing levels of resiliency.

When things reach the point where work is intruding into other areas of a person's life and there is never a time when they are able to disengage, it may be time to stop and consider getting help. If they are out to dinner with friends and rather than relaxing they are thinking about all they need to do, they need to pause, reassess, and refocus on taking care of themselves.

My advice to those working in the care, rescue, and welfare of animals would be to plan ahead. Don't wait until you are experiencing symptoms or suffering to take stock and practice self-care. Begin by assessing what you are experiencing or feeling along with your self-care routine. It is a process of self-awareness and self-honesty that can begin by taking the Professional Quality of Life self-assessment online (or any other similar assessment and checklist) to help evaluate where you are at.

For those who feel they are already in the throes of compassion fatigue, it is imperative that they determine if seeking professional support might be helpful or necessary.

There is a natural tendency for those in impacted communities to tell their stories, share their experiences, or simply have their experiences or trauma validated. It can be quite therapeutic provided they do so in a safe place and with safe people who are free of judgment, pity, or pressure.

Self-care tools should not overload the individual or feel like a barrier for them to do the work they love. Rather, they should bolster a person's resilience and support them when they are feeling overloaded.

It's important that people not wait until they feel the impact of compassion fatigue to start developing self-care techniques. Having a metaphorical "go bag" of behaviors that embrace the whole person, body, mind, and spirit/soul, can include:

- Support systems: Surround yourself with people you trust and with whom you can share your story when you're struggling.
- Relaxation: Facing stress in a more relaxed state or manner helps you respond, rather than react, with more thoughtfulness and intention.
- Self-care activities: Seek and choose healthy activities that help you relax, release stress, treat your whole self, and support you.
- Look at your worldview: Understand that you have control over your perceptions and assumptions about the world. Understand how your worldview might impact or be impacted by a stressful situation. What perception do you have that might get in the way of self-care?

Practice the contents of your "go bag" before an emergency, just as you would practice fire drills because this will help you continue to do more of the work you love. Consider it to be like the oxygen mask on an airplane, remembering to put your mask on first so that you can in turn help those around you.

I have found many in the animal community are more apt to focus on caring for a dog than on their own self-care. We need to encourage one another to practice self-care so the work can continue. If someone in your office or rescue is frequently fatigued, putting in a lot of hours, or avoiding talking about difficult situations, consider starting a conversation by saying, "I see you're tired and frustrated. Tell me what's going on and what you've been doing." Try to get them to open up by providing them with a willing ear and the time, space, and permission to talk or relax. Suggest they take a break by going for a walk or to a movie.

While it's important to talk about compassion fatigue and discuss it before issues arise, it's the practice that is tough. Find methods that allow you to continually take stock of how you are feeling and how you are dealing with your daily life and practice those methods frequently. Do a conscious

Dr. Johnson's four Cavaliers: Sophie, Rupert, Humphrey, and Beatrice Joy

full-body scan starting at the top of your head and going all the way to your toes. Be aware of areas that are tight, as they will indicate where you are carrying stress. Once you locate those areas, focus on implementing relaxation techniques to release the stress. The more relaxed we are, the better we can respond to situations with intent and purpose rather than with a knee-jerk reaction.

Doing regular body scans can become a tool of self-regulation and a way to check on where you are throughout the day. It is also important to take care of your body through proper nutrition, staying hydrated, getting adequate sleep, and regular exercise. Integrating your pet into your exercise routine can have additional benefits since further healing can occur through our relationship and interaction with our pets.

The simple act of petting your dog is relaxing self-care and releases oxytocin, the "feel-good" hormone. It is also a great way to reconnect, be in the moment, and engage with your dog.

Rescuer Therapy is a program that provides free time-limited compassion fatigue treatment to people working in the animal care community as well as free on-site training and groups geared toward bringing compassion fatigue and self-care into our community dialogue.

Compassion fatigue is manageable, but when left unrecognized and untreated, its consequences can be life-shattering. By learning the tools to recognize our own level of stress and burnout, knowing when we are at risk, and implementing self-care strategies for reducing our risks, we can improve our lives as well as the quality of care we provide without cost to ourselves or the animals.

Chapter Four
DELAWARE VALLEY GOLDEN RETRIEVER RESCUE

Delaware Valley Golden Retriever Rescue (DVGRR) was part of Kristy's and Mary Jo's stories so I continued to connect the dots. One bright, sunny April morning, I hopped in my car and headed several hours west into Pennsylvania.

DVGRR is located in Lancaster County, Pennsylvania. Sometimes called the Garden Spot of America, Lancaster County is also home to one of the largest Amish settlements in the United States. On the day I drove there through the bucolic countryside and past the well-kept, pristine Amish farmhouses, I had no idea the area was also well-known for puppy mills. While at DVGRR, I learned they are changing the lives and futures for displaced goldens as well as for puppy mill dogs.

The first person I met was John, DVGRR's Executive Director. John joined the organization in 1994 as a volunteer and said the best way for me to understand DVGRR was for him to show me all they did by way of a personal tour. We started by walking toward a one-story building. The sign next to the door read Golden Gateway. As we walked in, John began to fill me in on the past and present of DVGRR.

JOHN

DELAWARE VALLEY GOLDEN RETRIEVER RESCUE BEGAN BACK IN 1986, in large part as a result of one woman trying to find a home for one golden retriever. After she joined forces with others, an all-volunteer, foster-based grassroots organization was formed, which ultimately led to the formation of DVGRR in 1994. By 1999, we had found homes for more than 800 golden retrievers. That same year, we were unable to help more than a dozen dogs because we no longer had enough foster homes to accept relinquished goldens and provide them with necessary training and consistent medical care. It became obvious that a facility was integral for our ongoing success.

In 2000, this property came on the market. It had five acres, a small house, and this building, which had been used as a boarding kennel. It was perfect for DVGRR, and thanks to the generosity of many people, our dream of one day having our own facility became a reality.

We restructured this building into a space where rescued dogs could receive physical and emotional evaluations, training, socialization, exercise, and love. We created a separate area for dogs needing isolation due to medical or health issues. Workers assigned to that area wear protective clothing and scrub down before and after leaving the area so as not to cross-contaminate any other dog or person.

Golden Gateway is the first stop for every dog that comes to DVGRR. The length of time a dog stays at Golden Gateway depends on their individual needs. While the typical stay is from three to six weeks, those who require more intense training or physical rehabilitation stay longer. Once a dog comes to DVGRR, they are here for as long as is necessary to receive the care, training, and support they need before being released for adoption.

Our daytime staff begins every morning at seven o'clock by taking the dogs out for a potty break and a short romp in the yard before breakfast. Morning meals and medication are prepared in advance by our evening staff, and in turn, the daytime staff prepare evening meals and medication.

At night, every dog gets a Kong filled with peanut butter. The dogs come to learn the Kong signals bedtime. By then, they are usually ready to go to sleep because throughout the day, they have numerous opportunities to play, go for walks, and interact with staff and volunteers for training and socialization. We do everything we can to keep every dog happy and healthy.

People are amazed and constantly comment that despite the presence of somewhere between thirty to fifty dogs, there is absolutely no odor. That can be attributed to two things: our high standards for cleanliness and a great staff who constantly and consistently clean and sanitize the kennels, the dogs' bowls and Kongs, and their work space.

John and I exited Golden Gateway and walked toward a small blue building with a ramp at the entrance. It also had its own fenced-in, covered outdoor kennel and play area. The sign next to the door read BARK: Buddy's Animal Rescue Klinic.

BARK is our on-site hospital and veterinary facility. Before BARK, staff members drove dogs back and forth to the vet on a daily basis, which was not only time consuming but also stressful for the dogs. Having BARK on site meant a huge savings in staff time and overall costs as well as decreased stress for the dogs. It also allowed us to provide the dogs with better and more immediate medical care.

We have a small surgical suite, and several times a week a veterinarian comes in to perform spay and neuter and other standard surgical procedures. There is digital X-ray, dental, and blood testing equipment so we can do chest and abdominal X-rays and a 23-panel blood chemistry. Since we get many of the tests results immediately, it allows us to get dogs on the road to recovery much quicker. It also allows us to address concerns about a dog's health, which, in turn, improves their chance of being adopted sooner. This has been especially true for our seniors.

Leaving BARK, John pointed to a ranch house atop a small rise a short distance from the Golden Gateway.

That is the original house. It became our full-time caretaker's home and initially housed an area for Project Home Life, a program that helps us transition puppy mill dogs from their former conditions to life in a normal home. Although our dogs come from private owners, shelters, and other rescues, we also take in dogs from large commercial breeding kennels since Lancaster County unfortunately has become known as the East Coast capital for puppy mills.

Turning, we followed a path to another ranch house at the opposite end of the property. On first appearance, the interior looked like someone's home. Framed pictures and dog-related sayings decorated the walls. The kitchen counter was lined with a coffee maker, dog bowls, and a treat jar. A television quietly played in the background. Leading me down a short hallway, John stopped in the doorway of a bedroom. The two dogs in the room jumped up on the Dutch door to greet John, but seeing me, they backed away. One headed into the closet; the other stood back from the door, eyes diverted.

We walked to the next bedroom where a senior dog relaxed on a dog bed while another dog relentlessly circled the perimeter of the room. John quietly described what I was witnessing.

The circling, retreating, and diverted eyes are very common for puppy mill survivors. For many years, we did all we could to help puppy mill dogs, but when this property came on the market in 2014, we purchased it and created The Lynne Glennon Sanctuary for Senior Goldens and Puppy Mill Survivors. The Sanctuary has exponentially increased our ability to help these dogs recover from their experiences and reality at the puppy mill. It allowed them to live in a home environment 24/7, something they had never experienced. It allowed them to get accustomed to the sights and sounds of a home and family: people going in and out of the house throughout the day, the clanking of pots and pans, the smells of cooking, people talking, and the sound of a television in the background.

We removed the closet doors and placed dog beds in those spaces to give the dogs a quiet place to retreat and relax. We replaced the standard bedroom doors with Dutch doors to keep the dogs safe in the rooms while letting them observe and hear activity and people in the house through the open top half of the door. We created a Thunder Room in the basement for dogs who are reactive to lightning or thunder. It is soundproof and windowless, and the furnace and water heater in the adjoining utility room help create white noise.

Exiting the house, John led me toward a large barn-type building adjoining a large fenced-in grassy area. This was the Thomas and Marian Ludwig Adoption and Activity Center, their most recent addition.

We have meet-and-greets on the second Saturday of every month. In the past, we had them here in the yard, but we were always at the mercy of the weather. Bad weather meant low attendance and undesirable conditions for the dogs.

All of that changed when we completed the Adoption and Activity Center. It is a 40-foot by 140-foot temperature-controlled building that allows us to have our monthly meet-and-greets, educational seminars, training classes, fundraisers, and other events regardless of the weather, and, in nice weather we can use the adjoining yard.

AMY

John ended our tour at DVGRR's administrative offices where Amy, DVGRR's Intake, Boarding, and Transportation Manager, shared her story with me.

I'M FROM LANCASTER COUNTY AND WORKED IN DOGGY DAY-care. I also volunteered for United Against Puppy Mills, a Lancaster County organization committed to educating and raising awareness about puppy mills. I knew about DVGRR and was thrilled when I was given the opportunity to join their staff.

Three months after I started working here, a woman called to tell us their mini goldendoodle puppy, Gibson, had been tied to their barn for a month. She said her children were done playing with him and asked if we could come get him.

Our kennel manager picked up Gibson. He was petrified when he got here and didn't want to get out of the crate. They carried his crate into the yard and left him there to relax. After a while they opened up door and Gibson ran out, across the yard, and as far away from everyone as possible. He stood motionless and petrified, so I finally knelt down and quietly said, "Hi, Gibson." He walked over, jumped in my lap, and licked my face—and I think you know what happened from there.

Gibson came home with me Thanksgiving weekend. It helped that I had Zoe, a twelve-year-old dachshund, because she and Gibson got along really well. Gibson has calmed down but he is still very afraid of men, especially tall balding men. We believe the children where he originally lived as a puppy may have pulled him around by his tail because he also doesn't like anyone to touch his tail.

In recent years, we have seen a

Gibson

decline in the number of goldens needing rescue, which may be due to a combination of the strong educational efforts of the Golden Retriever Club of America and, in our area, because of our highly trained staff and the education, support, and resources we provide. This decline has allowed us to open our arms a bit wider to accept Doodles and Labs.

We can also bring in goldens from other areas, including Puerto Rico and Turkey where purebred puppies are both fashionable and desirable. However, once that cute little puppy begins to grow or becomes too much work, people abandon the dog on a beach, in the forest, or on the street where the dog has to fight to stay alive.

Dogs from Puerto Rico arrive by commercial airline at Philadelphia Airport, where they are met by our transport team. In a typical year, we handle approximately 150 dogs from Puerto Rico. Puerto Rican goldens tend to be a little smaller than goldens here in the continental United States but they also have the sweetest temperaments. They are absolute cuddle bugs and typically don't have any aggression problems.

Every three months or so, eight to ten goldens from Turkey arrive by commercial airline at JFK Airport. Since it is a two-day journey, the dogs spend the first night at a facility where they are bathed and can rest before continuing their journey to us.

Working here means dealing with a variety of people, circumstances, and situations so it helps that I have a degree in psychology. It can be incredibly difficult and emotional for people who have to give up their dog due to a change of circumstances, financial difficulty, health concerns, or a divorce, so it is important that we support and help both them and their dog.

We recently got a call from a woman whose sister had stage 4 cancer and two dogs: a mixed breed that was taken by a family member and a golden.

I sent a seasoned volunteer to the woman's house to pick up her golden. She sat with the woman and showed her pictures of where her dog would be going, assuring her that her dog would be safe, well-cared for, and loved.

An hour later, at the exact moment the volunteer and dog pulled into our parking area, we got a call that the woman had passed. We all stood there crying, knowing she had been waiting to pass until she knew for certain her dog would be safe and loved.

Calls like that are heartbreaking, but I'm thankful we were able to give her that assurance so she could pass in peace. I am thankful we are here to help dogs and people. Regardless of the circumstances that bring a dog to DVGRR, in every single case I stay focused on the fact that we are here to help get every dog into a better situation.

CINDY

Thanking Amy, I exited the trailer and saw John standing with a group of people seated at an outdoor table. He motioned for me to come over and explained it was a Life Skills class and introduced me to the instructor: Edna. This was Leeward's Edna, who Kristy and Mary Jo had talked about. Once again the dots were being connected so Edna and I confirmed plans to meet the next day.

Pointing to another woman walking out of the Golden Gateway, John said, "There's Cindy. I'd like you to meet her."

Cindy and I walked into a room in the Golden Gateway. At the far end of the room, a golden was curled up, sleeping. Cindy explained that the dog was undergoing medical treatment and was being kept in the room since it was quiet. As Cindy began to share her story, the dog began to quietly snore.

GROWING UP ON A FIFTEEN-ACRE FARM, I HAD COLLIES, A PET crow, and a pet raccoon. I was always rescuing animals and dreamed of becoming a veterinarian, but instead I got married, had kids, and became a stay-at-home mom.

When our oldest son Zack turned four, he wanted a dog so we got a golden retriever. That began our passion for goldens because they are such happy dogs. Even if they are sick, goldens are still always happy. All they want is someone to throw a ball or pet them.

After our youngest went off to school, I applied for a job at DVGRR and have been here for ten years. I suppose my official title would be DVGRR Jill-Of-All-Trades because two days a week I help in the kennels and two days I assist Marie, our vet tech, in our on-site hospital. I have been trained to groom and I also help my son Zack, who is the DVGRR Director of Adoptions. I might not make a ton of money, but I wouldn't trade it for the world. I knew DVGRR was a great place and I feel so for-

Leroy

tunate to work here. In the ten years I have been here, we have adopted five golden retrievers.

Maggie, our first, arrived in pretty rough condition. She didn't have any teeth and was thunder-phobic. I adopted her when she was eleven and only had her until she was fourteen, but those were honestly the best three years of my life. Maggie truly was the best dog in the world. She was always happy and smiling her golden smile. She greeted everyone with her tail wagging and would just stand there waiting to be petted. Just seeing Maggie made people happy.

Our next dog, Leroy, came to DVGRR from a puppy mill when he was only twelve weeks old. He was absolutely terrified of everyone and everything. For the first three months, he hid under the table in our home and eliminated every time the doorbell rang.

While the puppy mill probably knew Leroy had health issues, they never disclosed them to DVGRR. When our vet checked him, they found a heart murmur and other heart-related issues. We were told that as Leroy grew, his heart would be unable to keep up with his growing body. Despite our concerns over his health, Leroy was always happy, loved to play, and was always getting into mischief. Once he learned he could trust us, he relaxed and truly enjoyed people and his life. When he was one year and one month old, Leroy fell over and passed at our home.

Even though he was with us for such a short time, everyone who met Leroy said he was special. He had that certain something that can't be put into words; it was something you felt. I believe Leroy came to teach us the importance of forgiveness. When you consider all he had been through, Leroy should have hated people. Instead he loved every person and animal he ever met.

I currently have three DVGRR dogs: Winston, Lady, and Crystal.

Winston came in as an owner-surrender when he was eight months old. The owner tried to train Winston to be a service dog for a paraplegic without knowing how. He wrongly thought Winston would simply know what to do. When he didn't, he beat Winston with a newspaper. The first time I laid eyes on Winston, something about him spoke to me and I

Lady

adopted him. He is now ten and still gets upset if he sees a man with a hat and sunglasses.

Lady was found tied up in someone's backyard. She was unable to bark, which we learned was due to a cancerous mass in her throat. We had the mass removed but it grew back one month later. All signs indicated that Lady wasn't going to live very long—three months at best—so I took Lady home on hospice care. Eight years later at thirteen, she still can't bark and still has cancer but she is still like a puppy and still happy every single day. She is also, hands down, the boss in our house.

Crystal arrived at DVGRR from a puppy mill when she was six weeks old. One of her eyes looked like it had burst and she was completely blind in that eye. The puppy mill knew they couldn't sell her and that keeping her with her litter might scare away potential purchasers so she came to DVGRR. The plan was for me to foster Crystal until she was twelve weeks old, but by that point we loved her so Crystal became my first foster failure.

I love fostering puppies. It's fun to watch them come into our home and integrate with my pack who, in turn, teach the puppy the rules and guidelines of being part of a family and being a great dog.

Even though I lived in Lancaster County my entire life, I had no idea what a puppy mill dog was until I started working here. I had no idea how it impacted a dog's life. I had no idea a dog would hide in the back of their kennel, be afraid of people, or refuse to take a treat from you because their only contact with humans, up to that point, was negative. Seeing the look in a puppy mill dog's eyes when they first arrive always breaks my heart.

On the other hand, to be able to witness their transformation is astounding. To see a dog go from being frightened of people to a dog that just enjoys people changes you. It has changed my entire family. If someone tells my daughter they got a puppy, she immediately asks them, "Where did you get it? From a pet store? From a farm?" She has become an advocate against puppy mills and has now begun to educate others.

HEATHER

Next I spoke with Heather, the Manager of the Sanctuary and the Director of Project Home Life. I was eager to talk with her to learn more about the work she was doing, especially as it related to puppy mill dogs.

WHILE I GREW UP WITH AND ALWAYS LOVED DOGS, IT WAS MY sister who worked with animals at a vet hospital. I was more interested in music. After getting my bachelor's degree in music from Lebanon Valley College, I worked in a music store, played in several rock bands, and was a live sound engineer, but over time, I got burned out on the music industry. I knew to truly make it in that world meant moving to either New York or Nashville, but I wanted to stay in this area. This was home, so I stepped back to reassess, which led to years of working odd jobs.

In 2005, my mom adopted two dogs from DVGRR and the following summer I was hired as a part-time kennel worker. A year later, the caretaker position opened up, so for the past nine years I have been living on the property as the full-time caretaker. I am responsible for ensuring that any dog who needs assistance overnight receives it, which often means helping dogs that are thunder-reactive get through a thunderstorm. I also help train and groom dogs to get them ready for adoptions and meet-and-greets.

Up until May 2007, I fostered dogs but didn't have a dog of my own until a puppy mill dog named Mel came to DVGRR. Shortly after she arrived, Mel gave birth to eight puppies.

Since we didn't have a history on Mel, there was no way to know she had canine herpes virus (CHV). Also known as fading puppy syndrome, CHV is a viral infection of the reproductive organs of adult dogs. Adults can carry the virus oftentimes without showing any symptoms. While it is not a death sentence for an adult dog, it is fatal to puppies less than two or three weeks old.

This was my first experience with a dog giving birth and my first experience with CHV. We suddenly had eight cute little helpless puppies screaming in pain. We rushed them to the emergency vet, but only one puppy survived. It was the most traumatic experience I have ever been through.

Mel was adopted and I took the last surviving puppy to my house so as not to risk exposing any other dogs to the virus. I adopted the puppy and named him Satchel. He was my first dog as an adult and was very special to me. Satchel turned out to be a wonderful, healthy dog who loved people and food. He was always getting into trouble in an attempt to get food wherever, however, and from whomever he could.

When Satchel was seven months old, we adopted Jilly, a very sweet eleven-month-old golden who came from a Florida rescue. She soon became known as Silly Jilly because she was a happy, wiggly, silly dog. From the moment Satchel and Jilly met, they bonded and would lay with their heads next to one another. She truly was the perfect match for him.

Sami

My next dog, Sami, was a nine-year-old, one-eared puppy mill dog. While no one at DVGRR knew for certain what happened to Sami's ear, she was in rough shape, and based on the wounds on her side, she may possibly have been in a dog fight. Sami constantly spun and pooped in her crate, which can be fairly common with puppy mill dogs since they have spent their entire lives up to that point living in a kennel. Sami would lay and nudge invisible puppies, another PTSD behavior we see in many puppy mill dogs.

And then along came my fourth dog, Lance, who came from a hoarding situation in Virginia. The lady had 297 animals—dogs, cats, horses, goats, and every other kind of animal you can imagine—in what she called her "animal sanctuary." A golden retriever rescue finally convinced her to allow them to take Lance, who she had found in a box on the side of the road when he was only five weeks old. He was at least five years old by then, and by all indications had spent those five years tied outside living under a tarp with a bunch of other dogs. The woman was ultimately charged with animal cruelty and her "sanctuary" was permanently shut down.

Lance is the most fearful dog I have ever worked with. He wouldn't take food from anyone. For the first four months, I knelt down next to his kennel so he couldn't see me to try and give him a piece of cheese. He was deathly afraid of men and still doesn't like them, but it was also tough for women to get Lance to come in and out of his kennel. He simply didn't want to be touched by anyone.

After eight months, Lance had begun to make progress with some people, but not others. I had built a bond with him and anytime he saw me he would bark and bark—then bark some more. It was a happy bark, but it was nonstop so I finally decided to take Lance home and work with him. Even after he was in my house, it took a long time for him to calm down. It took at least one year before he was completely comfortable with me, although it helped that we had Sami, Jilly, and Satchel because Lance loved playing with them.

I've had Lance seven years now and have developed such a deep bond with him. Even though it took a long time, he is a completely different dog now. He has come such a long way and is a total mama's boy.

Jilly, Lance, Satchel

One afternoon, we were all in the yard running around when Satchel stopped, fell over, and died. I was with him and saw the whole thing. It was truly the worst day of my life. He was only seven and I had taken him to the vet two weeks earlier where he had been given a clean bill of health.

Then Silly Jilly developed a cantaloupe-size tumor and died. Shortly after turning fourteen, Sami developed kidney failure and died. A month later we adopted Lola, a chocolate Lab. While it was probably a little too soon for us, Lance was really depressed. He was used to a house full of dogs and we knew he needed another dog. Three months later, Lola started having seizures. We found out she had a brain tumor and she died two months later.

After Lola passed, we got Leia, a Puerto Rican golden. As is typical of

Leia, Lance, and Lady

Puerto Rican goldens, she was smaller and weighed only forty-two pounds. Leia was a really sweet dog and helped heal our hearts since she allowed us to just be.

Lance was getting older, and with Leia only being three and wanting to play, we decided to get another Puerto Rican golden mix named Lady. Leia and Lady became best friends, which took the pressure off of Lance.

My passion is for the puppy mill dogs. I connect with them possibly because most of them are shy and I was once incredibly shy. Ten years ago, I wouldn't have been able to talk with you like we are talking today, but this job and the dogs have changed me.

Project Home Life came about after I was asked to implement a program to help transition puppy mill dogs from a kennel environment to a home environment. To understand the importance and scope of that transition, it's important to consider what their lives were like as puppy mill dogs.

A puppy mill is essentially a large-scale commercial breeding facility. Female dogs are typically bred at every heat cycle with little or no recovery time between litters. Since profit takes precedence over the well-being of the dogs, they are kept in overcrowded, unsanitary conditions, oftentimes without food, water, or adequate ventilation. They spend their lives in cages, which many times are stacked in columns. They are not allowed out to play or potty and their feet are never given an opportunity to touch the ground or grass. The wire crate flooring they stand on all day injures their paws and legs.

Socialization doesn't exist for these dogs since they have little to no interaction with humans, and what little contact does exist is often abusive or inhumane. Likewise they receive little or no veterinary care, making their puppies particularly prone to congenital and hereditary conditions such as blood and respiratory issues or heart disease. The puppies, sometimes removed from their mother and littermates at a young age, often suffer from fear, anxiety, and other behavioral issues and are typically sold to pet stores, over the internet, through newspaper ads, or at flea markets.

When the adult dogs are no longer able to reproduce, they make it to rescue—if they are lucky. Otherwise, they are killed or taken to auction.

When creating Project Home Life, I took all of that into consideration. It started in a small room the size of a closet where volunteers sat and quietly read books to the dogs and gave them treats. We also kept a television on to allow the dogs to get used to the sound.

We eventually moved the program into the apartment in the basement of the caretaker's house, which gave us more space and more options. In March 2014, we opened the Sanctuary, which has been a blessing for these dogs.

When a puppy mill dog first arrives, they spend the first few days in our Special Care Unit at the Sanctuary since the shock of going from a confined wire kennel into a home can often prove to be too difficult for them. Once the dog begins to settle in, our volunteers (who are known as Compassionate Caregivers) begin working with the dog both indoors and outdoors. They slowly introduce the dog to gentle petting and brushing. The dog is encouraged to approach people and take treats and slowly they become accustomed to normal household noises. Compassionate Caregivers oftentimes read books to the dog, which has proven to help them relax.

During the next stage, we focus on building the dog's confidence. They learn to walk through doorways, balance on unstable structures (to make riding in a car easier), and master basic obedience skills. Many of these dogs are fearful of a collar or leash since they may have been dragged by a farmer to be bred, so we work on them gaining confidence and being comfortable wearing a harness.

As the dog's confidence grows, we begin to see a formerly terrified dog starting to approach people and situations without fear. The difference for the dogs—as well as for our staff and volunteers—is truly life changing.

Before opening the Sanctuary, the dogs would spend a few hours every day in the caretaker's house before returning to the kennel. Now the dogs live in the house all day, every day, so we try and provide them with every experience they would hear, see, smell, and encounter in a home environment.

They live in bedrooms and with other dogs, which helps them progress since they learn from one another—especially if we can match a shy dog with a dog that is more confident around people and has more normal behavior.

Matching a senior dog with a puppy mill dog has also been a great combination. The senior dogs make themselves at home and, for the most part, are pretty relaxed. Many times this has a calming influence on the puppy mill dogs.

A perfect example is Olivia, the dog you saw earlier today circling in the bedroom. She is a very shy girl but we have paired her with a calm senior dog, which gives her the ability to see and learn normal reactions. It has helped Olivia calm down, although many times when I am making Olivia's meal, or if she gets nervous or excited, she begins circling.

Circling is a typical behavior for puppy mill dogs. Before they came to us, their life was lived in a wire cage or kennel. Since that is the only space they have, and since they aren't allowed out of it, they begin to habitually pace or circle.

Before Project Home Life, a puppy mill dog typically stayed at the rescue six to eight months. After Project Home Life, it went down to four or five months. Now, with the Sanctuary, the average is thirty-eight days! The only ones who stay longer are the ones who are really shy.

Puppy mill dogs can be very shy or shut down and you can't do too much with them too quickly. If you look at them, they will shake or tremble. They won't walk around the property and are afraid of a leash. A bath would be traumatic.

In the beginning, we just exist with them. We make sure they get outside six times a day and we slowly work with high-value treats like chicken or meatballs. Little by little, with patience and by giving them space, things begin to change and slowly they begin to learn that being with us is a really good thing.

At DVGRR, we try not to focus on where a dog has been but rather on what they can become and where they are going.

Chapter Five
JOJO AND SAM

Out of the corner of my eye, I saw a woman getting out of her car with a golden retriever. As they slowly began walking in our direction, Heather said, "That's JoJo and Cano." Person after person walked over to greet them. As we watched them slowly head in our direction, Heather began to tell me about Cano.

CANO'S LIFE BEGAN IN PUERTO RICO. HE WAS OWNED BY A FAMILY who operated a security company, and when the son no longer wanted Cano, the father tried to train him to be a guard dog. His training method was having his Rottweilers and German shepherds attack Cano to make him more aggressive. He still bears scars on his legs and a large scar near his eyes that we believe are from being attacked.

Cano's life consisted of being kept in a dirt lot behind a chain-link fence with little to no positive human interaction. We suspect he was possibly beaten with a pole because he is terrified of any kind of pole, including a broomstick. They may have also used a shock collar on him because he is reactive to certain tones.

When it became apparent it was simply not in Cano's nature to be aggressive, the owner decided to euthanize him, but a rescue organization in Puerto Rico saved his life. They placed him on a flight from San Juan to Philadelphia where DVGRR transport team volunteers picked him up. Most dogs arrive at DVGRR after their journey and jump out of the travel crate to discover their new surroundings—but not Cano.

Cano

When Cano arrived, he definitely wasn't in a good place with people. After all the failed attempts to make him aggressive, Cano had begun to completely shut down. He hid inside the crate shaking. The DVGRR staff carried his crate into a secure area and left the door open so Cano could wander out whenever he felt safe.

I and another staff member, Tara, began working with him, and Cano grew to love Tara. Even though she has since moved away, to this day whenever Cano sees Tara he is completely overjoyed. I have never seen a dog with a memory like his—which is unfortunate for Marie, our veterinary assistant, since Cano tested positive for heartworm and she was the one who had to give him the heartworm shots.

Dogs can suffer from post traumatic stress disorder (PTSD), and when Cano arrived from Puerto Rico at two years of age, he had PTSD. He was terrified of any new person, so we took our time and very slowly introduced him to our long-term volunteers. After being here a month, Cano moved into the Sanctuary and after one week decided he loved it. It helped that he met a female dog named Bessie, who very quickly became his girlfriend and roommate.

All seemed to be going well until a few weeks later when Dennis, our Kennel Manager, visited the Sanctuary. As soon as Cano saw him, he barked, groaned, put his head down, and cowered as low as he could.

To help him associate men with good experiences, one of our male volunteers, Dave, began spending time every Friday working with Cano. Several weeks later, Cano stopped barking and groaning when Dave approached and instead began rolling over so Dave could give him belly rubs. Dave continued speaking to Cano in a soft voice and kept their sessions light and happy while providing him with plenty of high-value treats.

That was the beginning of Cano's journey. The rest of his journey belongs to JoJo and Sam and it is their story to tell.

JO JO

I watched as the woman and dog took the last few steps before reaching us. I got up to greet them. "I'm JoJo," the woman said, shaking my hand. "And this is Cano." Cano was a handsome golden sporting a tuxedo with a skull and crossbones bowtie. He crawled under the table to relax while JoJo told me the rest of his story.

THIRTEEN YEARS AGO, WHILE VOLUNTEERING FOR A SERVICE dog program, I met the director, a woman named Sam, and we rapidly became best friends. When a divorce left her without a place to live, I asked if she wanted to be my roommate to split expenses. She moved in, along with her golden retriever, a wonderful dog she'd had since its first breath because it was literally born right into her hands.

After moving in, her dog battled cancer for two years, ultimately passing away at the age of fifteen. Since we lived in the area, we started coming to meet-and-greets at DVGRR to get our golden fix. We were happy to support them but weren't ready to adopt.

In November, not quite a year after Sam's golden died, we began to think about getting a dog. We came to a meet-and-greet and saw the Sanctuary dogs, including Cano. We had heard about Cano but when we walked by him, he hid behind one of the volunteers and wouldn't come out to greet anyone.

By the time we came back for the December meet-and-greet, we had been preapproved to adopt. We looked at a puppy who already had a whole list of potential adopters, but since we were unsure if we could commit to a puppy, Heather and Tara gently guided us to visit with Cano.

This time our meeting with Cano went very differently. When we knelt down, he immediately came over, greeted Sam, and licked my cheek. The volunteers were surprised and jokingly said we must be dog whisperers.

Heather encouraged us to take Cano into one of the play areas to visit with him off-leash. He was shy and kept his distance, running the perimeter of the fence. We kept looking at him and one another, unsure we had the skills to work with such a shy, fearful dog. We decided to visit with other dogs. Then, with only five minutes left in the meet-and-greet, we started talking about Cano again and decided to find out more about him. After signing a form expressing our interest in Cano, we left the event uncertain what we were getting ourselves into.

Several days later, we received an email stating we had been approved to adopt Cano—and our journey began.

Since Cano was still very afraid of new people, we decided that we would give him time to get to know us before bringing him home. For the next few weeks, we visited Cano at the Sanctuary for about an hour twice a week.

At our first visit, Cano sat in the corner of the room and stared at us in true stranger-danger fashion. Sam and I both work full time so my parents were going to be Cano's daytime caregivers. Over the weekend, we brought them along to see how Cano would react around my father. At first, Cano was a bit timid with my father, but we came prepared with high-value treats Cano only got when he approached or was near my father. The treats worked amazingly well and Cano began looking for the treats every time my parents visited.

Since everything was going well, Heather, Tara, Sam, and I decided we would bring Cano home just after the holidays. We immediately began to prepare our house, trying our best to simulate the space Cano had been living in at the DVGRR Sanctuary house. We set up a crate in our kitchen, placed a bed alongside it, and put gates up to section off the room.

The first night, Cano refused to leave his crate and actually hid inside it and stared at us. We decided to leave him alone and sat in the family room with the television on to provide quiet background noise in a further attempt to simulate what he had gotten used to in the Sanctuary. Thankfully, we were able to get him out of the crate once to potty before we went upstairs to bed.

That continued for about a week—until Cano realized he could go upstairs. After that, he started taking turns sleeping one night in my bedroom and the next in Sam's bedroom.

During the day, my parents watched Cano and we all tried to keep the same daily routine he had at the Sanctuary. Wanting him to continue being comfortable with men, my father gave him his afternoon piece of cheese at naptime. Every night, Cano got a peanut butter-filled Kong before bed, just like he had gotten at the Sanctuary.

We have an in-ground pool, and the first year we had Cano, he had a pool party for his birthday. We invited all of his friends from the Shy Dog Park, including a dog named Leeward. As soon as Leeward got to the party, he and his sister Hope—another shy dog—immediately jumped in the pool. The next thing we saw was their human, Mama Edna, jumping into the pool in her clothes to grab them and show them the way to the steps to get out.

Leeward was a good friend to Cano. Leeward started a tradition of wearing a tuxedo for special occasions so every time Cano wears a tuxedo now he is doing it in memory of his friend Leeward.

In March, we enrolled Cano in a beginner obedience class. This decision was deliberate because we felt a puppy/beginner class would be a more socialized situation with less threat from larger dogs. Cano excelled. After the second week he was allowing strangers to approach him and was calm around baby strollers. On weekends, we took him different places around town. At first, we would leave him in the car so he could watch us walking around and going in and out of stores, but over time we started bringing him into new places and introducing him to new situations.

He did great in the intermediate obedience class and excelled in the advanced obedience class. When that ended, we had him tested for AKC Canine Good Citizen. Once again, he passed with flying colors. Little by little, with every experience and every success, Cano's personality was beginning to shine.

Our previous golden had been a therapy dog through Therapy Dogs International (TDI). While we weren't sure if

Cano

Cano was ready, we decided to challenge him. We spent the next few months working with him at home then drove to Philadelphia for the test without any formal preparation class. TDI requires the handler and dog be tested as a team. Since Sam and I would both potentially be working with Cano, that meant he had to take the test twice—once with each of us—but he passed both times without any problem.

As a therapy dog, Cano visits two different nursing homes. One is very close to our home. The other is further away but going there is a personal mission for us. There is a DVGRR volunteer who worked with Cano at the Sanctuary and her mother lives at that nursing home. Visiting her is our way of giving back for all the time her daughter gave to Cano—and it is Cano's way of giving back to those who believed in him. It is full circle for all of us.

Last September, we organized a Dog Festival in downtown Lititz complete with vendors, dog games, contests, and a food truck. It was a lot of fun and the entire event was a fundraiser for DVGRR.

Sam and I also began volunteering two Sundays a month at the Sanctuary. While there one Sunday in November, a staff member named Jess carried out a three-month-old puppy mill dog named Autumn. Handing her to me, she said, "This one is extremely afraid. You're really going to have to work with her."

I held Autumn but the poor little puppy continued to shake uncontrollably. While it's common for puppy mill dogs to be afraid, Autumn was from a puppy mill that had previously surrendered dogs to DVGRR and every dog from that puppy mill had a pattern of fearful behavior. It was suspected that some of Autumn's fear may have actually been inherited rather than learned. Autumn also had health issues the puppy mill never addressed.

Having begun to plateau with Cano's training, we had started to think about getting him a packmate. Holding this frightened little puppy, I got the feeling Autumn might be the one for Cano, so I walked over to the adjacent yard where Sam was working with another dog, held Autumn over the fence, and said, "What do you think?"

Sam looked at her, then at me, and said, "Maybe." We tried to play with Autumn but she just sat and continued to shake. In the meantime, Sam had fallen in love with another dog named Kissy she thought might be a good match for Cano so we went home to discuss our options.

Two weeks later we made arrangements for Cano to meet Kissy with Autumn as a backup.

Early one Saturday morning, Zack, the Director of Adoptions, met us at DVGRR and we took Cano into the Sanctuary yard. Zack brought Kissy out, but much to Sam's dismay, she snarled and snapped at Cano. She didn't want anything to do with a male dog.

Next, Zack brought Autumn out, and in true puppy fashion, she began chasing Cano and biting his back leg. Cano wasn't sure how to react but took it like a perfect gentleman and didn't snap, snarl, or react in any way. After watching them interact for about a half hour, we decided Autumn would be Cano's new sister. We fostered Autumn for sixty days while some of her health issues were addressed. In January, we officially adopted her and changed her name to Kenzie.

On the ride home after signing the official adoption paperwork, Kenzie curled up next to Cano and put her head next to his, which was our sign this was a perfect match. They play in the backyard, go on adventures together, and have become inseparable. They are so bonded that we actually purposely separate them from time to time so that when they are apart they don't get too upset.

We knew Cano would be Kenzie's mentor and watched as he taught her and she followed his lead and guidance. Kenzie took three obedience classes, and at each class, Cano sat on the bench and watched her. She passed all three classes. Eventually we will test her for CGC and for therapy dog certification. Right now, she's not ready because she is still a little too fearful, so we work with her every weekend, just like we did with Cano. She has an incredible personality, a lot of energy, and is a really funny, sweet girl.

If we take Kenzie downtown, she doesn't even want to get out of the car. She is fine with people but is afraid to go into a new environment. Cano is the complete opposite. He is willing to go into a new environment or situation but can still be hesitant around someone he doesn't know.

In Chinese philosophy, yin yang describes how seemingly opposite or contrary aspects of the same phenomenon can actually be complementary and interdependent. Our two shy dogs are complete opposites on their spectrum of fear, but the wonderful thing is that they support and balance one another. Cano and Kenzie are our real-life yin yang.

Cano and Kenzie

Chapter Six
EDNA'S DOG HOUSE

After leaving DVGRR, I checked into a nearby hotel and met a high school friend, Kris, for dinner. We had a wonderful time, and the next morning, I awoke refreshed and excited to meet Edna.

Kristy, Mary Jo, JoJo, and several people at DVGRR had described Edna as both remarkable and amazing. More than once I heard, "Edna takes the dogs no one else wants."

As I pulled into her driveway and got out of my car, I heard dogs barking, followed by a woman's voice saying, "The front door is open. Come on in. There are three dogs in the house but everyone is friendly."

Walking in, three golden retrievers stood, tails wagging, happy to greet me. The back door opened and a woman walked in, followed by two more dogs. Walking toward me, she smiled and said, "Welcome to Edna's Dog House. I'm Edna."

For several hours, Edna and I sat on her screened-in porch, and with her dogs milling around us, she told me stories about The Dog House.

OVER TWENTY YEARS AGO, I GOT ROOKIE, A GOLDEN RETRIEVER-shepherd mix when he was a little over a year old. As a puppy, Rookie survived distemper, which is extremely rare. However, even if a dog survives distemper, they can sometimes be left with neurological problems, which happened with Rookie. He continued to have seizures throughout his life, although the last four years of his life we had fairly good control of them.

When Rookie was nine, I met a five-week-old golden retriever puppy. When she was old enough, I adopted her and named her Eden. She was the first dog I ever raised from a puppy and I credit Eden for getting me involved in rescue work.

After Eden, I adopted Magellan, a six-month-old golden retriever, and then along came Murphy, a three-month-old golden who was born without a tail, making it difficult for the breeder to sell him.

Eden was diagnosed with hermangiosarcoma, an aggressive cancer that occurs almost exclusively in dogs. After she passed, I wanted to rescue another dog, so I started going to meet-and-greets at Delaware Valley Golden Retriever Rescue and got preapproved to adopt. I am someone who falls in love with a dog because it looks like my dog that just died. When I saw Princess, I thought she looked just like Eden so I filled out the application before learning Princess had already been placed with another adopter.

Princess was an older, sweet, gentle dog, which made her an easy placement for the rescue. A dog like that does well in any situation and with people who don't have a lot of dog experience—and that is exactly where she went. It was a perfect fit.

Dogs with bigger challenges often result in a rescue having to work really hard to match them with the right home and person. That was the case with Riley, an eight-year-old former puppy mill breeder dog. I inquired about Riley and made arrangements with DVGRR to bring Magellan and Murphy to meet him. The visit went really well so I adopted Riley and he became my introduction into the world of puppy mill dogs.

Riley did not like to be restrained or crated, had a fear of big open spaces, and was also noise-phobic. Anytime I took Riley to PetSmart, there were too many smells and noises for him and he would immediately go into sensory overload and have a panic attack. He would begin to pace and look for a way to flee. The impact was visible not only in his body language (with ears down and body low) but also through the visible stress on his face. To desensitize him, I started taking Riley for very brief visits to a variety of places, and over time, he did really well.

Shortly after turning nine, Murphy was diagnosed with lymphoma and began chemotherapy. He sailed through the treatments without incident or side effects. He never had any nausea or diarrhea or any issues with eating or sleeping. The only thing that happened was he lost his whiskers and undercoat.

Even though he was doing fabulous, I created a bucket list for Murphy and we started doing all the things he loved. Every Sunday we went for a drive since he loved going out in the car. We visited the Smoky

Mountains, several NASCAR tracks, and, since Murphy loved the beach, we made several trips to Cape Henlopen State near Lewes, Delaware. We went through a lot of McDonald's drive-thru's for Happy Meals and walked endless miles at state parks.

One year after his diagnosis, Murphy finished his first round of chemotherapy. One month later, the cancer came back and they resumed treatment, but this time Murphy couldn't tolerate it. He got violently ill after the first treatment. Knowing he wouldn't be able to handle another round, I stopped treatment.

Shortly after Murphy passed, Riley started limping. We tried treating the symptoms, but when he didn't improve, we did additional testing and found out Riley had plasma cell cancer. I promised Riley before he passed that I would start volunteering at DVGRR in gratitude for bringing us together.

In three years, I lost three dogs. It was just Magellan and me in the house. For the first time in her life, she was the only dog but it was way too quiet for both of us. I started going to meet-and-greets at DVGRR again, and that's where I met Hope.

Hope was a former puppy mill breeder dog who came to DVGRR with her twin littermate, Faith. Faith passed from mammary cancer after being at DVGRR one week. Since they were bonded siblings, there was obvious concern about Hope.

Having come from a puppy mill, Hope was put in the Project Home Life program at DVGRR. When she was ready, I brought Magellan over to meet her. Hope was still really shut down but Magellan is very social, outgoing, and dog- and kid-friendly and was deemed a good mentor dog for Hope.

I wasn't overly concerned about bringing Hope home since it would be fairly quiet with only her, Magellan, and me at the house. However, when we got home, I learned Hope had problems with doorways. She refused to go through the door to go outside so I had to carry her in and out to go to the bathroom. After a week, she finally followed Magellan outside for the first time, and I was so excited that without thinking I yelled, "Yay, Hope!" and she shut down for another week before going out again. All things considered, it could have been worse, but that was in large part because of all Project Home Life had done for Hope.

Four years later, Hope still has issues with certain noises. She still circles, although they have now evolved from small, tight circles into large, loose, lazy circles. When I look at Hope I can't help but be grateful that she is now living in a home where she is cared for and loved.

The first Sunday of every month, DVGRR holds a Shy Dog Park. It was begun by Heather at DVGRR and is an extension of Project Home Life. It is for any puppy mill survivor or shy or fearful dog that has been preapproved by Heather.

Shy and fearful dogs like Hope don't do well in public dog parks or big open events. Shy Dog Park provides dogs like Hope the opportunity for two hours once a month to come and play off-leash with other dogs. It gives them a chance to just be a dog. The program has been running for three years now and we have had up to thirty-five dogs together at the Shy Dog Park and never had an issue.

The first time I brought Hope to Shy Dog Park, there was a puppy mill hutch in the corner and she hid under it the entire two hours. She didn't come out and we didn't push her. The next time, she started to interact and play with some of the other dogs. We have found that the dogs heal one another. As humans, we do what we can but the dogs take the healing to another level—and it has been wonderful for Hope.

Riley passed in November and I adopted Hope on the first of December. That Christmas, I decided it was time to keep my promise to Riley and began volunteering at DVGRR. From the first day I volunteered, I absolutely loved it.

One day while volunteering, the Adoption Manager called me over and pointed to an old red golden with a big white head. "That's our big sweet Annie," he said. "She's fourteen and we don't think she has much time left. We were wondering if you would consider taking her home on hospice."

I had heard about a woman named Sara who took a dog named Trixie home on hospice; she passed three days later. I always admired what Sara did for Trixie but that was the one and only time I knew of someone providing hospice care for a dog. Until Annie, I had never thought about providing hospice care for dogs.

Annie had been a breeder dog and was kept in an outdoor pen. When the owner surrendered Annie, he said it was because they wanted her to be a guard dog but she just wasn't good at it. We all knew it was because she could no longer breed.

I brought Hope and Magellan to meet Annie and it went great so I brought Annie home. Annie was incredibly frail but all she wanted was for someone to touch her. She just wanted to be with you. Annie truly had the purest heart and was the purest soul of any being I ever met in my life.

A month after bringing Annie home, a dog named Casey was dropped off at DVGRR by her owner. When the owner came in with Casey, he glanced at the puppies in the front room. He told DVGRR that he'd had Casey since she was an eight-week-old puppy, then handed her off and immediately walked over to inquire about the puppies. DVGRR never approved him to adopt the puppies or any dog and never even gave him an application.

Casey was an eight-year-old female golden with broken teeth and big patches of hair missing. From the back, Casey looked like an armadillo. She had a massive lump the size of a Nerf football attached to her lungs, which made it inoperable. We nicknamed it the Lump of Love, and every night Casey slept under the covers up against me with the Lump of Love on top of me.

Despite all of that, Casey had the biggest smile and was a fun dog. She desperately wanted to play, but as a former puppy mill dog, she never had the opportunity to play and didn't know how. Since Hope had never learned how to play either, they invented their own form of play, which for Casey usually involved throwing her Lump of Love on top of Hope.

Casey was with us four months when one morning a brown liquid started pouring out of her. The vet determined it was pyometra, a life-threatening uterine infection. Casey's case was severe and untreatable. I promised Casey I would be with her until the end and I was. When it was time, I held her, told her I loved her, and said goodbye.

It was the twenty-third of December, two days before Christmas, and I was scheduled to walk dogs at DVGRR that night. Instead, I drove there, rang the doorbell, and when they answered I stood there crying, saying, "She was a good girl." When I finally calmed down, I told them I wasn't going to be able to walk dogs that night because I needed to go home and have a good cry.

The next day, Christmas Eve, I went to DVGRR. As soon as I arrived, a young man who worked in the kennel stuck his head out and asked if I knew how to birth puppies. There we were on Christmas Eve delivering puppies. The first came out shortly before I got into the room but I helped deliver the second one. We named it Casey.

For the next year, I had Hope, Annie, and Magellan. That is a long time for me to have only three dogs. One day, Gina, a DVGRR volunteer who lives in New Jersey, sent me a message saying: "OMG! There's this dog in New Jersey. He's your dog. Contact Intake and tell them there's a golden in desperate need. He's gotta be your dog!"

There is a big circle of people who are connected by a common love of golden retrievers. Two people in that circle, Kristy and Mary Jo, had pulled the dog from Animal Control, posted his information on Facebook, and everybody was going crazy over this dog. He had been found in an abandoned house and was in really rough shape. His ears were bloody, he was missing huge patches of hair, had tested positive for giardia and Lyme disease, and, to add insult to injury, he was crying. No one knew for certain whether the dog was going to make it but they needed the best place for him to go and who knows goldens better than DVGRR?

The dog spent a night with Mary Jo and the next night with Kristy. The next morning, Kristy and her husband closed on a beach house on Leeward Avenue, so she named him Leeward before bringing the dog to DVGRR.

I was volunteering to walk dogs at DVGRR every Friday and Saturday, so I started visiting Leeward those days. One weekend, Gina sent me a message: "Can you let me know how Leeward is doing?" I sat on the kitchen floor and looked over at Leeward. He had big dark circles around his eyes and big bloody ears. Leeward got up, came over, and put his head on my shoulder. I just said, "Awww, buddy." Even as sick as he was, there was something about Leeward.

The next day, Heather showed me an overnight surveillance video that had been taken in July, just one month after Leeward came in. The video was of Leeward and Teddy, a gigantic golden who had needed surgery. Every night Leeward would reach his paw out to touch Teddy while they slept. During the day, Leeward curled up next to Teddy.

When the video stopped, I turned to Heather and said, "Let me ask you a question. They said they don't know what to do for Leeward. His blood work is all over the place and his hair isn't growing back. You're filling up at the Sanctuary. If you would consider hospice for Leeward, I would love to bring him home and see if I can get him into better shape."

Hope, Annie, and Magellan met Leeward, and although Leeward remained aloof, there was no aggression or growling so I brought him home. Within days, we all started to itch: first Magellan, then Hope, and then me. We finally determined Leeward had mange, which in humans is called scabies. There are two types of mange: demadex, which is non-contagious; and sarcoptic, which is extremely contagious to other animals and humans. Leeward had sarcoptic mange.

After six weeks of treatment and constant vacuuming and steam-cleaning the house, we kicked it. In the meantime, I put Leeward on a really good diet and began giving him coconut oil. Before long, he started putting on weight and his hair grew back. He went from dead dog walking to a dog with an absolutely gorgeous triple coat and a personality to match.

One weekend while at DVGRR, several people asked about Leeward. I told them he was still on hospice but that everything was going really well. One of the people looked at me, smiled, and said, "I think Leeward belonged to someone." I looked at her quizzically and she said, "Let me show you something."

She put Leeward on a leash and began walking with him as if they were in a show ring. When she stopped, Leeward stopped and stacked, a position a dog is trained to do in the show ring. Again, she walked and stopped and Leeward stopped and stacked. I was stunned.

The truth about Leeward was that he genuinely enjoyed being with people and people naturally gravitated to him. He had this big beautiful block head you just wanted to touch. Heather always said when Leeward smiled he looked like a jack-o'-lantern because of the big gaps in his teeth, but you couldn't help smiling when you saw him. There was something absolutely infectious about Leeward—everybody saw it and everybody felt it. It was undeniable.

That year, Leeward went to the DVGRR Gala and had a great time. He arrived in his tuxedo but an hour into the event I replaced his tuxedo with a "Donor" vest and Leeward started to work the room. Actually, he *owned* the room. Walking around that night, he never once begged for food because food was never his motivation. Leeward just enjoyed being around and engaging with people. He loved it and got a lot of donations for DVGRR.

When Heather was grooming Leeward before the Gala, she noticed a problem with his hip, so after the Gala, I had him checked. It turned out that Leeward had soft tissue sarcoma: cancer. The vet also found an egg-shaped lump behind another leg, and before long, lumps started popping up everywhere. He had six lumpectomies to have them all removed but they all came back as cancer.

I'd only had Leeward less than eight months but I knew how old he was and knew we were fighting an aggressive cancer. I knew what chemotherapy would do to him and knew that radiation was painful. I didn't want to put Leeward through any of that, so instead we started him on some Chinese herbal therapies and acupuncture and he responded really well.

In the meantime, Annie had grown old and frail. She was somewhere around sixteen and honestly just wore out. When I looked at her one day while helping her up, she still had a spark in her eye and I knew she wasn't ready. The next day, the spark was gone, and I knew it was time so I called the vet.

From the day I brought Leeward home, it had always been Annie and Leeward. Within the first five minutes of coming home with me, Leeward curled up with Annie. He always had to have his paw over Annie's or just be touching her somewhere. Annie once had a cyst removed from her foot. That night, she began bleeding out and Leeward came and woke me up, saving her life. Leeward loved Annie.

After Annie passed, Leeward and I were both a little lost. We slept a little more, and while I'm not sure if my sorrow exacerbated his, there were definite signs that Leeward missed his sweetheart.

Then I got a call from my friend Sarah at the Animal Rescue League. Sarah knew I wanted my goldens to raise a pit bull puppy and she started telling me about a three-legged pit puppy who had been found chained in an abandoned lot with his mother, brother, and sister. It was suspected they had been beaten in an attempt to get them ready for dog fighting.

The puppy, a little over three months old, had human bite marks on his face. His leg had been broken at the elbow, but since it was never repaired, it had to be surgically removed. Sarah didn't want him to recover at the shelter and wondered if I would foster him.

Two days later, Summit came here, and within five minutes was curled up with Leeward for comfort. Leeward was very tolerant of Summit and his puppy ways. He helped Summit heal, and in turn, Summit helped Leeward heal his broken heart.

Realizing I had all these old dogs, I began looking for a playmate for Summit when along came Woody, a white pit bull who had been found on Woodrow Avenue in Reading, Pennsylvania. I am not a trainer or animal behaviorist but just someone who loves dogs. After spending time with him, I told Sarah I thought Woody was simply a dog who was afraid of everything.

Fearful dogs aren't always afraid of just one thing. At the shelter, Woody sat in his kennel as far away from everyone as he could, his body pressed against the rear wall of the kennel. He shook and barked, and if you approached him, he tried to back away even further.

He did fine walking on leash until he saw someone approaching. At that point, he would pant, shake, and desperately try to get away.

I introduced Woody to Summit and they did well together so I brought him home to foster. I made sure he played and was outside as much as possible with Summit. In the beginning, I didn't try to approach or pet him and essentially ignored him for a while. Before long, Woody was lying in bed with Summit, Leeward, and me. He always made sure he was never far from Summit and walked much better on a leash if Summit was alongside him.

While Woody can be standoffish with strangers, once he has met someone he will come right up to them. I still can't pick Woody up but he now lets me hug him and he likes to snuggle. The more I was with Woody, the more I understood him. I knew he wanted to engage with people but that the stress simply got in the way. I started taking him out in the yard, holding my arm straight out at shoulder height, and say "Touch." Woody would jump up to touch my hand with his nose and then excitedly give me his paw. When he isn't stressed, he is incredibly smart, focused, and wants so much to please. Little by little, he is learning how.

I volunteer to teach a Life Skills course at DVGRR along with a staff trainer. In the middle of one of the classes, I saw an eight-year-old Lab being brought in. A street dog from Puerto Rico, Bennie had been hit by a car, which resulted in an injured leg and spondylosis, a degenerative condition of the spine. DVGRR immediately began giving him injections. While I had never been a Lab person before, I asked Zack, the Adoption Manager, to keep me updated on Bennie.

From the moment they met, Bennie and Leeward were best friends. Having lost Annie, I had room to bring Bennie home. It is amazing to me how I bring dogs home and it works, but that's not me—it's them. My pack was growing. I laughed and told people I finally had a six-pack: Magellan, Hope, Leeward, Bennie, Summit, and Woody.

In the beginning of March, I walked into the living room and only counted five dogs. Leeward was nowhere to be seen. I finally found him sleeping behind the couch, which was something he had never done before, so I knew something was going on. I took him to the vet and X-rays revealed the worst news ever: Leeward was loaded with cancer.

The next day, Leeward and I started working on his bucket list, starting with a trip to the beach. I sat next to him, looked into his eyes, and said, "I don't know if you've ever been to the beach or seen the ocean, Leeward, but you're going to see it today."

Our first stop was at the Rutter's convenience store down the street from my house where I got myself a cup of coffee and French toast sticks for Leeward. He loved them, and from that point on, Rutter's French toast sticks became his special treat and the official travel treat for all of my dogs. We drove to Cape Henlopen State Park and Leeward and I walked on the beach and played in the ocean.

Since he loved the beach, I took Leeward and Hope to Long Beach Island, New Jersey, to visit Kristy, the woman who had originally rescued him and named him Leeward. I took a picture of Kristy and Leeward under the Leeward Avenue street sign and we all had a wonderful time together.

We went to the Bass Pro Shop and the Field & Stream store. Everywhere I went, I took Leeward. I could feel time slipping away and needed every second I could get with him.

On Easter Sunday, eighteen days after discovering the cancer again, we all got up and, like every other day, all the dogs went outside to potty before breakfast. Leeward was a little slower due to the advancement of the cancer but he was still able to get up on his own.

Once everyone was back inside, they all sat and waited while I mixed up their food and medication. Leeward walked up to his bowl, briefly sniffed it, then walked over to lay back down. He had no interest in eating, which happened some days because of an upset stomach.

After breakfast, everyone except Leeward went back outside. By seven o'clock, everyone was back in the house. A few minutes later, Leeward went over to his leash and bumped it with his nose, which was his signal that he wanted to go for a walk or a ride. We hadn't been walking very much since he tired so easily, but I thought maybe a little walk would be good for him. I put on his leash and together we walked out the gate and along the outside perimeter of my backyard fence. We only walked about ten steps when Leeward stopped. I looked down at him and said, "I know you're tired. Is that it, buddy?"

Leeward looked at me and smiled. As we both started to take a step toward one another, Leeward sat down—but it was a different kind of sit. It was the kind of sit you do at the end of a long, exhausting day. Looking up at me one more time, Leeward smiled, and before I could reach out to touch him, his eyes rolled back and he collapsed. Leeward was gone.

I immediately began CPR while dialing the vet's office. It was early and the vet wasn't in but the office staff suggested I drive there. The office was twenty-five minutes away. I got a faint pulse, but before long, Leeward died. I crumbled to the ground cursing God for taking my dog, but the truth is Leeward went the way he wanted to go.

The weekend before Leeward passed, a photographer named Susan, who I met through a mutual friend, sent me a message. As part of Leeward's bucket list, Susan wanted to take pictures of him for me. The day Leeward passed, I posted one of her pictures on Facebook along with this message: "Leeward: Rescued, July 2014; Adopted November 2014; Got his wings March 27, 2016. I will always love you. A piece of me goes with you. Rest now, my gentle friend. My life was better with you than it will be without you."

My phone and Facebook page blew up as people around the country and around the world began reaching out to me. I got messages from people in Australia and Tokyo. It was because of Leeward that I ended up with so many friends on Facebook. People who never met him and only knew him from his pictures and stories were in love with Leeward. When he passed, they cried like I cried.

There have been many suggestions, possibilities, and conjectures on

Edna and Leeward: "My life was better with you
than it will be without you."
Photo courtesy of Susan L. Angstadt

how Leeward came to be found in that abandoned house, but the truth is we will never know. The only thing everybody knew for certain was that there was something special about Leeward. There was something inexplicable that drew you to him. When I saw your term "magical dogs," it made me smile because I always said Leeward was magical. There was something enchanting, something special, something that simply could not be put into words. It was something you felt deep in your heart when you met him and anytime you were with him.

I have a friend who lives in Annapolis, an amazing woman in her own right, who just wanted to touch his head. "I have to touch his head," she would tell me, "because when you touch it, it's magic." Leeward impacted so many people and so many lives. Leeward truly was a magical dog.

People talk about their heart dog, but with Leeward, that word doesn't even come close to describing it. Even saying he was my soul dog doesn't come close to describing it. When I look at the picture Susan took of us, he was that, but the truth is, there simply are no words to describe that or what he meant to me.

After Leeward passed, I worried about Summit. Leeward had raised Summit and was his male role model. Summit was only a year old when Leeward passed and I didn't know how his passing would impact Summit. While Summit was a little lost at the outset, he recovered fairly quickly, which was good because three days after Leeward passed I got a call from Mary Jo.

"I know this is really soon," she began, "but there's an eleven-year-old golden. Her owner has dementia and has been moved to a facility. He is the only owner she has ever known and no one in the family will take her. She's on her way to a kill shelter."

When Mary Jo told me the dog was lumpy and had a huge lipoma, I said, "Mary Jo, I'm not sure what you're asking me. Are you asking if she should go to DVGRR or are you asking me to do hospice for her?"

My eyes were still swollen shut from crying for days over Leeward but the truth is that goldens do not go to kill shelters on my watch. I got in my car and drove to Allentown, Pennsylvania, to meet Mary Jo, Gina, and a dog named Rosita. While her paperwork said she was a therapy dog, we were never able to find any documentation to support that claim. Rosita is sassy, brassy, demanding, and a perfect fit here at The Dog House.

A few weeks after Rosita arrived, I found out Bennie had cancer. We had been doing acupuncture on his spine and three legs, and during one of the sessions, the doctor commented on the size of his belly. I simply looked at the doctor and asked how long. He said, "I don't know. It's pretty big. A couple of days or weeks."

I went home and immediately started on Bennie's bucket list. Just like with Leeward, we began with an order of French toast sticks from Rutter's.

There were so many things I wanted to do with Leeward but we had run out of time, so I started doing them with Bennie. I took him on the Lehigh Gorge Scenic Railway, which is a scenic train tour in Jim Thorpe, Pennsylvania, you can enjoy with your dog. He rode the train and had ice cream and hot dogs. We went to Gettysburg where Bennie became an honorary Park Ranger. We stopped at Rutter's, got a bag of sliders, and ate lunch together on the battlefield. We went to Becky's Drive-In in the Lehigh Valley and that night the movie was *The Secret Life of Pets*. Everything we did was inspired by Leeward, and everywhere I went, Bennie went with me.

They had given us weeks with Bennie but we were lucky. We got seven-and-a-half months. As Christmas approached, Bennie was having mostly good days but he tired easily. I bought him a special cart so he could to go to the DVGRR reunion, and even though he rode around the reunion in the cart, it still took him a week to recover because he was just so tired.

Knowing a traditional Christmas would be too tough for him, I decided instead to have "A Very Bennie Christmas." I invited people to join us for a few minutes at a specific time on Christmas night for our first Facebook live event. I put up lights and a dozen inflatable figures in one corner of our backyard. When we went live, everything was lit up. The first thing I did was focus in on Bennie to let everyone know he was still kicking cancer's butt. I told everyone how much Bennie and I appreciated the outpouring of love and support we had gotten. That Christmas there were no trees, no presents, no rushing around—just a very grateful, very Bennie Christmas.

Almost two months later, on February 16, I went into the basement to get Bennie a clean comforter, and when I came up I looked at him and knew. I got down and held Bennie until he took his last breath. He passed very quickly, didn't suffer, and when he passed, Bennie had a smile on his face.

Once again, I worried about Summit because he slept with Bennie every night, but it turned out that Hope took it the hardest. She curled up on the floor with her head next to Bennie and didn't move for two hours. She just laid there with him. It was like she was completely shut down so I just sat there and waited.

After Bennie passed, Hope's muzzle began to turn dark and tests determined she had a weakened immune system. She was put on medication and regained some of the weight she lost. At thirteen, she is currently in the best condition we can expect considering her age.

Each of my dogs has a theme song. Annie's song, obviously, is John Denver's "Annie's Song"; Bennie's is "Benny and the Jets" by Elton John. Eden was ticklish and whenever you tickled her she crinkled up her nose so her song is "Bubbly" by Colbie Caillat because it talks about crinkling her nose. Rookie's song is "Put Me In, Coach" by John Fogerty; Riley's is "Greatest American Hero" by Joey Scarbury; Casey's is "Funny Face" by Donna Fargo; Rosita's is "Big Noise from Winnetka" by Bette Midler; Megallan's is "Calypso" by John Denver; Summit's is "You'll Never Walk

Alone" by Elvis Presley; Hope's is "All the Animals" by Jewel; and Woody's is "Pure Imagination" from the Willie Wonka movie.

Leeward loved Beyoncé. Anytime I put the music channel on the television, if Beyoncé came on, Leeward would just sit in front of the television and stare. His favorite Beyoncé song was "Halo." I will forever think of Leeward when I hear it, but the theme song I chose for him is Beyoncé's "I Was Here." The song begins by talking about being here, living, loving, and doing everything they wanted. It ends by talking about how life was more than they thought it would be and about leaving a mark so everyone will know they were there. That song is Leeward.

The truth is I bring home the dogs nobody wants, the ones that might not get adopted, and I truly believe that is what I am meant to do. What these dogs have given me in turn is indescribable. It wasn't until I had them that I realized they are my official unofficial support system. I have difficulty talking in crowds, but if I have a dog with me, I am fine. I have great difficulty being somewhere without a dog. I need them as much as they need me.

Individually, the dogs have taught me so many unique, incredible lessons. Casey showed me that despite what people think, how you look, and regardless of your past, life is to be celebrated. She found so much joy in just waking up or rolling in the grass. The food she was eating today might be the same as what she ate yesterday but her attitude was, "Isn't it great?!?!"

Sweet Annie, whose heart beat not just to give her life but also to give others love, was a living, breathing example that love, and the ability to love, is deep within everyone—even an old white-faced dog.

Riley was the reason I began volunteering with DVGRR. I promised him I would, and in keeping that promise, it led me to rescuing dogs and ultimately to the rescue work I do now.

Bennie was the definition of hospice. He was the poster child for giving compassionate care to another being who needs it and allowing them to enjoy every minute. He taught me that dying doesn't mean not living.

Eden showed me the simple, never-ending, indescribable joy of being with dogs, and through her, I began to learn about unconditional love.

Leeward was the dog that completed me. When you lose such a big piece of yourself, time and memories are what remain. I still grieve for

Leeward and haven't been able to absolutely define his lesson for me. Maybe it will come at the end of my life.

Leeward
Photo courtesy of Susan L. Angstadt

I try not to overanalyze what I get from my dogs because if I do, I might miss the true lesson. When they are sick, especially with cancer, they don't know it. They have taught me that here in my Dog House, we need to live for now rather than worry or think about whether there will be a tomorrow.

Chapter Seven
LET'S PAWS: PUPPY MILLS

During interviews for this book, the subject of puppy mills came up re-
peatedly, making me realize it was an important topic to pause and discuss.
For some, it may be a difficult discussion. Puppy mills aren't pretty or fun;
they are heartbreaking and inhumane. The good news is the more we know
about puppy mills, and the more we can spread the word, the greater the
possibility we can change the lives and reality for these dogs. We will begin
with Jackie, the President of United Against Puppy Mills (UAPM), a Lan-
caster County–based organization.

UNITED AGAINST PUPPY MILLS

UNITED AGAINST PUPPY MILLS (UAPM) WAS FOUNDED IN 2005 BY
residents of Lancaster County, Pennsylvania. Our primary mission is to
promote awareness and provide training for anyone interested in affect-
ing positive change for the elimination of puppy mills.

I was led to UAPM after hearing about a breeder in Strasburg, Pennsylvania, who repeatedly paid thousands of dollars in fines only to immediately return to breeding. She didn't care about the fines because
breeding was so lucrative.

While wondering what, if anything, could be done to stop her, I saw
an ad for UAPM. I began as a volunteer and am now the president of
UAPM.

One of the most important things UAPM does is educate people
about puppy mills. People love puppies, but *before* they get a puppy, we
encourage them to investigate not only where the puppy lives but also,
more importantly, where the puppy's parents live.

If a breeder refuses to let you see the parents, tells you the parents
don't live there, or says you can't see the dogs because they are afraid you

might spread disease to the dog, these are all huge red flags! If they allow you to see the parents, watch how they react towards the people in the house. If the dogs appear skittish or fearful around anyone in the home, you need to question why.

A responsible breeder will always allow you to meet the puppy's parents and see where they all live, and they will always take the dog or puppy back regardless of how old or young it is. A reputable breeder will breed a dog once a year. Period. A reputable breeder does not sell their dogs online, in pet stores, or through classified ads and always wants to know where their dog is going.

People think purchasing a puppy from a pet store means they are saving it, but it's not just about the puppy—it's about the puppy's parents, especially the puppy's mother. Since almost every dog in a pet store comes from a puppy mill, buying that puppy simply puts more demand on that puppy's mother to keep breeding while continuing to live in horrific conditions.

Puppy mills are governed by the United States Department of Agriculture (USDA), the federal department responsible for developing, overseeing, and executing federal laws that relate to farming, agriculture, forestry, and food. It is also the umbrella under which our companion animals fall. Why are they governed by the USDA? The short answer is because there was no place else to put them.

We constantly receive questions from people asking about a particular breeder. Since our focus is mainly on Pennsylvania, we maintain a link on our website to the Pennsylvania Department of Agriculture's database of kennels, which includes boarding kennels and nonprofit shelters that do not breed dogs.

In Pennsylvania, every commercial kennel is given a kennel license based on the number of dogs they have on their premises in a year. A K-1 license is given to kennels that have between 26 and 50 dogs, while a K-5 is issued to kennels that have between 251 and 500 dogs. The new CK-6 classification license is for kennels that see more than 500 dogs on their premises in a year. It is up to whoever inspects the kennel—typically the dog warden—to count every dog.

A reputable breeder is unlikely to house more than fifty dogs per year, so the more dogs a kennel has on its premises, the more likely it is that it falls into the category of being a puppy mill. Since breeders often give the public a different kennel name, owner name, or address than the one their license is registered under, we encourage people to search the database in a variety of ways.

The puppy mills have lobbyists. We would love to have lobbyists but they cost a lot of money. We and so many other organizations are fighting an uphill battle, but we all do what we can to get new legislation passed and to educate the public.

I am constantly amazed at the number of people who do not know about puppy mills. While our focus is on educating people about puppy mills, we also try to get them to consider what they are doing by buying that puppy.

To understand the daily life of a puppy mill dog, I tell people to imagine they have a puppy named Logan. What if instead of living in your home, getting regular meals and affection, and playing in your yard, Logan was a puppy mill breeder dog? Logan would spend his life in a crate stacked among other crates being peed and pooped on by other dogs. Logan would get little to no fresh water, would never be petted, would never know love, and his feet would never even touch the ground. No animal lover or compassionate being would want that for Logan, but that is the life and reality for a puppy mill dog.

We have used billboards to educate the public. We put one up that had a picture of puppy mill dogs with the caption: "Before the pet shop, your puppy lived here. His mother still does. End puppy mills. Don't Shop; Rescue or Adopt."

Jackie and Duncan

We put a billboard up in Brick Township, New Jersey, a while back. It cost $2,000 to make and an additional $2,000 to keep it up for three months, but the payoff was tremendous. When the residents saw it, they took it to their zoning committee and got an ordinance passed so that no new pet stores were allowed to open in Brick Township (although existing stores were allowed to remain open).

I currently have three Italian greyhounds and a Chihuahua, all puppy mill dogs. Duncan, one of my Italian greyhounds, was saved when he was two years old by Healing Hearts Italian Greyhound Rescue. He had to have all but two teeth pulled because of a rotted jawline. He had scars and wounds from living in crowded conditions. He now suffers from thyroid issues and tracheal collapse, problems that are typical of senior dogs, but Duncan is only three years old.

Lancaster County is the East Coast capital of puppy mills. Back in 2008, Governor Ed Rendell signed Act 119, which called for the elimination of deplorable conditions in puppy breeding and commercial kennels. The bill addressed the health and welfare needs of the dogs housed in these facilities and set stricter rules and regulations, including physical standards for cage size and flooring.

Lots of puppy mills immediately went underground to avoid being investigated. The legislation wasn't strictly regulated or enforced and monies allocated to institute the law went elsewhere.

There is one kennel that has been noncompliant for years. Dog wardens and inspectors have to wear gas masks when they go there due to the acidic pH of the environment. These kennels house big-eyed dogs, like pugs, who are particularly sensitive to acidic conditions. It can create lesions in their eyes, which attract dust particles that result in eye infections leading to blindness or a need for their eyes to be enucleated. And yet these kennels are still allowed to produce puppies.

Ten years ago, I had an Amish puppy mill breeder come up to me after one of our presentations and tell me he didn't care how many dogs were euthanized a year because, in his own words, "As long as there's a demand, we'll supply."

Another breeder in Lancaster County, after being convicted of animal abuse and learning their veterinarian's license was rescinded, told me to "Get the hell out of our county." Another breeder walked up to me and said, "I hope you're happy. You city girls need to mind your own business." I told him I wasn't a city girl, had been brought up by my grandparents on a one-hundred-acre cattle farm, and could plant tobacco and throw hay bales like the best of them. He listened, sneered at me, and said, "I'm from New York. If I ever see you in New York, I'll come get you."

Despite the threats and the setbacks, we still remain hopeful. UAPM will continue educating and spreading the word. Our hope is that people coming to Lancaster County to buy a puppy understand exactly where they are getting that puppy from. They need to understand that, while the puppy might be getting out, its parents will remain behind living in deplorable conditions probably for the rest of their lives.

THE PUPPY MILL PROJECT

Next I interviewed Cari, the founder of The Puppy Mill Project, an educational and advocacy organization dedicated to fighting puppy mills and puppy mill cruelty based in Chicago, Illinois.

THERE'S NO QUESTION I WAS BORN WITH A LOVE FOR DOGS IN MY heart and my soul. I have never been without a dog for even one day my entire life. I currently have three rescue dogs, including one from a puppy mill.

Before I knew about puppy mills, I bought an Eskipoo from a pet store outside of Chicago. She had a face like a Samoyed, her hair was crazy, and when I first saw her, I thought, "What a sad-looking puppy." The pet store had reduced her price so I bought her and named her Freddi. She was quirky and would jump up and sit in the middle of the kitchen table. If you didn't stop her, she would kiss you and literally continue kissing you for hours. Freddi grew into the most beautiful, wonderful dog and has become my heart dog.

One night, I was in bed on my computer. Freddi was lying next to me and I truly believe she guided me to an article on puppy mills. Looking at Freddi, I began reading—and was sickened by what I read. I could not believe these cruel, horrible places were legal, that no one was doing anything to stop the cruelty, and, even worse, that most people didn't even know they existed.

As I continued investigating, I decided to do something to stop the horrific cruelty of this multi-billion dollar industry. In 2009, I started The Puppy Mill Project. We educate the public about puppy mills, facilitate rescue, and advocate for change.

Puppy mills are a huge industry. There isn't a state in the country that is untouched by puppy mills. Even if they don't have a puppy mill in their state, they have pet stores. People need to understand that, despite what they are being told, reputable breeders don't sell to pet stores. Unless a pet store has been transformed into a humane location that only has dogs from a rescue, the puppies in that store are coming from puppy mills.

To sell to a pet store, a breeder must obtain a USDA license, but the fact that a breeder has a USDA license does not provide assurance of humane breeding. It simply means it is held to a very minimal standard of care and is most likely a puppy mill.

The people who operate the puppy mills are millers. I refuse to call them breeders because that's not what they are or what they do. They are millers who have been lying to consumers for years and relying on consumer ignorance.

Our mission is to find a way to stop this and cut off the pipeline. People often ask me why we don't just shut the mills down. If we could have, we would have, but there are 10,000 puppy mills in this country. Approximately 3,200 of them are licensed by the United States Department of Agriculture (USDA), and the ones that aren't licensed are often hidden down some back country road out of sight.

A handful of USDA inspectors are assigned to go around the country to inspect anything having to do with agriculture on an annual basis. Maybe the inspections happen; maybe they don't.

Typically the millers get a slap on the wrist by the USDA inspector and are told what they have to do to correct any violations. The inspector may—or may not—go back to ensure the corrections are made. We know of puppy mills that have had repeated violations over the years yet are still allowed to remain open.

There was a licensed miller in Illinois who had beagles. When the USDA inspector showed up, there was one part of the barn that needed to be fixed. The inspector told the miller to fix that part of the barn because it was impacting the health and welfare of the six beagles in that section. She wrote it up and surprisingly went back the next month to check on the repairs. What the inspector found when she returned was that not only had the repairs not been made, but that the six dogs were missing. When she asked the miller about the dogs, he said he had hit them over the head with an iron pipe. Instead of fixing a section of the barn, he chose to kill the dogs.

To make matters worse, the USDA inspector never reported it to the

State of Illinois. When we found out, we took it to the attorney general in that area who went after the miller. He was fined and lost his license. We got a beagle rescue to go in and take the rest of the dogs he had, but I heard recently that he may be back in business so now we have to be vigilant again. This work is nonstop.

To add to that is the unbelievable cruelty of what these dogs experience. The Animal Welfare Act, which was signed into law in 1966, is the only federal law to regulate the treatment of animals in research and exhibition. While it governs the mills, it is also very vague. It essentially says animals need to have adequate food, shelter, and water, but what "adequate" means to you or me means something very different to a miller.

Two months ago, someone reached out to me about a miller in Indiana who had multiple violations and was not supposed to have dogs, but she had ten Shih Tzus living in an old underground bunker with very little air and no light. She also had two bulldogs chained to a pile of garbage and another bulldog and a black Lab running free. Someone got wind of what was going on and Animal Control rescued the dogs. We were able to place them with several wonderful rescues.

Every single one of those dogs has a great home now, but on the day they came out of that underground bunker, they couldn't see. They had never been outside or in the light. Two of the workers were hospitalized because of the incredibly poor air quality inside that bunker.

People don't realize the cruelty and the horrors these dogs endure—and believe me, that particular situation is far from the worst we have seen. People need to understand that this industry places profit over the health and well-being of the dogs. Veterinary care, humane living conditions, and adequate staffing all cut into profit margins so they are kept to a minimum—if they exist at all. Even after the millers are busted and their dogs are taken away, they typically pop up elsewhere because this is so lucrative for them.

To add to the inhumanity, there are the dog auctions where millers sell the breeding dogs they no longer want. They hold the dogs up like livestock and sell some for as little as a penny. You can have a dog with two legs and one eye and the miller says, "She's good for one more litter." That poor dog has just left one hell for another because other millers buy these dogs, and on the way out, they are given an AKC certificate for the dog. There is no confirmed lineage so I have no idea how they get the certificate—but they do.

This industry is like an onion: you peel back one layer and you get to another. It is an enormous industry—and is enormously cruel, valuing money over morals. They crank these dogs out without concern for their health or well-being.

In 2009, when we started, there were only two ordinances—in New Mexico and California—regarding the sale of companion animals in pet stores in the United States. Since then, over 225 ordinances have been passed in municipalities across the country. When ordinances were passed in Chicago, it stopped 2,000 puppy mill dogs from being brought in from Iowa and sold in pet stores.

Two pet stores filed a lawsuit against me and The Puppy Mill Project claiming the City of Chicago pet store ordinance impacted them. They lost, appealed, and lost again, so the two pet stores created a phony 501(c)(3) and said the dogs they were selling for $2,000 to $3,000 were rescue dogs. What rescue ever charges $2,000 for a dog? These are puppy mill dogs with a rescue label. These are people who will do and say anything to keep the money pouring in.

There's a misconception, often reinforced by the pet stores, that you can't find purebred dogs or puppies at a rescue, but that is absolutely not true. Almost every rescue or shelter will have purebred dogs and there are also breed-specific rescues.

We work very hard to educate people but people who don't listen or simply don't care are an ongoing frustration. They go into a pet store to "just look," but how many people can walk out of a pet store without something tugging at their heart strings? Pet store staff assures buyers that their puppies are from a private breeder and that they have AKC paperwork to prove it, but it's all a lie. It is only after they have brought that precious puppy home that the dog's physical, emotional, or psychological problems surface. We constantly receive emails about puppies people brought home that died or are at the emergency vet. Our frustration is how to get people to understand and care.

One person recently told me they knew the puppy was from a mill but that "buying from a pet store is so much easier than going to a rescue." I know there are people we won't reach. I know there are people who think, "It's easy, I want it, and I want it now," but in getting that puppy, they are putting money in a miller's pocket, have potentially purchased a sick puppy, and are keeping the whole industry going.

We, along with organizations around the country, are trying to get word out that if people stop shopping in pet stores, we can cut the head off the dragon. I believe that as people get more educated they will no longer want to go to a pet store to get an animal. I believe the winds of change are here.

Three years ago, I went to volunteer at the National Mill Dog Rescue in Colorado. Before we left, I told the people I was traveling with, "No dogs for me. None. Get it? I can't bring any more dogs home."

The first morning I walked in and saw Millie and her sister. Millie's eyes looked a lot like Freddi's but she was a hot mess. She had been there two weeks and you couldn't go into her cage. She constantly walked side to side in her cage or circled.

I decided to spend the three days we were going to be there with Millie. I wanted to hold her and try socializing her. Even after Millie let me hold her, she remained very tense. Every time I approached her crate, she would go into a corner or hit the ground in what we call a pancake position.

On our last night, we all went out to dinner and everyone asked if I was going to adopt her. I reminded them I couldn't, but the next morning, I changed my mind. "I can't go home without Millie," I told them. "Millie is mine."

Cari and Millie
Photo courtesy of
Karen Morgan Photography

Since she wasn't spayed and didn't have a health certificate to travel, I had to leave Millie there. Three weeks later, a pilot on Southwest Airlines took her on board his flight and brought her to me.

Millie was from a Kansas puppy mill. For eight years, she had lived her life in a cage as a breeding dog. She had already had thirteen teeth removed and had to have a hysterectomy. Chronic ear problems resulted in permanent hearing loss so she could no longer hear very well.

When Millie came to us, she wouldn't

look at us, which is common with puppy mill dogs. Part of their survival mode is to avoid looking directly at a person. They will look past you or beyond you but never directly at you or into your eyes. It was months before Millie looked at me.

Puppy mill dogs are not your average rescue dog. They are special needs. They haven't been socialized and have never walked on the ground. They have spent every day of their lives sitting in cages, in barns, or outside. Some live in darkness and only come out when the miller grabs them to put them in the cage to be bred. As a result, they are typically terrified of human beings since all they have ever known or experienced from humans has been cruelty. As a result, they are not cuddlers or cozy little lap dogs. For some dogs, it can take a year before they even want to be touched.

Some puppy mill dogs are runners and will try to flee. My guess is that because they have never been free. they will bolt any chance they get. The first day I had Millie, she tried to run to the house next door.

I had to be careful how I approached Millie so as not to frighten her. She is still not completely housebroken, but Millie is a gorgeous, sweet, angelic dog. The other day she gave me a kiss for the first time. We had a big celebration because moments like that are huge for dogs like Millie. It's a sign they are beginning to embrace their new life.

The Puppy Mill Project recently created Millie's Mission, where any rescue anywhere in the country who has a legitimate 501(c)(3) and is rescuing mill dogs can apply for grant money from us for vet bills or to get a mill dog into shape. We do this to encourage rescues to pull more puppy mill dogs, because the truth is there are just too many.

I do this every day and it's a lot. I could go sell shoes somewhere and walk out of work every night at five o'clock and be done for the day, but then I look at Millie curled up next to me and know that will never happen. I look at this little girl who still, after all these years, cannot walk down the stairs and will pancake flat on the ground if anyone unexpectedly comes up behind her.

Millie's health and other issues are from years of neglect so how, after knowing what I know, can I stop fighting for these dogs? Why are millers allowed to do their own C-sections and other horrible things to these dogs? How do we live with that? Why are puppy mills even allowed? I cannot turn my head and heart off. I feel a huge responsibility to these animals.

We have a campaign called "It's Not Cool to Be Cruel," that we take into the schools to teach the younger generation that it's just as important to be kind to their dog, cat or any animal as it is to be kind to their brother, sister, parent, or any person.

We want all generations to understand that everything begins with a thought. People need to understand they *can* do something. The public has the power to close this horrible industry down. People can do it; the consumers can do it.

Get involved by starting in your own community. Is there an organization you can align yourself with? Are there pet stores selling dogs in your town, and if so, where are their dogs coming from? What are the pet stores telling consumers? Educate yourself and educate others.

If there are pet stores selling puppy mill dogs, go to your legislators and educate them. Explain that this isn't a business you want or need in your town. Suggest that pet stores in your town "sell" rescue dogs rather than importing dogs to your state. Why breed and import puppy mill dogs when there are millions of dogs being killed every year?

People get upset about cruelty toward one animal—and they should—but how do you wrap your mind around the abuse of thousands of dogs? We need to ferret out legislators who won't take a stand against this immoral industry. The truth is you can't pass more laws to govern the mills or have more inspections to make a puppy mill better because there *is* no way to make a puppy mill better. You are not going to make a difference in the lives of these dogs as long as puppy mills are allowed to remain open.

Puppy mills are one of the largest systemic forms of animal cruelty in this country. They are an industry that must be stopped, permanently, and The Puppy Mill Project is working every day to make that a reality.

I don't know how these dogs survive and keep going, but they are my heroes. My mantra has always been not to focus on where these dogs came from but on where they are going. Otherwise, I would never be able to get out of bed in the morning.

BAILING OUT BENJI

Finally, I reached out to Mindi, the founder of Bailing Out Benji. What began as a small nonprofit based in Iowa has now grown into a nationwide organization dedicated to changing the world for companion animals by educating and raising social consciousness about various animal welfare issues—specifically puppy mills.

MY SISTER AND I LOVED ANIMALS AND WERE ALWAYS TAKING IN stray cats. We promised our mom we would find the cats a home but they usually ended up staying with us.

When I went away to college, I was homesick. To deal with it, I would go to the local Petland to see the dogs. On one visit, a Siberian husky puppy caught my eye and I kept going back to visit him. The employees, sensing a possible sale, started painting a picture in my mind of the two of us together. They would let me take him into another room to play and would come in and ask me, "If he was your puppy, what would you name him?" I told them I would name him Ozzy but reminded them I was a nineteen-year-old starving college student—and that the puppy cost $1,200. Not surprisingly, they had a solution to that problem as well: a store credit card.

I used their store credit card and bought Ozzy. I was in heaven. One week later, a local news station did a story on puppy mills—and focused on the store where I had bought Ozzy. I had never heard of puppy mills before and was devastated when I realized Ozzy had come from a puppy mill. I worried about his health, but thankfully he was healthy.

Two years later, something happened that made me understand puppy mills were a much bigger problem than I first realized—and one I could no longer ignore.

At the time, my now-husband and I were living in Ames, Iowa, and had adopted two rescue Labs. One of them, Ellie, was pregnant and soon gave birth to ten puppies. Around the same time, I saw a story about a woman who was staying in a hotel with a black Lab and her nine puppies. Having a mama dog and puppies ourselves, I was empathetic to what this woman was going through. However, as I continued following the story, I learned that the dogs weren't being properly cared for, were

Mindi with Ellie,
mama of the ten puppies

living in filth, and that the puppies were drinking their own urine to survive.

After seeing the television segment on puppy mills and doing my own research, I was appalled at what I learned. I learned that, despite the filth and horror that mother dog and her puppies were living in, based on the laws in Iowa, the woman would just get a slap on the wrist. I learned that someone could shoot their dog in Iowa and get the same slap on the wrist. I learned that Iowa was consistently ranked forty-ninth in the nation for laws that support animal welfare.

All of this created the perfect storm for me to have my aha! moment and start a blog. Since everyone at the time was talking about bailing out the banks, but no one was doing anything to bail out or help these dogs, I called the blog Bailing Out Benji.

People commonly ask, "Who is Benji?" They assume that Benji was my dog or a specific dog, but the truth is that Benji is *every* dog who has spent their life in a puppy mill or chained up in someone's backyard. Benji is every dog who has ever suffered and died without ever having a name or knowing kindness, dignity, or love.

Through Bailing Out Benji, we are not only giving those dogs a name and a voice but we are also serving as a constant reminder to those who insist on hurting innocent creatures that we are watching.

My goal was to create posts that were educational without being graphic. For some people, seeing a sad or emaciated dog gets them fired up, but other people, like me, are very empathetic and seeing things like that can cause them to turn away. I didn't want to turn anyone away so the only graphic photos you ever see are when we go in to save the dog. While those photos may show the hell the dogs were living in, at the end it is a happy post because we save them from that hell. Our focus is always on kindness and compassion.

For years, the United States Department of Agriculture maintained breeder data on their website that included the breeder's address as well as their USDA inspection reports. Last February, there was a USDA blackout, and during that time, they took that data down saying it was a breach of privacy for the breeders. It didn't matter that the breeders were a public business and selling to the public—it was all removed.

We had a hunch they were going to do that, so our volunteers worked overtime in advance of the blackout and saved all of the USDA data. Based on that data, we were able to create puppy mill maps so that you can see the number of puppy mills in your backyard. There is also information on pet stores who buy their dogs from puppy mills along with the name and location of those puppy mills.

There is a common belief and statistic tossed around that the Amish run 20 percent of the puppy mills. The data showed us that the percentage of Amish-run puppy mills varies by state. Here in Iowa, approximately 22 percent are Amish, but in Pennsylvania the number is closer to 63 percent. According to the USDA statistics, in Ohio over 98 percent of the puppy mills are run by the Amish. Keep in mind that number can change year to year since some mills go out of business while others open.

We had been doing this for four years when we were filmed to be part of a documentary called *Dog by Dog*, which is currently available on Netflix. Being in that documentary helped us get volunteers in other states. As we grew, we got the attention of the puppy mill owners. Some of them chose to give their dogs to us when they were done breeding them, starting with one helper at an Amish breeder here in Iowa.

Every year, the Humane Society publishes a Horrible Hundred List that lists the worst one hundred puppy mills in the nation. Every year, without fail, Iowa and Missouri make up half the list. The Amish breeder that helper worked for was on the list.

The helper sent us an email saying, "We have dogs we don't want anymore. Would you want to find them a home?" I honestly thought it was a joke, but my husband and I went over there anyway and ended up taking the dogs he wanted to get rid of. Since that time, my husband and I have gotten over sixty dogs from this one Amish breeder.

His dogs are always in horrible condition: long nails, matted fur, dirty, heart conditions along with genetic conditions that are being passed on to their puppies. To add insult to injury, the man and his son aren't nice to the dogs. The dogs have no emotional value to them and have a horrible life and existence. When we started getting dogs from him, he had over 150 dogs on his property. He is slowly downsizing and getting rid of the dogs since he has decided to finally go out of business.

The thing we all need to understand is that the people who run the puppy mills believe it is a dog's purpose to have litters and it is their purpose to sell the puppies. They have no empathy for these animals and don't think what they are doing is wrong.

This year alone, we have rescued 312 dogs from puppy mills and we helped three puppy mill breeders close their doors for good. It's hard because our volunteers take any dog the breeders give us and then we need to vet them, foster them, and get them adopted or to one of our rescue partners.

The recurring theme over the last year is that a lot of the breeders are saying they can't sell anymore because they're on lists or people are sharing information about puppy mills. Pet stores are being held to a higher standard, and in some towns you can't buy from a breeder if they have a violation. Some of the worst breeders are shutting down because they have no place to sell the dogs.

That's wonderful because one of the most important things we need to remember is that rescuing is just a Band-Aid. The idea of "Adopt, Don't Shop" is ideal and wonderful, but we are never going to adopt our way out of this problem so educating the general public is critical.

People are wrapped up in their own worlds. That means we need to make our information readily available, and having access to social media and the internet makes that easier than ever before. If we can get the information to people and have them do their research *before* they get a dog, the demand will go down.

No one wants to know that their dog came from a place where dogs are being tortured or treated inhumanely. We all want to know our dog and its parents were well cared for before we got them. At the end of the day, we need to have a coalition of reputable breeders, rescuers, and animal advocates standing up against the puppy mills.

The rescue world knows there are reputable breeders who aren't milling out their puppies, who love and properly care for their dogs, and hate puppy mills. To see real change, it can't be an us–against–them mentality; we need to work together. Puppy mills are making billions of dollars and one of the reasons they can is because we remain divided in our efforts.

Auctions are another little-known facet of the puppy mill industry. Just like a car or farm auction, there are dogs upon dogs upon dogs you can bid on. If a breeder is going out of business, he may have five dogs up on a table, and if you win, you have the option to take as many of those five dogs as you want.

In 2015, an Iowa breeder who was one of the Horrible Hundred was closing and decided to sell their dogs rather than give them to rescues. Out of 300 dogs at this particular auction, there was one black Lab. Since my husband and I love black Labs, we went.

The auctioneer's catalog said the Lab was eighteen months old and had already had three litters of puppies. The inspection report said she had open wounds and scars from dog fights. This tiny puppy had been living in an outdoor kennel with bigger male poodles so she could produce the next litter of Labradoodles. While giving birth to and caring for her puppies, she was repeatedly attacked by the male poodles, so she spent her days trying to protect herself and her puppies.

I knew we weren't going home without her—and we didn't. Lola has been with us for three years, and to this day, she still has flashbacks. If there are baby bunnies in the backyard, she goes out and protects them. If we foster puppies, she is always very protective of them. In those moments, Lola goes back to being that mama trying to protect her own puppies.

Every puppy mill has the same smell. It is a combination of filth, feces, urine, hormones, and stress. It is the weirdest smell and it never leaves your nose. When we come home from a rescue, Lola is super snuggly and more loving because she can smell it. She knows where we have been and what we have done. She knows we have saved another dog. Every day, Lola reminds me why I am doing this.

Chapter Eight
MONKEY'S HOUSE

Several weeks after visiting Lancaster County, I was the keynote speaker at a state hospice conference since I am a Certified Alzheimer's Educator, author, and former Alzheimer's caregiver.

Over lunch, I sat with a wonderful group of hospice staff and volunteers. Our conversation was lively and diverse. At one point, we discussed hospice care for animals and someone mentioned Monkey's House, a sanctuary that provided hospice care to senior dogs.

A few weeks later, I contacted Michele, the co-founder and Director of Monkey's House, and arranged for a visit. The day I arrived, Michele came out to welcome me and instructed me to walk in the house, ignore the dogs, and head into the family room.

I did as Michele instructed, and once I was seated, Michele gave the dogs a signal. As if by magic, they all stopped barking. Several casually sauntered over to smell me.

There were dogs relaxing and sleeping everywhere on dog beds, daybeds, chairs, quilts, and the floor. Other than a couch and a few pieces of furniture, this was a home that clearly existed for the comfort, care, and well-being of dogs. Much like Edna's home, it was—in the best sense of the words—a dog house.

Three small dogs clambered up a small ramp in front of the couch where Michele was seated. One curled up in her arms, another next to her, and the third behind her. The two dogs sniffing me decided instead to curl up at my feet. With everyone now settled, Michele began to tell me about Monkey's House.

I HAVE ONLY INTENTIONALLY GONE TO A SHELTER TO ADOPT A dog twice in my life because somehow dogs always seem to find me. Emmy is a perfect example.

Emmy was an Australian shepherd mix a close friend gave me after I was involved in a car accident. I had amnesia, and my friend thought Emmy would be a great project for me. Emmy was much more than a project. She was a great companion and friend and truly meant the world to me.

Emmy developed chronic pancreatitis when she was thirteen and I lost her quite suddenly. Every time I walked into the house and Emmy wasn't there, the silence was deafening. My home, life, and heart felt incredibly empty, so I contacted a friend who worked at a shelter and told her, "Get me a dog. It can be old, ugly, I don't care. Just please get me a dog." She explained she would be happy to help but I needed to fill out an application, get approved, and then come meet some dogs.

When I filled out the application, I stressed that I wanted to see dogs that other people might not want. After I was approved, my friend called and said she had a few dogs she wanted me to meet.

The first dog was Poncho, a seven-year-old, fourteen-pound terrier mix who smelled horrible but had a crazy smile. I instantly fell in love with Poncho and adopted him. The next dog was McKenzie, an incredibly sweet thirteen-year-old Shih Tzu. My original intention was to only adopt one dog, but I didn't want a senior dog left at a shelter so McKenzie came home with me too.

While Poncho and McKenzie didn't lessen the pain of losing Emmy, they helped me move forward, and I was grateful for the joy they brought into my life. In gratitude to the shelter, I started dropping towels off on a regular basis. When my coworkers found out, they started giving me supplies for the shelter too.

Next I began fostering, and my second foster was Goldie, a golden retriever. When I picked her up from the shelter, they told me she had an appointment with their vet on Wednesday to have a tumor removed.

I brought Goldie home and soon instinctively knew there was something else wrong with her. Fosters agree to use the shelter's vet. If a foster takes a dog elsewhere, they assume the cost. I wanted a second opinion so I made an appointment for Goldie with my vet at my own expense. He also felt there was something else wrong but without extensive testing there was no way to know exactly what it could be.

I called the shelter and tried to explain that something was very wrong with Goldie but they told me to stick with the original plan and drop her off at their vet for surgery on Wednesday.

Shelters have to approach situations from a different perspective because many times they simply are not set up to do everything they can for a sick or dying dog. Often they have to face the reality that they can do a community rabies clinic for the same cost as treating one sick or dying dog so they have to make a choice.

I had to make a choice as well, so I called the shelter's vet and made an appointment using a false name and information. It was completely out of character for me but I didn't want them to know it was me—or Goldie—coming in.

I sat in the vet's office that day struggling with what I was doing. Honesty, ethics, and my credibility are everything to me but here I was outright lying to them. By the time they brought us in to see the vet, I immediately burst into tears and the truth poured out. I admitted I was there without the shelter's knowledge and didn't want to get her into trouble, but I was concerned there was something really wrong with Goldie. I took a breath and said I was paying for the appointment and assumed full responsibility for my actions.

The vet smiled and said, "You're not lying. You're being a dog advocate." And with that, she began to examine Goldie.

Goldie had a brain tumor so we adopted her. She was with us for a very short time and was euthanized here in our home. I still have her ashes because I am not ready to let go of them. I just want her here.

After Goldie, my husband, Jeff, and I began fostering and caring for sick and dying dogs. Before long, we started adopting them and spending our own money to get them the care they needed.

Jeff and I were both working, and while he was on board with what I was doing, we both knew we couldn't keep going on like that forever. We decided to simply adjust our lifestyle, starting with no longer taking vacations and only taking in as many dogs as I could properly care for.

We continued to help two or three dogs a year, and I also began to enroll in every dog and behavior class I could find. I wanted to learn everything I could so I could figure out how to take care of really sick dogs.

In the fall of 2013, a shelter called us about a stray dog named Monkey. Possibly a Pekingese–Chihuahua mix, they estimated Monkey was about nine years old. He had a cough the shelter determined was caused by a severe heart murmur, which made him unadoptable. When the shelter asked if I would foster Monkey, my answer was an immediate, "Sure!"

Monkey had a respiratory rate of eighty. With my background in nursing, I knew a

Michele and Monkey

rate that high makes it feel like you can't breathe. In addition, whenever he got excited, Monkey's gums turned blue and he got extremely uncoordinated and collapsed. Knowing it was a quality of life issue for Monkey, I asked the shelter vet for medication, but he refused and told me, "Just take him home and enjoy him for a few weeks."

Instead, I adopted Monkey and took him to my vet and then to a cardiologist. Every visit to the cardiologist cost five hundred dollars. I knew we couldn't afford it but I also knew we weren't going to stop. Once again, we tightened our belts and adjusted our lifestyle, thinking that after Monkey passed, we would take a break to rebuild ourselves and our rapidly disappearing finances.

Once Monkey's heart issues were under control, we then faced a mouth full of teeth in horrible condition and breath that was simply horrendous. The pain from his mouth often caused Monkey to be grumpy and forego eating so we coordinated his dental surgery with the cardiologist. Monkey was left with only his canines—and we were left with a grateful, happy dog.

In the midst of dealing with all of Monkey's health issues, I attended a seminar where I met Dr. Judy Morgan. I pummeled her with questions about dogs and nutrition and she had answers for them all, so I made an appointment for a nutritional consultation for Monkey.

When we walked into her office, Dr. Morgan reached out to check Monkey but I immediately stopped her and said, "You can't touch him. He's not user-friendly." I will never forget the look on her face but the truth was that Monkey bit. He only had four teeth so he couldn't do any damage but he still bit.

For the rest of the exam, Dr. Morgan pointed to whatever she wanted to see and I would pull back his lips, paws, or whatever she needed. It was also the beginning of a great friendship.

One of my concerns was that Monkey had become reclusive, hiding upstairs in our closet. I was afraid his reclusiveness was because he was suffering. We had begun to think about putting him down if we were unable to improve his quality of life.

When I told Dr. Morgan about Monkey hiding in our closet, she immediately asked what happened in May. I told her my horse had died, and since all of our horses and dogs are older and uninsurable, we had spent our emergency fund to take care of the horse. The result was that we were forced to switch some of the dogs' diets to save money.

"You don't want to do that with Monkey," Dr. Morgan said, and went on to tell me I needed to feed Monkey beef heart, eggs, and sardines. Deciding I had nothing to lose, I followed Dr. Morgan's recommendations. Within a few days, Monkey was back to being himself and happy.

As a traditionally trained, science-based nurse, you question these things, but the proof was in the pudding. Everything Dr. Morgan told me to do for Monkey worked, and the more I adjusted the dogs' diets, the better their response and quality of life. I started seeing dogs getting relief from arthritis. I witnessed dogs becoming happier and more active. Looking into the backyard, I saw dogs zooming around with Frisbees in their mouths and thought, "We found the missing link. The nutritional aspect is what we need to help these dogs."

Dr. Morgan helped give Monkey a great quality of life. Everything sent him spinning in happy circles. He was filled with such joy and loved walks and car rides. She also added to his longevity. Here was a dog we were supposed to take home and "enjoy for a few weeks," but instead he made our life amazing for seventeen months.

Losing Monkey was the worst. We had loved many dogs but there was something about Monkey. He had become the center of our universe and we were beyond devastated.

My husband and I decided to take a break from fostering or adopting dogs to replenish our finances. I knew that if we let our grief simply be about constant tears it would be a waste of energy, so we began to talk. We knew the desperate need for these dogs and we wanted to do something to honor Monkey, so we decided to open Monkey's House.

A lot of really wonderful, generous people stepped up to make it happen. An attorney helped with the 501(c)(3) and another friend helped us write by-laws. Dr. Morgan agreed to assist and also helped us get volunteers and funding. She also became our first foster home—and foster failure—because that is the kind of vet, friend, and person she is. To see someone who has been a vet for over thirty years so in love with these older, stinky dogs still amazes me. They aren't easy dogs but they rock her world.

We were still two normal people living in a normal house and that had to change, too. After a lot of brainstorming, we began transitioning our house into a home for sick and dying dogs.

Early on, the majority of dogs were coming from a kill shelter in Philadelphia. As an open intake shelter, they can't refuse any dog, but with fifty kennels and 300 dogs, it doesn't bode well for many of the dogs at the end of the week. They are forced to time-stamp, which is when you read a post about a dog that ends with: "The dog has until eight o'clock tonight." When you read that, it's tough.

It's also difficult to choose an older dog with cancer hanging off its side and leave behind a two-year-old dog whose only problem is that he has long nails and tartar, but I have to accept that is not what I have chosen to do and that the senior dogs are my specialty. If I fell in love with and took in the young ones, it would mean not helping the ones I believe I was meant to work with.

I think the easiest way to continue telling you about Monkey's House is to tell you about some of the dogs that are here with us, starting with this dog curled up next to me on the couch.

This is Buck. He was our third pull from the Philly shelter. He had bad skin, dental disease, flea dermatitis, and his paperwork said he had a grade 3 heart murmur, making Buck a perfect dog for Monkey's House.

Buck had two seizures in the car on the way home, and when we got here, we found out he wasn't good with other dogs. If he got excited, he would stumble and pass out, so I kept him in the quiet part of the house. Dr. Morgan was away so I gave him a bath to get rid of the flea problem. Having learned about cooling foods from Dr. Morgan, I started chipping away at some of his problems through his diet.

By the time Dr. Morgan saw Buck, I had determined he couldn't see very well and was almost completely deaf. She determined he actually had a grade 5 heart murmur and was in pretty bad shape.

We got Buck neutered and had dental work done. Healing his mouth infection helped his heart and cleaning up his diet got the inflammation under control and improved his quality of life. We added supplements to slow the growth of a cancerous tumor, and two years later, Buck is still with us. He is completely blind now but he doesn't know he's blind. He's happy and has a great quality of life.

When I first saw Buck, I thought he looked a lot like Monkey. I was worried about that but honestly, it's been fine. Buck has such enthusiasm in just being alive that he spins in circles when he gets excited, just like Monkey. All of that warms my heart and is very healing to my soul. I'm so thankful Buck is still with us.

The little Chihuahua in the dainty pink dress quietly sleeping on the other side of the room is Daisy. She was found wandering the streets in Philly. It was believed she had survived by eating twigs and the resulting lack of nutrition caused her to lose her hair. Her nails were so long that they had actually grown in circles. She had two large hernias and some of her internal organs were, quite literally, hanging outside her body. She had a grade 5 heart murmur and it was suspected she was feral. In short, she was a hot mess and had been time-stamped.

Dr. Morgan performed surgery on Daisy and did an incredible job. Two years later, while her heart disease is progressing, her quality of life remains quite amazing and she has gone from being a suspected feral dog to being quite domesticated and loving.

The small cream-colored poodle lying next to Daisy is Fifi. When Fifi's owner died, the family took her to the shelter, and the shelter time-stamped her. We often tell the shelter that if a dog is time-stamped to put us down as a last resort. That means if no one else steps up before the dog's time is up, the shelter calls us to come get the dog.

We were a last resort for Fifi. The shelter said she probably wasn't going to last another day and delivered her to us. When she arrived, her little body was covered in urine and she had blood clots hanging from her mouth. I cleaned her up but I knew she needed to see Dr. Morgan.

It was a long drive to Dr. Morgan's office and the entire way it felt like Fifi was dying. Dr. Morgan made a list of everything that was wrong with Fifi: her teeth were a mess, she was on the verge of pyometrea (a uterine infection), sepsis, and dehydration. Her blood work revealed diabetes and her breath had an acetone smell, which made her suspect for a diabetic emergency—and possibly on the verge of a diabetic coma.

I have a nursing background so Dr. Morgan loaned me an intravenous pump and we turned our bathroom into a mini intensive care unit. We no sooner finished getting everything ready than Fifi slipped into a diabetic coma. For the next few days, Fifi fell in and out of consciousness. I sat and held her the entire time, because if she was going to pass, I wanted it to be in my arms being loved. I continued giving her IV fluids, antibiotics, insulin, and kept her hydrated.

While I was busy with Fifi, incredible volunteers came over and put dishes in the dishwasher, did laundry, walked dogs, and helped run things at Monkey's House.

Then one day, Fifi just woke up. My husband came home from work that day, saw me sitting in the family room, and asked, "You're out?" I nodded.

"Who's that?" He pointed to the dog lying next to me.

"Fifi."

"It can't be."

I assured him it was. She was still fragile but we continued to monitor her. Once she was well enough, Dr. Anthony pulled out twenty infected teeth.

Fifi is an insulin-dependent diabetic. Her blood sugar suddenly drops very low for no reason. I can usually tell when it's about to happen so I rub syrup on her gums and wait for her sugar to stabilize. It's a challenging disease but something we can live with, and we can still give her a lot of love.

Fifi was fifteen when she was surrendered. She's now sixteen and a half. She is a very cool dog and a complete mush head. I believe she was loved in her previous life because she loves to snuggle and will actually hug you. I believe her owner is smiling down, grateful that her dog is with us—and I know we are grateful Fifi is with us.

Jeff and Fifi

Pumpkin is the Pomeranian lying on a quilt on the floor in front of us. She was brought to a shelter at closing time. The staff had already locked the door so his owner just left him lying on his bed in front of the shelter and drove away. He left no information, no note, nothing. The shelter is on a busy highway and Pumpkin probably wouldn't have made it through the night except someone from a large dog rescue was leaving the shelter and saw him.

A small dog can be an inconvenience for a large dog rescue, but this rescue worker still took Pumpkin home that night and contacted our friends at Tiny Paws Rescue the next day. Tiny Paws took him to the vet and learned there was a lot wrong with Pumpkin. The vet believed he was near the end of his life and recommended humane euthanasia but instead Kim, the founder of Tiny Paws, called me.

A mutual friend introduced Kim and me, and over the years, we have helped one another—and our dogs.

Kim also has a nursing background and explained that Pumpkin wasn't suffering, but she was unsure if their foster was up to providing hospice care. Hospice care can be difficult for many people because of the intensive level of care and the often greater challenge of waiting for the inevitable end. So Pumpkin came here.

He has a mass on top of his heart and is in end-stage heart disease. He also has a tumor that bleeds from time to time, and when it does, his body becomes flaccid. I have emergency Chinese herbs that bring him out of it but it usually takes around eight hours. I hold him the entire time. I know that rushing him somewhere won't change the end or the amount of time we have together, and I also know this is where Pumpkin wants to be.

Pomeranians are quirky and full of piss and vinegar, and Pumpkin is no exception. When I am making breakfast, he comes over and stands by me and barks. When he barks, the front of his body comes off the ground and, when he lands, he catches his breath and barks again.

Pomeranians also typically have a long fiery-red coat, but from Pumpkin's coat you can tell his body is burned out. I am grateful we have the resources to diagnose dogs properly because now it is about giving Pumpkin what he needs and sending him out in the way he wants.

In my early life, I was very quiet and strait-laced but I'm now known as the place for dogs to go and have fun. For Pumpkin, and for all these dogs, I'm honored to be the party girl for dogs.

The small white dog lying next to Pumpkin who just picked her head up and looked at me is Sugar. A volunteer from Tiny Paws was at the Philly shelter when Sugar was surrendered by her owner. The woman at the shelter explained in painful detail to Sugar's owner what the dog's future—and death—would look like. The owner listened, looked down at Sugar, and said, "Okay." She bent down, kissed Sugar, told her to be a good girl, and walked out. The shelter worker said it was absolutely heartbreaking to witness.

People ask why I drive so far to see Dr. Morgan and Sugar is a perfect example. When Sugar came to us she was in severe liver failure. We changed her diet, gave her milk thistle to support her liver and subcutaneous fluids to keep her hydrated, and six weeks later, all of her liver functions were normal. An ultrasound of her liver only showed some age and fatty masses.

When Sugar first got here, she didn't like people and would swing around to bite you, but now she just melts in your arms. She has a little bit of dementia but still finds ways to let me know she is still loving life.

This tiny dog sleeping on the tiny bed on the floor in front of me is Bea who was surrendered by her owner too. She came to us last July and was allegedly sixteen at the time but she may be twelve. Who knows?

She had a big hernia, a heart murmur, and was blind and deaf. Her hip is chronically dislocated and X-rays showed old breaks and unhealed things in her body, all signs that her previous life wasn't very good. As a result, Bea isn't very social. She doesn't walk very well but she knows where her bed and her water dish are located. If she has to go to the bathroom, she knows where the door is, and if no one lets her out, she goes to the pee pad in the other room. She also walks into the crate in the other room to sleep, so even though she's blind, she knows her way around.

She has a brain tumor and was having frequent seizures. For a while, we controlled them with anti-seizure and anti-convulsant medication but her last round of tests showed she is probably in end stage. There really isn't much we can do except care for her and love her.

At Monkey's House there are three reasons we have for putting an animal to sleep: pain we can't control; breathing problems; or seizures we cannot stop.

I think Bea is grateful to just have her independence and free will. She can get up and go for water. She enjoys lying outside in the sun. Two weeks ago, one of our volunteers took Bea for a car date and took her to Arby's for roast beef. We know Bea's clock is ticking but we are giving her every single day and as much love and joy as we can.

The black and white hound who greeted you when you came in is Bull, short for Bullwinkle. Bull has cancer of the anal glands, which is a very aggressive cancer. He was at the York County SPCA but they didn't want to adopt him out with that type of cancer so he came to us just before Christmas.

Bull can't hear a thing, doesn't see much, and has a very bad heart murmur, but he's also a very sweet dog.

All of the dogs are on a home cooked or raw diet, which is very similar to a person eating a clean diet. Thermogenics and a food's cooling or heating properties also come into play when choosing the right food for a dog, so Bull is on a special anti-cancer diet that won't feed the cancer. Dr. Morgan also cut out all of his lumps and bumps.

We recently found Bull confused, cold, lying in a pool of saliva with his eyes rapidly darting back and forth from side to side. Those are all signs of vestibular syndrome, an inner ear malady that older dogs can get. He was so dizzy he couldn't find the ground to sit or lie down so he now wears a heavy-duty harness and is on meds for nausea and dizziness. Today, as you saw, he actually walked.

Buck and Bull

I used to think how it stinks that Bull made it here, we got so many of his problems handled, and now this happened, but the reality is we are not going to stop spending money or doing what we need to for Bull. We will actually amp up what we do for Bull. Since he lies down all the time, we will make sure he has the softest sheets. We don't have that long to change a dog's perception of humanity so while Bull is here he will get accelerated unconditional love.

Here in my arms is Mattie, who came in as a stray to the Burlington County Animal Shelter still wearing her collar and tags. When the shelter called the owner, she said she didn't want her back, so Tiny Paws got her into foster care right away. They found out she has end-stage heart disease, and despite being on medication, she continued to get dizzy and pass out every day. Kim decided it was time for her to go off to the party rescue—which is us.

Mattie's heart was in rapid a-fib. A heart in rapid a-fib is really not functional, because rather than all the chambers of the heart being synchronized and working together, each chamber works independently. The timing is off so the blood going through the system isn't properly oxygenated.

Dr. Morgan did an EKG and adjusted Mattie's meds and she now has a regular heartbeat and no longer gets dizzy. Her quality of life has improved to the point where she runs and trots around now. Mattie is a sweet loving dog but she still has a grade 6 heart murmur, which is about as bad as it can get before they leave this world.

Having a nursing background has helped many times because it allows me to recognize when it's a dog's time. It doesn't scare me when we are at the end. I'm glad we have the resources to know because I never feel "I wish we could have done this or that." We have already done it.

When it's Mattie's time, she'll be here in our arms.

There was another dog, a little beagle, who had a huge impact on so many people, not just here at Monkey's House but elsewhere. The dog was at a no-kill shelter, and when it was determined he was in end-stage liver failure, they immediately put him into foster care. His foster mom named him Bob, but he soon became known as Feisty Bob because he climbed up on tables, chased cats, went through garbage cans, and, when his foster mom wasn't looking, Bob ate her lunch right out of her purse.

When Bob came to us, we had him fully vetted. His liver was done for, and while he needed dental work, evidence showed he wouldn't have come out of the anesthesia so we decided to make life as good as we could for Bob. He stopped climbing up on tables and chasing cats, and before long, Feisty Bob became Relaxed Bob. We began posting pictures showing everyone what "Relaxed Bob did today . . ."

Bob's belly was getting bigger and bigger, and soon he stopped walking. When we bathed him, we had to turn him since he could no longer turn on his own. I called Dawn, his foster mom, to tell her he was going to the light and she immediately came over with a bag of Chik-fil-A—which, for our dogs, is forbidden junk food. She stayed with him, and that night he was incontinent like you would not believe.

Over the next few days, Bob released all the fluids in his belly. This is known as dieresis and occurs when the body releases fluids in response to a stimulus. The stimuli may have been caused by a sodium shift in his body. Whatever it was we called it "The Chik-fil-A Miracle." Because of The Miracle, we discovered Bob's inability to walk had nothing to do with cancer. It was simply that his belly was too big and he couldn't carry the weight. Now, Bob started walking—and once he came back from the dead, all he wanted was more junk food. Every day, while everyone else ate free-range this or organic that, Bob ate pancakes, macaroni and cheese, and peanut butter pie.

The first time Dawn brought him peanut butter pie she put Bob in the back seat of her car. Bob grabbed the pie out of her hands and started eating it before it was completely unwrapped. We were laughing, crying, screaming, and trying to wrestle it away from him so we could get the rest of the wrapper off it. It was such a magical moment. We all needed a good belly laugh and Bob gave it to us.

Bob became a peanut butter pie–addicted beagle, and even though I tried making them from scratch, Bob only liked the store-bought ones.

The next few time Bob's belly filled up, we got it drained again. Draining wasn't without risk, but we felt it was worth it to give Bob a few more months of quality life and great adventures.

Bob had "those eyes," so people on Facebook changed his name to Much Loved Bob. When Much Loved Bob passed and we saw people's heartfelt comments, we realized how much Bob had impacted people's lives and hearts.

Even though Bob was in a no-kill shelter, chances are he would never have been adopted and would have spent the rest of his days in a cement shelter. Instead, Bob was with us, and for seven months, Bob's life was filled with fun, adventures, peanut butter pie, and a lot of love. Over 37,000 people mourned the loss of a little beagle that, up until then, had been invisible his entire life. It was incredible.

When Bob passed, I was on one side of him and Dawn was on his other side and we were playing music from "Through a Dog's Ear," an album of therapeutic pet music. Even though Bob was deaf, he could feel the vibrations, which comforted him. We held the music up against him, and with Dawn loving him on one side and me loving him on the other, Bob just passed. The only thing that would have been more perfect was if he lived. Then we would have just been two crazy ladies crying.

And that brings us to Bugsy. Bugsy is in a crate in the next room because he is afraid. He is afraid because you're here. He is afraid of most people and many situations so we let him relax in the next room.

Bugsy was in a kill shelter in Kentucky. The volunteers at that shelter are compassionate, brave people because there is no help for them in that part of Kentucky. They have to bring their own collars and leashes to walk the dogs and the system down there doesn't support them or the animals. Sometimes a dog can have a confirmed rescue and the shelter will still kill it. There is no reason and they don't offer an explanation; they just do it.

Through Facebook I had connected with Keesha, one of the volunteers at the shelter. She was a photographer and would take photos of the dogs in the hopes of getting them into a home. Keesha is just an amazing soul and would fight tooth and nail for any dog she could help.

Keesha took a picture of Bugsy, a fourteen-pound Boston terrier–pug mix (thus the name Bugsy) who was covered in bed sores. The minute I said I would take Bugsy, Keesha pulled him.

Bugsy's vetting didn't go well because in addition to his weight and bed sores, there were at least twenty other things wrong with him. I told Keesha, "That's okay. I can handle anything but high energy."

Bugsy came to us in 2014, before we had Monkey's House, so all of his medical expenses were out of our own pocket. He was also high energy. He is now seventeen, twenty-eight pounds, and still high energy—but, most importantly, he is still with us and he is happy.

This tiny dog lying behind me on the couch is Fiddle. Kim at Tiny Paws called me one night and said, "A little dog was just surrendered. Her owner said she's full of cancer and the shelter is going to put her down. Can she come die at your house?" Conversations like that happen every day and are normal here at Monkey's House.

Around ten o'clock that night, Fiddle arrived. While she couldn't walk and appeared to be paralyzed, I knew from looking at her that she wasn't full of cancer.

We gave her subcutaneous fluids, and three days later, after one laser and chiropractic treatment and some medication, we had her up and walking.

During her spay surgery, they removed bladder stones. Laser therapy treatments three times a week for a month helped us get a handle on the inflammation in her body.

Fiddle now has a great home and great life and is incredibly spoiled. The fact that her previous owner betrayed her like that blows my mind. The only reason that she's still alive is because Kim was there and we were able to intervene for her. The stars lined up that night to save Fiddle.

These two tiny beagles dashing across the room in our direction, barking, are Lucy and Peebody. They were brought into the Philly shelter by their owner who said they were eighteen and too old to hunt. Trust me, they are not eighteen. They also were not spayed, neutered, or socialized.

When they got here, they were absolutely terrified. We tried several times to bring them into the house but they were too nervous and refused to eat. We have an area in the horse barn where they could be alone, warm, and safe. It had a twelve-foot by twelve-foot covered area where they could go out so we began by keeping them there. Various volunteers spent time with them so they could get acclimated to different people.

Many months later, we were having our annual Christmas picture taken, and through a simple miscommunication, Lucy and Peebody ended up in the house. It turned out to be a blessing because they did pretty well, so slowly we began bringing them into the house for longer and longer periods of time. Now Lucy and Peebody are complete couch potatoes.

For so long, they were afraid and unhappy, but now they are happy and content. It's adorable to watch them walking together in the yard because their tails wag in a synchronized motion.

The sweet dog who just came over and leaned into you is Holly. She came here in November by way of the Philly shelter. Kim was at the shelter when a man brought her in the back of his pickup truck saying she was a stray. If a dog is brought in as an owner surrender, the owner pays a surrender fee of ten dollars; if they say the dog is a stray, there is no fee. So even though everybody knew the dog was his, he said it was a stray to avoid paying the fee.

Holly was the skinniest dog I had ever seen. At twenty-seven pounds, she wasn't just skinny—she was emaciated. After a brief checkup, Dr. Morgan said Holly's problem was that she had worms and was being starved.

Holly's problems were a simple, inexpensive fix. Knowing that for $110 and a recommendation to a food bank, Holly could have been healthy and happy instead of in her current condition was utterly heart-wrenching.

When Holly came here, she was terrified of other dogs and cats and had no use for people. She growled at me and whenever my husband and I were in the room, Holly would stand and stare at the wall.

A trainer came out and started by rearranging the room and putting up fencing so Holly was in a small area where she could see three other calm dogs. We pack-walked her with the calm dogs, and she has become reasonably good with the other dogs. She has also come to accept and understand that there is good in people.

Holly is a sweet dog. I try not to ever look back at where dogs came from, but I can't help wondering sometimes why someone didn't help her back then. I guess the good news is Kim and we did. As a result, Holly went from being deathly ill and emaciated to being the happy dog that had always been inside her waiting and wanting to come out.

Before leaving, I spoke with Trudy and Susan, two volunteers who had been holding, loving, and tending to dogs the entire time Michele and I were talking. I began by speaking with Susan.

I have a twelve-year-old mini-dachshund who is totally incontinent. One morning, while changing her diaper, I heard a story on the news about Monkey's House. I did some online research and sent a donation, but since I have a senior dog, I decided to volunteer.

I live about an hour away and driving here my first day I didn't know what to expect. When I arrived, I found a home that is a dogs' house. Michele and Jeff just live here. It was incredible.

Mealtime is impressive because the dogs aren't just tossed some food in a bowl; they get specific food for their individual needs. Some get raw food, some get their food smashed up against the side of the bowl. Some eat out of metal dishes while others eat out of paper bowls. Then there is the medication and supplements for each individual dog. It is truly an incredible task but look at them! They are all so happy.

The dogs may not look sick but that is because of the care they get. It is because of Michele, Jeff, Dr. Morgan, and the volunteers.

Being here restores your faith in people because these are dogs that were not cared for. Many of these dogs were mistreated and unloved, but then they come here and their world and lives are changed. Even with all the dogs we have, there is something very calming and peaceful here at Monkey's House. We can feel it and I know the dogs feel it. They have a beautiful quality of life and they know they will be cared for and loved for the rest of their lives, however long that may be.

Trudy, the other volunteer, by her own admission is shy but still wanted to share her thoughts about Monkey's House.

I had been working at a shelter but the stress was too much for me. A friend told me about Monkey's House and asked if I wanted to come along with her. I will never forget the first day I walked in and saw dogs and dog beds everywhere. My first thought was, "This is home." That was two months ago and I'm so happy to be here. I love taking care of dogs and every dog here gets exactly what they need: good food and a lot of love. They are all getting the care and love they probably never had before in their lives, but they definitely get it here at Monkey's House.

As we walked out to my car, I asked Michele how many dogs they can comfortably handle at Monkey's House and how she makes it all appear so effortless.

The number of dogs depends on what medical and behavioral issues we are dealing with, but typically we average around twenty dogs.

As for the effortless part, that happens because of our volunteers. Meals alone take over two hours to prepare, but we have over fifty incredibly dedicated volunteers. Ten volunteers come every week without fail. Others help with events and we have someone who handles the legal work and writes grants. It takes a variety of skills along with a team of people to make this work, and we are very lucky to have a team with the dedication to make it work for the dogs.

Three weeks ago, fifteen of us took all the dogs to a park. Some dogs were in wagons, others were pushed in strollers, and others walked. Those kinds of trips are important because so many of the dogs are blind or deaf but in a new environment they are surrounded by different smells. It's stimulating for them, and at the end of the day to have that many dogs come home exhausted and happy is uplifting for us. Field trips like that are possible because of the volunteers.

When we are all together in the same room, it's magic. Some people may think we are all crazy dog people, but if we are all crazy, we are all crazy in the best possible way.

When I started Monkey's House, I planned for everything I could and said prayers for the things I couldn't—and there's also been some magic along the way. There are also gifts the dogs have given me over the years that I never planned on or expected.

I truly believe Monkey's House benefits us as much as it does the dogs—if not more. They give us the gift of learning to live in the moment. In human hospice, there is so much we look back on. We think about this being our last spring or that we aren't going to see that friend again. Dogs aren't like that. Their thoughts are, "Breakfast was awesome and lunch looks pretty good. Oh look! That lady just dropped a crumb!" Dogs are really good about living in the here and now. They believe in making today awesome even if it's cloudy and rainy, which is both remarkable and inspiring, because if today is their last day, they are going to go out with a smile.

Chapter Nine
✦ JUDY MORGAN, DVM

Since so much of the Monkey's House story involved Dr. Judy Morgan, I asked Michele to connect us. After doing my own research, I learned that in addition to receiving her Doctorate of Veterinary Medicine, Dr. Morgan is also a certified and accredited veterinary acupuncturist, chiropractitioner, and food therapist. Her veterinary practice offers an integrative approach that combines holistic medicine with traditional Western techniques. She is a wealth of knowledge and experience and I am honored to share her story with you.

WHEN I WAS TWELVE, MY SHOW PONY BECAME LAME AND WAS no longer able to be shown or ridden. Our hope was for him to live out his life in the field with the other retired horses, but he was no longer able to walk across the field without being in a great deal of pain.

My riding instructor's daughter was an equine veterinarian and told me the pony needed surgery to remove the nerves in his front feet. My parents agreed to pay for the surgery and the veterinarian allowed me to assist and taught me how to provide aftercare for him. I was completely enamored with everything I saw and learned and thought it was the coolest thing ever. I followed the vet around all summer and, from that point on, my sole focus in life was to become a veterinarian.

Living in New Jersey, where there weren't any veterinary schools, I ultimately chose the University of Illinois. My focus was on equine medicine but I still had to study other animals: chickens, dogs, cats, pigs, cows, and wild animals. In my senior year, I began an internship at an equine practice in New Jersey. It was January and brutally cold. I hate cold weather and began wondering if working outside with horses all winter was what I really wanted to do. Working in an equine clinic also

Dr. Judy Morgan with her dogs (left to right):
George, Pookie and Shayna

meant being on call 24/7, a schedule that wouldn't afford me time to ride and show horses, which I loved.

My next internship was at a small animal clinic. I enjoyed the work, and with heat in the winter and air-conditioning in the summer, I began to think this might be a better fit. The chance of getting hurt doing equine work was also staggeringly high in comparison to working in a small animal clinic. After weighing all my options, I ultimately took a job at a small animal clinic and have never looked back. It has been a good fit for me.

The first ten years of my veterinary practice centered around the traditional Western methods I was taught in veterinary school—until the day something accidental happened.

My partner in the clinic did orthopedic surgery, so when I learned about a course that promised to help pets heal faster following surgery, I thought it would be a good addition to our practice and registered. When I arrived and found out it was a course on chiropractic care for animals, I almost left because I didn't believe in chiropractic. To me, it was fairy dust.

Thankfully, I stuck it out. When I began using what I had learned, what I saw amazed me. After one chiropractic treatment, animals that had to be carried into my office were walking out without any help or assistance. With one healing therapy making such a difference, I decided to research other alternative treatment modalities.

I began studying homeopathy but soon realized it would take me three lifetimes to learn everything there was to know. I learned enough that if someone was already using homeopathy, I could work with them and fine-tune their remedies but, from there, I jumped into a year-long study of acupuncture.

Acupuncture was just beginning to gain ground in both human and veterinary communities, and when I realized acupuncture and chiropractic points matched up, everything started to fit together for me. I completed the course and began using acupuncture along with chiropractic and started seeing tremendous changes in my patients.

Then I learned about another branch of Traditional Chinese Medicine: food therapy. Food therapy took hold of me and changed the course of what I did for the next twenty years.

I discovered that many pet foods were made by big companies and corporations—the same ones that had basically paid for some of my training. In school, we learned that a dog with kidney disease should be prescribed a KD diet. For heart disease, we should use the HD diet. It was called the alphabet soup diet, and for years it was the only thing being researched or taught to veterinarians. We simply picked it off the shelf and trusted it would take care of the problem. For the most part it did; however, many of those diets are expensive and are also made with poor quality ingredients that ultimately left the pet deficient in the long run.

With food therapy, I found I could cure about 70 percent of my patients simply by changing their diet. A real whole food diet would totally change the course of their life. Dogs that were obese no longer had a weight problem. Dogs with mobility issues were suddenly running around playing. Dogs with cancer miraculously had increased longevity. While dogs with diabetes couldn't be cured, we were seeing a drastic reduction in their insulin needs. The changes I saw in my patients—and in my own pets—blew me out of the water, so I made it my mission to educate myself and pet owners about the importance of food. It has totally changed my way of thinking as well as my approach to veterinary care.

Since graduating from veterinary school in 1984, my practice has evolved to using integrative medicine, which is a blend of traditional and holistic medicine. Certainly if a dog is hit by a car we use traditional medicine, such as intravenous fluids, surgery, and pain medication, but we also incorporate cold laser, acupuncture, chiropractic, herbal therapies, and sometimes herbs instead of antibiotics. With more tools in my toolbox now, I can truly make a difference and enjoy it so much more.

A year after graduating from veterinary school, I got my first Doberman. My son and daughter grew up with Dobermans but when my daughter Gwen was a preteen, she wanted her own small dog.

Even though I had never seen a Cavalier King Charles spaniel, I had been recommending them for years as family pets due to their even temperament, wonderful personalities, and because they are great with children.

Gwen overheard me talking about Cavaliers and began researching the breed. After seeing a show about Cavaliers on *Animal Planet*, she decided that was the dog she wanted. What she didn't know was that the price for a well-bred Cavalier was between $3,000 and $4,000. I calmly explained to her that I was not going to spend that kind of money on a dog when we could go to a shelter and give a dog a home.

Gwen remained undeterred and continued searching the internet and applying to rescue groups. She explained that her parent was a veterinarian, but no one would approve her application since she was only thirteen. I offered to help but she wanted to do it on her own.

Then, amazingly, Gwen saw a story on the news about a raid at a puppy mill in eastern Pennsylvania where more than 300 dogs had been seized. The majority were adult dogs that had spent their entire lives in cages too small for them to walk or even stand, leaving many with broken and deformed limbs and untreated medical conditions. When my daughter heard there were ninety-five Cavalier Kings Charles spaniels among the dogs seized, her reaction was immediate. She confidently came in and said, "I finally figured out how we can get a Cavalier!"

Since there was a court case pending, the dogs were considered evidence and were being housed at shelters until the legal issues were settled. It was estimated it would be eight or nine months before the red tape was complete and the dogs would be available for adoption.

Months later, while sitting in the drive-thru at the bank listening to the radio, I heard that the case had been settled. The court had decided the dogs would not be returned to their owner and that shelters would start adopting them out. There were already 500 applications to adopt a Cavalier so our chances of adopting one were slim to none. I went home and told Gwen but she remained confident, undeterred, and convinced that she was going to get her Cavalier.

The next day, while telling one of my friends the saga, she looked at Gwen and asked, "Do you want a girl or a boy?" We looked at her, confused, so she explained she worked at one of the shelters that had some of the dogs.

Gwen raided her piggy bank and come up with the $140 adoption fee. The day we brought Delilah home, she was scared to death. She cowered whenever anyone approached her or tried to reach out to her. Having never rescued a dog before, I thought we had made a big mistake.

From Delilah's perspective, she had never been treated kindly by most humans, so for her, as with many rescue dogs, trust was a huge issue. My daughter was so incredibly kind and patient with Delilah. Just like baby ducklings and chicks imprint on their mother, Delilah imprinted on Gwen. She kept Delilah in her room and her transformation over the next week was like nothing I had ever seen. When Gwen went to school, Delilah laid on the bottom step and waited for her to come home. She went everywhere with Gwen and everyone loved her.

I was so enamored with Delilah that I decided to search for a Cavalier of my own to adopt. After finding an English Toy spaniel that had come from a puppy mill, I applied, was approved, and drove to Indiana to pick her up—and ended up coming home with two dogs.

One dog, Jasmine, was from an Oklahoma puppy mill and full of piss and vinegar. The other, Lora Lou, who was five, came from a Missouri puppy mill, and was very sick.

When a puppy mill dog is no longer able to breed, they are either killed or sold at auction. Lora Lou was purchased at auction for twenty dollars by a rescue group. She had hemorrhagic gastroenteritis, an acute condition that was causing her to vomit and pass blood. She also had infections everywhere, fleas, heart disease, and was extremely anemic and dehydrated. With so many health issues, she almost died the first week after her rescue. Fortunately her foster mom spent over $2,000 the first week on her medical care and saved her life. Since I was a veterinarian, I wanted to bring her home and try to restore her to full health.

Adopting Jasmine and Lora Lou together resulted in them bonding and taking care of one another. When I brought them home, my Doberman tried to play with them but they had absolutely zero interest.

After my Doberman passed, I realized it would be easier for me to care for smaller dogs as I got older. I started fostering, transporting, and assisting with medical care for two rescue groups: Lucky Star Cavalier Rescue and Cavalier Rescue USA. My learning curve with rescue was still steep but the rescue groups were really wonderful in bringing me up to speed on the mental, physical, and health issues that can come with a rescue dog.

Owner surrenders were heartbreaking because you watch the dog and they look around as if to say, "Wait. Where did you go?" Many of them are devastated their owner would leave them and are very withdrawn. Initially they can't figure out how to love someone else. It can take months before they come around, so often they go into foster care first because the people who foster are trained to help dogs overcome emotional trauma.

A puppy mill dog faces additional challenges since they have never been in a home. They aren't housetrained, have spent their entire life in a two-foot by two-foot crate, and have never had the opportunity to walk or run on a lawn. Many don't even know they *can* run. It took one of our dogs three years before she ran for the first time and I simply cannot put into words how it feels when you see a dog like that run for the first time.

Many will hide in a corner and won't interact with anyone other than coming for meals. It may take months before they make a sound, but then one day something happens and they find their voice.

There was a Cavachon named Myra whose owner had bought her from a pet store when she was a tiny puppy. They lived together in an apartment, went for regular walks, and were very bonded. Shortly after getting married, the woman's husband got a husky and then they had a baby. The husky didn't get along with Myra and the husband hated Myra. Over time, Myra developed horrible skin issues, bladder stones, and began having accidents in the house. Myra was afraid of the other dog and the husband. She began hiding in her crate, and when she continued having accidents in the house, the husband told his wife Myra had to go.

When the woman brought Myra to me to surrender her, she was crying. Through her tears, she said, "For spite, she'll pee on the floor sometimes." That wasn't Myra's fault. Based on the almost nonexistent medical records the woman provided me, I don't believe her husband allowed her to spend any money on the dog's medical care. In addition, the food she brought me was very poor quality. Myra was suffering with an allergic skin disease and ear infections and hadn't been feeling well for over a year, but rather than receiving help, she was constantly being punished.

Despite all of that, Myra was bonded and madly in love with the woman. We had nine other dogs, but when I brought Myra home, she didn't really interact with any of them and was never really part of the pack. She remained a loner. While she came for meals, she never interacted with anyone and never made a peep. Not one sound.

Three months after we got her, I decided to take Myra with us to an expo in Virginia thinking it would be good for her. While we were there, we discovered Myra liked squeaky toys, so we started squeaking toys as we walked around the expo. She immediately responded and began running in circles. There were certain tones she responded to more than others, so we bought her every squeaky toy she liked. By the end of the weekend, she had a mountain of squeaky toys.

When we got into the truck to go home, we heard a sound we had never heard before. We turned, and there was Myra standing up in her crate in the back seat of the truck barking at a goat in the petting zoo. Something that weekend reminded her of happiness from her past and it was a turning point in her life. From that point on, Myra talked all the time.

And that's what happens. At some point, something or someone ignites a spark in a dog and most will become very bonded to their adoptive or foster parent.

A few years ago, while working with the Cavalier Rescue groups, we got wind of a puppy mill in Alabama where over 150 King Charles spaniels were living with a woman in a single-wide trailer. Every dog had medical or health issues, but due to the sheer volume of dogs, the woman couldn't afford to provide them with the care they needed.

Sadly the woman was an AKC-registered breeder of merit who had undergone a recent inspection. I don't know the circumstances of how that happened, but when she found out rescue people were going to swoop in and take her dogs, she decided to send them to an auction in Missouri instead.

Lucky Star Cavalier Rescue needed someone to go to Missouri to provide transportation and veterinary care for dogs after the auction. My husband rented a cargo van and we borrowed crates, loaded them in the van along with medical supplies, and headed for southwest Missouri. We got to the auction around noon on Saturday and it was the saddest scene I have ever witnessed. There were dogs of all ages and every single one was

Dr. Morgan and Myra

scared to death. People from rescue groups were bidding on dogs who were thin and matted, many with ear and eye infections. There were also people from puppy mills, but luckily, rescue groups were able to get all the dogs out of there.

My husband and I took charge of twenty dogs. After loading them into the van, we drove all night and arrived at a friend's veterinary clinic in Tennessee at five the next morning. We started giving baths; performing examinations; doing spay, neuter, and tumor surgeries; and provided dental care for the first dozen dogs. Every one of the dogs also got recommendations for diet therapy. After working all day, my husband and I slept for twelve hours before loading six dogs in the van to bring back to New Jersey for their grooming and surgical procedures.

We got the dogs the weekend before Thanksgiving and the outpouring of love and support for those dogs was amazing. A group of volunteers sat with them in my office during their recovery while other people dropped off toys, leashes, and collars. A friend spent the Thanksgiving holiday with our family and helped groom them.

Between our dogs and the rescue dogs, there were sixteen dogs at our house that Thanksgiving and they all got along. It was very emotional and one of the most memorable things we have done in our lives. A lot of dogs were rescued that day in Missouri, which made a huge difference in the lives of a lot of dogs and the families who adopted them. It was a great, and very thankful, Thanksgiving.

Once I got rolling with rescue work, I started offering discounts to legitimate rescue organizations that had their 501(c)(3). I also began looking at every pet's diet, using food as a tool to help with their physical and emotional healing, and began speaking at seminars and conventions. At one of those events, a woman introduced herself to me as Michele. She explained that she was a trained critical care nurse who was fostering a lot of sick dogs and was doing home cooking for them but she didn't really know what she was doing. From the moment we started talking, I loved her. We both have a history with horses, a common love for dogs, and she was also easy to talk to and really funny.

One of the dogs Michele was fostering was a dog named Monkey. Michele had adopted him in order to treat his severe heart disease. She believed food therapy was the missing piece of the puzzle, so several days later, Michele and Monkey showed up in my office. As I approached Monkey to begin his exam, Michele immediately said, "I don't think you should do that. Monkey isn't user-friendly."

I looked at her and started laughing because that was one of the funniest things I had ever heard. I said, "You want me to examine him and tell you what to do but I can't touch him?" She nodded her head and we made it work.

Michele and I became friends. Before long, she started adopting bigger and bigger challenges, including a dog named Ziggy who had horrible allergies and skin problems. The first time she brought him in, she told me she got Ziggy *because* he was such a mess. She believed Ziggy would teach her how to handle dogs with allergies and that I would teach her how to treat allergies.

The truth is, to this day, I learn from every patient that walks through my door. Myra taught me so much about skin disease and bladder stones. I had always been told that it didn't matter what diet you used with a dog who had her type of bladder stones because it was guaranteed that the stones would return. But Myra never got them again, so thanks to her, I now knew how to fix that problem. Through a combination of food and herbs, we ended up making Ziggy look and feel phenomenal.

In February 2015, Michele called to tell me Monkey had passed. She said she wanted to do something in Monkey's memory—specifically, she wanted to help old animals like Monkey who were in a shelter with severe medical issues or unadoptable.

"They need a place to go," Michele told me. "I don't want them dying in a shelter or on a cold steel table but I need veterinary help. Would you be willing to work with me to start a sanctuary?"

I immediately told her I would love to help. I never stopped to consider that we lived over an hour apart or how I was going to help because the truth is I never thought she would actually do it.

Four months later, I got a message about two fourteen-year-old dogs in Tennessee that were on their last legs. The woman who owned them was in her sixties and had severe dementia. Her son, who was caring for her and her dogs, had posted on Facebook: "I can't wait until Mom dies and I can dump these two dogs at the local shelter."

Paula, a friend of mine, saw the post, knew the shelter, and also knew the dogs would never get out of there alive. When I saw the dogs' picture, one of them reminded me of Lora Lou and I knew I needed to rescue them. My husband is a bigger softie than I am, so as soon as I showed him the picture, he said, "Let's get the dogs."

I phoned Paula and told her if she could get the dogs from Tennessee to New Jersey, I would take them. There was a moment of silence before Paula said, "You do know they're cocker spaniels, right?"

"Oh," I said. I thought they were King Charles spaniels with bad haircuts. We already had a cocker spaniel with attitude and I wasn't sure having three would work out, but after only a moment's hesitation, I told her, "We'll take them anyway."

Paula drove over to the guy's house and banged on his front door. When he opened the door, Paula said, "Give me the dogs," and he did. No discussion; no argument. The dogs were a disaster. They had skin, eye, and ear infections. They were also blind, deaf, and covered with fleas and urine.

While a friend drove them to New Jersey, I called Michele and said, "I have your first two Monkey's House dogs. They're blind, deaf, and a complete mess."

Michele said she and her house weren't ready. I listened and said, "After the dogs get here, I still have to address their medical issues. That gives you two weeks."

When Scout and Freckles, as they were called, got to our house, my husband and I bathed them and spent the next two weeks treating them. They arrived with the dry kibble they had been eating and when we opened the container, the entire bottom was filled with maggots.

The man Paula got the dogs from had told her that Scout was a bad dog who growled and snapped at him. Scout is truly one of the nicest, sweetest dogs I have ever met, which was confirmed by an article I found in a Tennessee newspaper.

After Hurricane Katrina, Scout and the woman began visiting a shelter where men who had been left homeless as a result of the storm were living. The reporter was so impressed by what a wonderful dog Scout was that she wrote an article about him. Scout was a therapy dog who had served people his entire life, yet when he needed care he was thrown away. I was glad we had him.

Two weeks later, Michele called. "Okay," she said. "I'm ready. You can bring them over."

"Actually," I said, laughing, "they're staying here. Just consider them Monkey's House dogs that are in permanent foster care at my house."

And that's how it started. Within a week, applications started coming in. Realizing Michele could end up with hundreds of dogs sitting on her doorstop within two weeks, we set up criteria for a dog to be considered for Monkey's House. In general, a dog needs to either be on death's doorstep or qualify for hospice care. They can't just be an old dog with arthritis; they had to be an old dog with a life-ending or life-threatening illness or condition.

From there, it snowballed. Michele brought every dog to me for a complete exam. We try to snag them before they are given any additional or unnecessary vaccinations. We test them for parasites and heartworms and any dog that needs surgery—for example, for hernias or tumors—will have surgery. Even though they are seniors, the majority have never been spayed or neutered so we take care of that also. You can't have twenty-six dogs living in the same house and have some going into heat.

We look at their problems and design a diet specific to their needs. One of the major reasons they are thriving is that every dog gets an individualized diet. They come in on death's doorstep but nine months later they are still running around Monkey's House.

Most of the dogs have received minimal, if any, care, but Michele never holds back on anything they need. We recently removed a fifteen-pound tumor off a dog that had been tied outside to a tree her entire life before the people simply walked away and abandoned her. We don't know her history or exactly how old she is but Michele saw a dog in need.

No shelter would have done for that dog what Michele and Monkey's House did. She was also the first dog to ever go into heat at Monkey's House. Since removing the tumor was such major surgery, she couldn't get spayed at the same time.

That is one of the reasons Michele has separate rooms and spaces for dogs depending upon their needs on any given day and in any given moment. Multiple rooms also exist because Michele is very focused on the dogs' emotional well-being. She is exceptional at pairing dogs together because her focus is on keeping everyone happy.

While all of this has been good training for all of us, it can also be nerve-wracking. A couple of dogs came in with such severe hernias that their bladders were literally on the outside of their bodies. You can't let a dog continue to suffer. Yes, they're in hospice care, but we are not going to allow them to suffer in hospice care or just wait for them to die.

Our tag-line and motto for Monkey's House is: Where Dogs Come to Live. When you walk into Monkey's House you don't see a bunch of dogs who are dead or dying; you see dogs that are truly living. They may have heart failure or diabetes, or they may be blind or deaf, but when you walk through Monkey's House you would never know that. You see dogs that are happy and enjoying their life. They go on trips to the beach and the park. They go for hikes in the woods. In the back field at Monkey's House there is a peaceful pond where volunteers can walk dogs. Volunteers constantly snuggle with the dogs because Michele understands their emotional health is as important as their physical health. We have had dogs recover to the point where they leave Monkey's House and go into foster care or are adopted out through cooperating rescue groups.

For me, Monkey's House was something I didn't think would ever happen. I thought Michele had a big dream she would never fulfill. I'm thankful for those two dogs—not only because they are both sixteen years old and I absolutely adore them—but because they spurred Michele into action.

I am thrilled we can share the story of Monkey's House because it helps generate donations that Michele and the dogs need. It is very expensive to care for and feed these dogs the way we do. We aren't buying cheap kibble for them. They are getting top-of-the-line raw food. Allprovide, a raw food company in Georgia, donates sixty pounds of high-quality, grass-fed, free-range food every week to Monkey's House. They also send raw meaty bones for the dogs to chew as well as bone broth. All of that has been an integral part of getting Monkey's House off the ground.

Monkey's House educates the public about the quality of life a senior dog can have. A dog may be old or unable to see, hear, or walk, but there are still many things you can do—cold laser, chiropractic, food therapy, acupuncture, herbs and supplements—to keep that old dog going and to make them healthier and happier.

Too many dogs are euthanized, abandoned, or suffer in silence as seniors. Maybe they aren't getting up because it is too painful; maybe they no longer interact with the family or snap because they don't feel well. It's true that you can give them a drug for the pain, but drugs mask the symptoms, don't allow the body to heal, and oftentimes you need to add another drug to treat the side effects of the first drug. Over time, the dog's quality of life goes downhill.

One of our goals is to have a place where people can come after they've been given life-altering news. If they are told "your dog has cancer" or "your dog will be dead within a week," we want them to have a place where they can spend a few days to learn about diet and get treatments and emotional support while allowing their dog to live to its fullest throughout the rest of its life, however long that may be.

Last September, my husband and I learned Myra had lymphoma of the bowel, so we put together a protocol to handle it. We began with an oncologist who also had training in acupuncture and herbs. I handled the food therapy portion of her treatment, and in addition to the acupuncture and herbs, we gave her CBD oil. However, probably the most important thing we did was to look at Myra. She was happy. She was jumping around. She didn't know she was sick so we stopped crying and started playing with her and her squeaky dinosaurs.

We posted Myra's diagnosis on Facebook, saying, "We know we may not win this battle but we are going to fight hard with traditional and alternative medicine. We are also going to make every day special by going to the store to buy her squeaky dinosaurs because Myra loves squeaky dinosaurs." Before we knew what was happening, packages began arriving with squeaky dinosaurs. Every day, bags and boxes arrived and Myra had a blast opening them and running around the house with her squeaky toys.

Myra only lived for two months, but during those two months, we went to restaurants, took her shopping, and even took her to the Orvis store in Vermont to buy squeaky toys. She loved going to work with me and greeting the other dogs. Every day, we asked ourselves, "What does Myra want to do today?" and focused on her bucket list.

We were devastated when we lost her, but we did everything possible to stay focused on living rather than dying.

I have clients come to me who have taken their dog to six different veterinarians in two days looking for a cure after receiving devastating news. Sometimes there is nothing you can do and you need to stop and ask yourself, "Is my dog happy going from office to office being poked and prodded? Does my dog even know he is dying?" Chances are the dog doesn't know, so I tell people, "Go out and live!"

I had one patient with oral cancer who hadn't eaten in weeks, but the dog absolutely loved to walk. One morning, the woman looked at the dog and decided she would let her walk as long as she wanted. They walked for four hours. The owner honored who the dog was, what she liked, and what she wanted. When they came home, both the owner and the dog were prepared to allow the dog to move on to whatever her next life would hold.

These dogs have so much to teach people. Michele and I are constantly learning from them, and one of the main things they have taught us is that when you are given devastating news, you have the ability to choose what to focus on. You can focus on being sad and grieve the dog before it is gone—or you can go out and live!

Chapter Ten
KRISTIAN

Several days after visiting Monkey's House, Bonnie and Barnabas stopped by for a visit. Bonnie shared her story in the first Magical Dogs *book and Barnabas, her new rescue puppy, made a brief appearance in the epilogue of that book.*

As Barnabas and Ava began to play, Bonnie said, "We're on our way home from meeting with an incredible trainer named Kristian." Kristy had mentioned a trainer named Kristian who helped her with Mr. Pickles. What were the chances they were the same trainer? I poked around and learned that it was the same person, so I reached out to Kristian. On a beautiful spring day, he and I sat on his patio while his dogs intermittently played and lounged nearby, and he told me about his journey with dogs.

GROWING UP, I NEVER HAD A DOG. FORTUNATELY MY BEST FRIEND had golden retrievers, so I spent as much time at my friend's house as at my own. It is hard not to like a golden because of their nature, and so I vowed that when I was old enough, I would get a dog of my own.

My first dog was a golden named Kaiser. I got him when I was twenty-six and loved him from the moment he came into my life. When I learned about another golden, Zoey, who had been returned to her breeder after six months, I took her, too.

There are always great moments and events in your life, but in many ways, Kaiser and Zoey were a major defining point in my life and they changed me. From that point on, I looked at my life as BD (Before a Dog) and AD (After a Dog). While I have memories from my younger years, at this point the actual feeling or memory of not having a dog in my life completely escapes me. Now everything in my life is about my dogs and I typically have a dog attached to me 24/7.

My original plan was to go to medical school, but the woman I was dating at the time had an uncle who taught medicine at Brown University. He sat me down one day and told me to really think about whether that was what I wanted to do. I really took his advice to heart and instead ended up in Jay, New York, living in an A-frame in the middle of the woods using a woodstove for heat and working as a ski instructor.

One afternoon, I overheard my friend's brother having a conversation with someone. He and I were both in our early twenties but he was mature beyond his years. In the midst of their conversation, I heard him say, "Like any responsible person, I plan on giving back to society."

I was completely taken aback because, up to that point, my life had essentially been about me. Having Kaiser and Zoey made me responsible for something other than myself so I had already begun to shift my thinking, but the thought of giving back had never crossed my mind. His words really resonated with me and I began wondering if there was a way to combine my love for dogs with giving back to society.

While researching and exploring possibilities, I found The Seeing Eye, a guide dog school located in New Jersey that trains dogs to assist individuals who are blind or visually impaired.

Working there would combine my love for dogs with doing something positive. The only drawback was that I would have to move back to New Jersey. I applied anyway, and one year later I moved back to New Jersey and began working at The Seeing Eye.

Without a doubt, The Seeing Eye is a remarkable organization and one of the finest training institutions in the world. It takes three years of ten–hour days to become a certified trainer for The Seeing Eye and I loved working there.

There was a golden named Yazzie in the first string of dogs I helped train as an apprentice. While you develop a special love and bond with every dog you train, some dogs leave an indelible mark on you—and Yazzie clearly left her mark on me.

Sometimes a guide dog chooses whether or not they are going to continue doing their job or are going to give in to distractions (such as being petted or picking food up off the ground). This is no fault of the training, which is extremely thorough. Extensive testing is done with both the dog and their human companion, but the possibility still exists for a dog to, as I call it, "go to the dark side." When that happens, the dog goes back to The Seeing Eye for retraining, which is what happened with Yazzie. Several years after leaving The Seeing Eye, she became very distracted and she was back for retraining.

I loved being with Yazzie, so after I finished my work and Yazzie was finished training, I stayed in the kennel with her. One night I stayed so late that all the lights went off in the building.

When Yazzie was ready, she went back, but she again had difficulty with distractions. The day she returned to The Seeing Eye, a coworker who knew I loved her said, "Guess who's back and available?" I took Yazzie home that day.

So I now had Kaiser, Zoey, and Yazzie and three seemed like a good number for me.

Then, out of nowhere, I started having back problems. At night, the pain was so excruciating that I was unable to sleep, and it kept getting worse. One day, my supervisor looked at me and said, "Kristian, you look awful. I think it's time you take a leave of absence and take care of yourself."

For the next eight years, I went from doctor to doctor—from specialists in New York to psychologists—but no one was ever able to provide me with a conclusive diagnosis or relief from the pain.

Unable to work, but still needing to sustain myself financially in some way, I started doing general obedience classes for people and their dogs. To this day I feel conflicted about it because I know how much The Seeing Eye puts into their instructors and I did not want to be one of those people who gets trained and then leaves. Working there was an honor and a privilege, but I knew I wouldn't be able to keep up the pace.

The training business was growing slowly—then my dogs' groomer decided to sell her grooming business and wanted to know if I was interested in buying it. I bought it, which at the time was probably the stupidest thing I'd ever done because I suddenly had a business with employees and everything that comes along with that. I was also now trying to build two businesses simultaneously. As if that weren't enough, I had absolutely no grooming experience.

As my business and work life continued to change, so did the dogs in my life. For years I had my pack of three, but when Zoey was eight, she got cancer and passed. Zoey has the distinction of being the first dog I ever lost, but before long, Kaiser and Yazzie also passed. I went from a pack of three to no pack but it didn't take long for my next pack of three to find me.

The first dog was a male golden retriever named Klyde. He belonged to a friend who felt Klyde would be better off living with me. Klyde was followed by a female golden retriever, Daisy Mae, who belonged to an amazing local artist Bill and his wife. They were in their mid-eighties when they got Daisy Mae as a small puppy. Goldens are wonderful and puppies are adorable, but even with all my experience I don't think I would get a puppy in my mid-eighties.

Bill and his wife did their best with Daisy Mae, but after nine months, they realized they were outmatched. Bill asked if I wanted Daisy Mae, which was a two-second conversation. She came home with me that night and I have never looked back.

Then I got Isar, who is a relatively unknown breed called a Hovawart. Hovawarts originated in the Black Forest, a region of southwest Germany, and look similar to a golden retriever. Isar was the first Hovawart I ever met. His mother was from Austria and his father was from Germany so I named him Isar, after the Isar River that flows through both Austria and Germany.

Isar loved hiking, so in the summer of 2011, I decided to take a break from everything to take him hiking in the Dolomites. There was a young woman, Hilde, who worked at the hotel where we were staying. She was incredibly nice to Isar, and every day, I wanted to ask her for a cup of coffee—even though I didn't drink coffee—but every day I lacked the courage. Finally, on my last day, I got up the nerve, walked down to the front desk to ask her—and she wasn't there. I left a note for her along with my email, and we began emailing one another. That Thanksgiving, Hilde came to the US for a visit, and in January, I put my life on hold and spent three-and-a-half weeks with her.

Hilde has three daughters: the older two live in Italy and Switzerland and have families of their own. Her youngest daughter, Natalie, was only nine, and everything changed when I met her. I cannot put into words how very special Natalie is to me and how much I love her.

After I returned home, Hilde and I continued talking and emailing one another. One year later, we were married and Hilde and Natalie moved to the States. My business and life was all about dogs, but neither of them had ever had or wanted a dog. I have a theory that there are dog people out there who do not know they are dog people simply because they may not have met a dog who affected them—and that is what happened to Hilde and Natalie.

I loved training and was getting increasingly frustrated with the grooming business. I wasn't a groomer and did not enjoy having staff. As soon as I started talking about selling the business, Hilde said she would run it. I reminded her she didn't know anything about grooming dogs but she said she would learn. She enrolled in the Nash Academy for dog grooming and ended up with an instructor whose native language was German. Hilde had just moved here and her English was not very good yet, so the situation was perfect.

Hilde took over the grooming business and I went back to training dogs and everyone is happy.

The name of my business is It's A Miracle Training but the truth is there really is no miracle. It is a lot of hard work and consistency.

Earlier today, a woman was here with her dogs. She loved seeing her dogs playing and running around but she also loved that her dogs now come when she calls them. I love watching the owners watch their dogs, but even more, I love watching the dogs.

I love working with dogs because even if they are behaviorally challenged, they always give you complete and total authenticity. Dogs are straightforward creatures; they are not deceptive. People often tell me their dog "did something out of the blue," but a dog will always show you what they are going to do. The problem is that most people don't understand their language.

I had a supervisor at The Seeing Eye who would tell me, "Watch that dog. I don't like the way he is looking." I couldn't understand what he meant because the dog seemed to be just fine, but without fail, the dog would begin acting out. Initially I thought it was a magic trick, but one of the most valuable things I ever did was sit and observe dogs. I watched how they played and interacted with one another. The more time I spent observing dogs, the more I realized there are ways to read a dog. Unfortunately, it takes years to develop and is something most people do not have the time, desire, or inclination to do.

Every dog I work with has one or a combination of the following behaviors: not listening; defecating or urinating in inappropriate places; destroying things; or aggression. Those behaviors are typically the four channels dogs choose to test their owners because the truth is dogs can push buttons and manipulate.

There are a number of reasons why behaviors occur. To try to explain them all as well as what to do to address and correct them would do the dog (and the handlers) an injustice and also be an oversimplification. However, one of the reasons behaviors surface is because it is part of a dog's nature and DNA to test a person or group for structure. It is part of their primal instinct for survival.

I use compliance-based obedience to satisfy and quell a dog's primal instinct to test structure. It addresses and remedies the behaviors without taking away from the dog's unique nature.

Normally, I go to the owner's home to train with them because much of what I do is designed to impact and enrich the relationship between the dog and owners. However, sometimes other arrangements need to be made, which is what happened with Sky.

I got a call from a couple about their one–year–old husky named Sky. They said Sky was chewing carpet, wouldn't listen, and also had horrible stool quality. Much of what Sky was doing was normal puppy stuff being done out of frustration, and since they were very busy, we decided I would bring Sky to my home and work with her.

Dogs typically come here for three or four weeks. The first week or two we don't do any formal training. It is actually a period where the dog detoxes from their family and is introduced to our "family." One of the reasons I keep several dogs is to have an established group that other dogs will gravitate toward. If you put a new dog in with a dog like Isar, who always comes when called, you can begin introducing them to appropriate responses and behaviors.

When Sky came here, she was a handful. She was the most adorable little pure white husky with beautiful blue eyes, but she was also a ball of tension and energy. I field-collar trained her and she loved going on hikes. We would go on five-mile hikes, but Sky was so busy running back and forth, that she would end up going five times the distance the rest of us went. That's simply the nature of huskies. They can be the friendliest, sweetest dogs but they love to run and run then run some more. They are extremely high energy and you need to appeal to the nature of who they are and what they want.

For the first time, Sky was able to be a dog and run around. By the end of the month, she was lying down, calm and happy, because she was being properly exercised. The problem was maintaining it.

A couple of weeks after getting Sky back, her owners realized they were in over their heads and called me. "After seeing her with you and the transformation in her, we realize Sky needs more than we can give her." There was a pause before they continued. "Can you help us find the right home for her?"

I agreed and the search lasted under ten minutes because as soon as Hilde and Natalie heard, Sky came to live with us and we were all happy and having a great time. Hilde took Sky with her to the shop and she was just an awesome dog.

In August, I was hiking with a group of dogs, including Sky. The leaves were still really thick and Sky, like she always did, ran into the woods. Thinking she was exploring, I gave her a few minutes then called her back, not realizing the trail was near a road Sky had already crossed. When I called her, Sky came running back like a bullet—and was hit by a school bus.

When I got to her, her leg was mangled. I rushed her to Crown Veterinary, a local emergency animal hospital, and started a recovery process that was nothing less than incredible. She had several procedures and surgeries followed by wet and dry bandages that had to be removed and changed under anesthesia. She also required several skin grafts.

Even with bandages and a cone, Sky was able to twist her body and get to the wound. Part of that was her trying to control the situation and part of it was sheer frustration. Nothing we did kept Sky away from the wound and every time she got to it, she opened it up and set back the healing process. Hilde and I started sleeping in shifts so someone would be with Sky and monitor her at all times. By Christmas, she had healed amazingly well, and while it wasn't completely healed, she had already begun to use the leg and was faster than many of my other dogs. We put a sleeve on the leg to cover the wound and continued to supervise her.

Then Sky developed a really nasty bacterial infection requiring drugs so toxic to her system that she needed dialysis. Twice a day every day Sky licked peanut butter out of Hilde's hand while I

Sky still recovering

ran the IV bag of drugs into her system. The amount of time, effort, and expense were mounting but she was worth it. Sky was our kid.

We were scheduled to be interviewed for a veterinary publication because of all that had happened with Sky. Her tendons had been sheared off in the accident, and for a dog with those kinds of injuries to make the kind of recovery Sky had was nothing short of a miracle. Dr. Ross, the veterinarian at Crown Vet, said they wanted to use it as a teachable moment so other veterinarians would understand amputation may not always be necessary.

One night, we were completely confident that Sky was healed and doing great so we decided to go out for pizza. We were only gone a short time, yet Sky managed to chew through everything and get to her wound.

Some dogs are prone to hyper-attachment issues. Sky had a touch of it from her last family, and with us spending so much time with her since the injury, it had gotten worse.

Once again, we repeated the process. A few months later, we went on a vacation to Lake Placid with several family members. Sky loved being in the snow and running around the trails. For the most part, she was healed, but we still kept her in the sleeve and cone as a precaution since there was a little bit of the wound that needed to heal.

The first night we went out for a very short period of time to see how Sky would do and she was a perfect angel. The next night we decided to try it again. We weren't out very long when we got a call from my parents. Someone had left a bag of cheese puffs in their room and Sky had found it. Since she was wearing the cone, as soon as she put her head in the bag it got stuck and she suffocated.

After all Sky had been through and after all that effort, for her to go like that was surreal. It is still really hard for me to talk about.

Calling her old owner was the toughest phone call I have ever had to make. She listened then said, "Kristian, it was going to happen anyway." She reminded me of the night before we were scheduled to pick Sky up at their house when Sky ingested several Percocet along with dark chocolate and ended up in intensive care. "Remember how I called you and told you I didn't think she was going to make it? Sky lived hard and fast— that is who she was—but she was also a well-trained happy girl and she lived longer with you than she ever would have with us."

I am still trying to make peace with what happened to Sky. I am the dog guy; I am the one people come to for answers and solutions to their problems. I vowed to love and take care of Sky like she was my own. She was a special girl and now she was dead because I wasn't good enough that day. People tell me I am being too hard on myself and how could I have known? It was my job to know. I knew she was mischievous and I should have looked for it. I believe that if there is a Heaven, I will answer for that one day.

Losing a dog is your come-back-down-to-earth moment. Anybody who has lost a dog understands what I mean. How many times do dog people talk about that moment?

When Sky died, I threatened I would never get another dog. I didn't want to go through that pain again. How do you move forward knowing one day your dog won't be there? How do you truly enjoy the present moment while remaining cognizant of the fact that they don't live forever? I wish I didn't have to live through that reality. I also wish I was better at living in the moment, because although I try my best, I often fall short.

Animals have the ability to authentically enjoy life in a way most people cannot. It is not that dogs have something we don't; it's what they *don't* have. They don't have baggage. They don't have a past they are reliving over and over again in their minds. They aren't thinking about their own mortality. They are living in and enjoying the present moment. I marvel at that.

Kristian with Daisy and Isar

For me, dogs make sense. I know what they want and I know I can provide a dog a good life—which is why we recently brought home two new puppies, Hannah and Hero. With them, we went from my usual pack of three to a pack of four. Isar tolerates them hanging off of him but Daisy can't stand them. If we had gotten one, it would not have gone well since I cannot be there all the time to play with them. But because Hannah and Hero have one another, it was the path of least resistance. While four is not my number, it's the lesser of two evils. When they are tearing it up around here, we just laugh and say, "Good thing we got two!"

People often tell me they don't know what to do for their dog, but people actually know more than they realize. If I were to give dog owners any advice it would be this: Trust your instincts. You know your dog. If someone is telling you something and you have a feeling it's not right, most of the time it isn't. If you have a feeling something isn't right for your dog or doesn't make sense, don't do it.

Chapter Eleven

LET'S PAWS: PREVENT PET SUFFOCATION

In sharing Sky's story, Kristian made me aware of the dangers of pet suffocation. When I mentioned it to others, they were also unaware of the dangers, so I reached out to Bonnie Harlan, the founder of Prevent Pet Suffocation.

Bonnie never knew a dog could lose their life from a seemingly innocuous nine-ounce bag of chips—until it happened to her dog Blue. In honor of Blue, she began Prevent Pet Suffocation and is dedicated to raising awareness about the suffocation dangers pets face from chip bags and other food packaging.

Despite gaining an international following, Bonnie still hears from three to four dog owners every week who have lost their pet to suffocation. By sharing this information with you, it is my hope that we can keep our pets safe from this danger. My other hope is that Kristian realizes he and Sky created this opportunity to educate others, and in doing so, will protect and save other dogs.

IT NEVER OCCURRED TO ME THAT I WOULD ONE DAY BE THE founder of the nonprofit Prevent Pet Suffocation. It never occurred to me that I would spend my days and time raising awareness about the dangers pets face from chip bags and other food packaging. More than anything, it never occurred to me that I would one day lose my beloved four-year-old rescue dog Blue to a nine-ounce bag of chips.

December 15, 2011, is a day that forever changed the rest of my life. I had been out doing holiday errands, and when I came home, Blue didn't greet me at the door like he always did. I thought that was odd.

Walking into the house, I saw a paper bag of trash scattered throughout our kitchen. Several Christmas decorations nearby were knocked over.

I called out for Blue, but there was no answer. I started searching in every nook and cranny and under every bed, thinking he was probably hiding because he felt guilty about making a mess in the kitchen. I continued calling for him but there was no answer. I checked the doors, thinking perhaps he had gotten out. Confusion turned to panic when I couldn't find him after several trips through the house. Then I saw him in the upstairs game room—lying motionless under a table with a Cheetos bag over his head, his body still warm.

Blue

I pulled the bag off, screamed his name, and checked for a pulse while frantically calling the vet. The vet told me to start CPR. Having never done it before, he walked me through it, but by that time, it was too late. It was only afterwards that I noticed the disarray in the game room—overturned lamps and the remains of where Blue lost his bowels in his last fighting moments.

It was too late for Blue, but it is not too late for you and your dog or for you to know the hazards that everyday packaging and bags create for your dog.

Many people erroneously believe that if a dog got their head stuck in a chip bag, they would simply be able to remove it with their front paws or tear through it with their claws, but that is not the case. Once the bag starts to seal around a dog's neck, it is extremely difficult to break the suction of the seal.

Every dog is vulnerable to pet suffocation, regardless of their size, breed, or age. It's important to understand that no dog—whether a tiny teacup poodle or a massive Great Dane—can win the fight against a chip bag or other plastic bag over their head once the bag seals and they start to lose oxygen.

It has become my mission for everyone to know how to keep their beloved pets safe from suffocation. I accomplish this through our web-

site, social media, television and radio interviews, written articles, and
speaking engagements. The website has a plethora of information including safety tips and pages dedicated to videos, articles, and info-
graphics. We maintain an active, online petition to one of the largest
makers of chips and snacks asking them to add warning labels to chip
bags. We are also a forum for emotional support for those who have lost
their pet to suffocation.

As part of that mission, I share the following tips and advice to help
you keep your pet safe from suffocation:

+ Keep all chip, snack, and pet food bags safely stored away from
  your pet.
+ Tear or cut up all empty chip bags and food bags after use.
+ Store chips, snacks, and pet food in resealable plastic containers.
+ Serve chips and snacks in glass bowls or containers instead of in
  bags.
+ Keep all trashcan lids tightly fastened, locked, or behind a cabi-
  net.
+ Keep the kitchen pantry door closed.
+ Learn pet CPR. There are a number of resources available to learn
  this, including online videos, a pet first aid app available through
  the American Red Cross, and the pet CPR video in the Blue's Blog
  portion of my website.
+ If you do not crate your pet when you are away, consider confin-
  ing them to one room or area of the home, away from the kitchen.
  My personal belief is that it is safer for a pet to not have free access
  to roam throughout the house when no one is home, because it
  only takes a minute for them to get into mischief that can cause
  them harm.
+ Alert your friends, family, pet sitters, and babysitters about the
  suffocation dangers of bags.
+ Be extra vigilant during family and holiday gatherings.
+ Lobby companies to add warning labels on snack, cereal, and dog
  food bags.

Chapter Twelve
TRISHA

Back in the '80s, my sons and I took a tour of The Seeing Eye. When Kristian mentioned them, I reached out to them to do an interview for this book. Despite emails and phone calls back and forth, we were unable to connect. I knew if it were meant to be, the dogs would make it happen, and I moved on to other interviews and stories.

Many months later, I got an email from a woman named Trisha telling me that someone at The Seeing Eye had mentioned my book to her. She wondered if I might be interested in interviewing her. When I left Trisha's house after her interview, I realized that once again the dogs had not only connected the dots but they also had found the perfect person to tell the story of how a guide dog changes a person's life.

WHILE CURLED UP ON THE COUCH WATCHING "THE BRADY BUNCH" one afternoon, I realized I had absolutely no vision in my left eye. I was only eight years old, so I didn't think anything of it, simply calling out to my mom in the kitchen, "Hey Mom, I can't see out of my left eye." My mother panicked and began taking me to doctors and eye specialists.

Several specialists determined I had a cataract in my left eye and another one starting to form in my right eye. After three surgeries on my left eye and one on my right, the cataracts were successfully removed. Although my vision was never 20/20, it was good enough that I could see regular print, which got me through grammar school. In high school, I developed glaucoma, and very gradually my vision worsened.

I was a teenager and afraid of what other people would think or say, so all through high school I hid my fading vision from everyone—including my mother. At times I walked into or tripped over things and people made fun of me, which only made me more determined not to tell anyone about my vision problems.

When I was old enough, I applied for my driver's license, knowing in my heart I couldn't pass. While I was still able to read fairly well, I was unable to see at a distance. However, I was still in denial about my vision so I decided to try anyway.

On my first road test, I drove onto the grass—and failed. The second time, I couldn't parallel park and failed again. After failing the third time, the officer told me to keep practicing and come back in a few months. I never told anyone why I really failed and pretended it was simply because I was nervous behind the wheel.

After graduating high school, my dream was to be a travel agent, so I went to Taylor Business Institute in Hoboken to study travel and tourism. It was tough for me to see, but I got books in large print, fudged my way through the classes, and ultimately graduated.

My first job was at Empress Travel in Fort Lee where I continued to fake my way through my work day and refused to tell anyone about my vision loss. Over time, it became increasingly difficult for me to cover it up, so I left and got a job at a day care center. It was the perfect situation for me because I could see the kids and was able to do everything required of me for the job. I loved it and worked there for the next eight years.

While working at the day care center, I reconnected with Dave, a young man I had met when I was fifteen years old. Dave knew about my vision problems and to him, it was no big deal. His approach was "It is what it is." With Dave I could be myself. He was always very supportive and realistic, and he was the person who allowed me to ultimately acknowledge and accept my vision problems without ever pushing me.

After Dave and I married, we adopted two children from Korea: a son, Andrew, and a daughter, Aimee. They were both four months old when they came home and I was lucky to be able to stay home and raise them. Taking care of them was never a problem since my vision problems at that point were mainly with reading and seeing at a distance.

When Andrew and Aimee went to high school, my vision took a turn for the worse. The doctors explained there are different types of glaucoma and mine was getting progressively worse. In 2005, they placed a tube in the back of my right eye to help regulate the pressure. Having already lost so much vision, my days and life continued to get smaller and more difficult until I found myself spending all day every day in my house. Going down stairs or crossing the street was a problem due to issues with depth perception. I refused to take the trash out for fear I might fall or trip or—even worse—that someone would see me and make fun of me.

It is amazing how things that happen to us as a young child can come back to haunt us as an adult. In high school, kids didn't know why I bumped into things and were mean. Now as an adult, those same feelings and fears were stopping me from going out.

My son and daughter were busy with their friends and school. While they were out enjoying their lives, I waited at home for someone to go out with me because I was afraid. I went from being an incredibly outgoing person to a woman who was spending her days alone, afraid, and trapped in her home.

And then I met a man named Danny, learned about The Seeing Eye, and my life began to change.

Danny, who had been totally blind since he was nine years old, invited me to join him at a convention for the National Federation of the Blind. I initially refused because I was unsure how I would get there but when Dave found out about it, he drove me to meet Danny. Danny and I went to the convention along with his Seeing Eye–registered dog, Sellers.

After the convention, I started using a white cane and taking mobility lessons. I hated the cane because having it meant people would know I couldn't see. After all those years, I still didn't want anyone to know.

Danny was and still is a true friend. He took me to workshops and talks, and I saw how he was able to get around efficiently and easily because of his dog. I realized that a Seeing Eye–registered dog would enhance my life. I researched schools and programs that offered training to visually impaired individuals who wanted to work with a guide dog, and while they all had different perks, The Seeing Eye was the best school for me for several reasons.

First, it was the only school in the US where you owned your dog outright when you finished your training. I was also impressed with their training and the people I met who already had their dogs. The Seeing Eye offered unending support for the lifetime of the dog, and it was in my home state of New Jersey, so I applied.

The Seeing Eye takes pride in matching the right dog to a person. Since dogs have different personalities just like people do, they wanted

Trisha and her
current dog, Astro

to know everything about me to make sure they matched me with the right dog.

The interview process included a three-hour interview in my home where they asked me about my life and my family, if I worked or volunteered, what I did and where I went on a typical day, and if I liked to travel.

After being accepted into their twenty-seven-day residential program, doubts and concerns surfaced. I would be living at The Seeing Eye in Morristown for almost a month. I knew my family would be fine but I was nervous and afraid, and I couldn't stop crying as Aimee helped me pack.

On September 1, 2007, I walked through the doors of The Seeing Eye for the first time and my life has never been the same since.

The first day we began with a variety of interviews and lectures followed by an introduction to Juno walks. In a Juno walk, you have an instructor on a harness instead of a dog. It sounds silly but it works. The instructor walks at your pace and mimics how a dog would react while you learn to use the harness to let the dog know what you want. You learn to test your strength and adjust it accordingly in the event the dog needs a correction. Through all of this, I began to find my pace and level of comfort.

The second day there were more lectures, introductions, tours, and Juno walks. On the third day, I was matched with my dog: a beautiful, gentle, kind two-year-old golden retriever named Rainy.

Rainy and I immediately started working together by going for walks around the building, then around the campus, and finally on the leisure path. We were given different routes and I learned to walk through town with a dog. We practiced stopping at curbs, going up and down stairs, and walking in and out of buildings. Eventually, we began going to the mall and supermarkets.

Together, Rainy and I learned to take the bus and go through security at the airport before heading off to the train station. We took the train from Morristown to Madison where we walked around before getting back on the train and returning to Morristown. While Rainy came to me completely trained, all our activities taught us more about one another and how we could best work together.

The next step was taking the train into New York City. On the train ride in, my mind went into overdrive. How would we navigate the streets? The people? The traffic? The closer we got, the more my concerns grew. We spent the entire day in New York City, walking around and through Times Square, and Rainy stopped at every corner and curved and swerved around people. We never once bumped into anyone or hit anything.

Then it was off to the subways. We rode them uptown and downtown. We did it all and it was the best feeling. My confidence in Rainy—and in Rainy and me as a team—was beginning to soar and I was getting my independence, freedom, and life back!

In order for us to remain focused on working with our dogs, The Seeing Eye creates an atmosphere where the only thing you have to take care of is yourself and your dog. Everyone is given a private room and bath, and housekeeping services are provided.

All of your meals are prepared for you. They are served in a beautiful dining room that is set up to simulate a restaurant, thus allowing us to practice eating out with our dog at every meal. The first week, students and staff eat together in the front of the dining room at tables of eight. We practiced getting our dogs situated under the table and having them remain quiet during the meal.

As the weeks progressed, the students and their dogs were seated in the back of the dining room and the staff was seated up front. That scenario provided us the opportunity to learn how to maneuver through a crowded restaurant with our dogs. Some days the food was presented cafeteria-style, which meant learning how to handle your tray and your dog. On those days, I made sure I got a bowl of soup, since that presented an additional challenge. Rainy and I did everything effortlessly.

Rainy—and all the dogs—were as good as gold. Unless you saw them walk in with us, you would have had no idea there were dogs in the room while we ate.

Seeing Eye–registered dogs are amazing. They are trained to ignore any food on the floor. Even when the staff purposely put food down, the dogs didn't go for it—and if they did, we were trained to correct them.

There were ongoing lectures every night to teach us about dogs and every aspect of life with a dog. Some lectures covered how a dog works and their senses; others were about how to keep the dog healthy and well groomed; and one even covered how to fend off and handle a dog attack. There were also lectures about the American with Disabilities Act and how to introduce your dog to your family.

Then it was time for nighttime walks. Even as a young child, nighttime was always difficult for me. Being unable to see, I never ventured out at night unless I had someone with me. Now we were heading out for walks at ten o'clock at night, but I had Rainy with me.

Every instructor was assigned to walk with two students. The first night, I and another student named Heather headed out with our instructor, Shannon. We got out of the van on a side street and Shannon told us to grab our dog's harness and go. I hesitated. Here and there I could see street lights, but for the most part it was pitch black. I was so scared and unsure of myself and Rainy, but knowing that I had to do it, I picked up her harness. Before I knew it, we were walking! Rainy stopped at every corner and did everything exactly as we did during the day, and soon we were walking at full speed.

You know as a kid the freedom you feel when you jump into a pool? That's how it felt. For the first time in a very long time, I was totally free. I knew I could do anything with this dog. From that point on, I had the biggest smile on my face—and to this day, it hasn't left.

The last week is called freelance training where the students tell the instructors what they want to do and learn. I and my instructor went to my home and for the next three days went everywhere in my town: the bank, Dunkin' Donuts, my mother's house, my in-laws' house, the nail salon, the hair salon. At every location, the instructor gave me helpful hints. For instance, at the nail salon, she told me a good place for the dog and me to sit.

The twenty-seven days I spent at The Seeing Eye were tremendously overwhelming—but in a good way. In the beginning, I was very emotional and it was nerve-wracking constantly wondering if and how it would work, but during those twenty-seven days I got my freedom, independence, and confidence back. Being able to work with a dog not only had an impact on the way I lived my life from that point on, but it also allowed me to finally accept my vision loss. I could finally say I was extremely visually impaired, and guess what? I am okay with it.

Working with Rainy gave me the courage to get out more, to travel, and to start working—part time at first and then full time. I now have the job of my dreams working with high school students who are blind. My high school years weren't ideal, so through my experience, I can encourage the students to find their courage and come out of their comfort zone to find their independence and understand they truly can do anything.

My hope is to help them accept their vision loss and understand that once they accept it, other people will accept it as well and their lives will fall into place. People shy away from what they don't understand, so many times it comes down to education, even within our own families.

I got Rainy in 2007. Rainy is a low-key dog and was fine when I was doing volunteer work and working part time. By 2011, my courage had reached a point where I was travelling more and Rainy was frightened by the loud noises on the planes and trains. She was afraid whenever I took her into the city to the point where she would shake. The Seeing Eye came out and worked with me to see if we could get her used to it, but regardless of what we did, Rainy continued to shake and continued to be afraid. They left the decision up to me, but knowing it wasn't in her personality to travel as much as my job and life required, I decided to retire Rainy.

With The Seeing Eye, when a dog is retired you have the option of keeping it or giving it back. If the dog is returned to The Seeing Eye, the first person they reach out to is the person who raised the dog when it was a puppy. In many cases, they take the dog back and love and care for it for the rest of its life.

I decided to retire and keep Rainy. She was happy being at home and was no longer anxious. I filled out the application to return to The Seeing Eye, and two months later, went back to begin training with my next dog, a black Lab named Harlow.

Even though I had been through the program before, the same emotions came up because every dog is different and it's a brand new relationship. The second stay was only nineteen days and Harlow and I did great but then she got sick. At first, she was diagnosed with Addison's disease but over time her symptoms changed. Unsure what the problem was, they began to look at Harlow's lineage.

The Seeing Eye breeds their own dogs, which allows them to breed out common problems such as hip dysplasia and to look at a dog's lineage to determine the source of a problem. However, the reality is that dogs can still get sick, and despite medical treatments, Harlow went from being a dog who loved walking several miles a day to a dog that was stressed to the point where she was starting to totally shut down. Again the decision was left up to me, and once again I decided to retire her.

Initially, Harlow stayed with us. At the time, Aimee still lived at home. She and Harlow were close, but when Aimee moved into her own home, Harlow began to act out. When I started working full time, Harlow went from a dog that never touched anything to a dog that was grabbing things off the counter and getting into the trash. Rainy was fine, but Harlow was clearly mad that she was being left alone. My father-in-law started coming over during the day to take Rainy and Harlow out, but soon Harlow began going to the bathroom in the house. I took her to the vet to see if there was anything physically wrong and the vet confirmed that she was just acting out.

The Seeing Eye contacted her puppy raiser who said they would gladly take her. When they came to pick up Harlow, it was so hard, but I kept telling myself I had to do it. It was what was best for her. As much as I loved Harlow, it wasn't right for me to keep her. She is now happily living with the family who first raised her.

My current dog, Astro, is utterly amazing and goes everywhere with me. I can give him directions where to go and by following my commands we get there. At the mall, if I say, "Astro, escalator," he finds it, hops on, and takes me up. If I don't know where the elevator is, I say, "Astro, elevator," and he finds it. He points his nose up toward the buttons and I follow his head and nose to find the buttons. Then I use the raised numbers or Braille to find the proper floor's button.

I have a little usable vision but a lot of how I navigate is by using my other senses. For instance, when we walk past the CVS pharmacy, it has a certain smell. As soon as I recognize it, I say, "Astro, inside left," and he takes me in. Once inside, he turns his head to indicate an aisle.

When walking down the street, Astro stops at every corner. He doesn't know if the light is green or red so I need to use my sense of hearing. Part of the training is to listen to traffic and traffic patterns. If I don't hear a car, I say, "Astro, forward," and he will step down, cross the street, and help me step up on the next curb.

In training we were told if our dog doesn't go, there is a reason. One day, Astro and I came to a crosswalk on Main Street in Hackensack. I listened and felt it was safe to cross, so I gave the command, "Astro, forward." He began to step off the curb but immediately slanted his body toward me and backed us both up on the curb—just as a car came zooming around the corner.

I love travelling and Astro is amazing on trains and at the airport. He is a Labrador retriever and tucks nicely under the seat. Many times people don't even know he is there until we get up to board the plane.

I took him to Las Vegas a few times and the very first time we stayed at Bally's. There were four banks of elevators depending on what floor your room was on, and to get to our room meant zigzagging through hallways to the very end of the corridor. I was with Dave, but we decided to let Astro do the work. After only being there one time, Astro took me through the casinos and a crowded mall area to the exact elevator and right to our room.

It still amazes me to this day. We always say The Seeing Eye is a magical place because they make dreams come true, but the dogs are magical as well.

Astro is different from the other dogs. Rainy and Harlow were fabulous, but Astro seems to be more in tune with me. If I sit on the floor or couch, he comes and lies by me. He is special not just because of the work he does but also because of his attitude and personality.

The instant his harness is on, Astro knows it is time to work and is at my side every second. When we come home and I take his harness off, he is free to play and lounge. He loves running in the yard but is always mindful of where I am and what I am doing. He follows me upstairs and downstairs, and if I take a shower, he sits outside the door. The minute I am awake, he runs over and is right there by my side. If I'm not ready to get up, I simply say, "Astro, back to your place," and he'll go lie down until I am ready.

Between the training, my stay, the dog's equipment, and the unending support, Astro is worth in the vicinity of $67,000. I paid $150 for my first dog and every dog after that has cost me $50. Veterans only pay one dollar, and if someone doesn't have the money, they will work out a way for them to pay. We are responsible for the dog's veterinary bills, but considering that these dogs have changed my life, that is not a lot to ask.

It is also why I volunteer for The Seeing Eye. I fundraise, do public tours, and anything else I can to educate the public about The Seeing Eye and service animals.

It is probably hard for people to imagine what it feels like for me to have this dog. What I tell them is to close their eyes and walk around their house by simply feeling around with their hands. Once they get a feel for that, I tell them to open their eyes. That's what it's like for me to have a dog. It's like having my eyes open.

Since the doctors put the tubes in, my vision has remained stable, but I still have good days and bad days. Today I can kind of see you, but not very clearly. I couldn't tell you what color your hair is. I can see the windows and the table and couches, but no longer care.

Somebody once asked me if I had one wish what would it be. I think they thought I would say, "I want 20/20 vision." But I don't feel like I have a disability. I would not trade my vision loss for the world because it made me who I am. I also feel like I have everything I need or could possibly want. I have a beautiful family. My kids are healthy and happy. We travel. I love what I do and have a job where I can help others.

So what is my one wish? I'd like a good singing voice because I would love to be a rock star.

Chapter Thirteen
BLIND DOG RESCUE ALLIANCE

After visiting Trisha and seeing the impact her service dogs had on her life, I started to wonder about visually impaired dogs. What if it was the dog that was visually impaired? How would visual problems impact a dog and their life? Were there people or rescues helping and rescuing visually impaired or blind dogs? Several weeks later, all my questions were answered when the dogs connected the dots for me at a pet fair in Quakertown, Pennsylvania.

Shortly after arriving at the fair, I met several volunteers for Blind Dog Rescue Alliance (BDRA)—and an amazing, inspirational blind dog named Quinn. A gentle rain had begun to fall, so Debbie, one of the BDRA volunteers, invited me to sit with her in their tent to talk about BDRA and blind dogs.

DEBBIE

WHEN I GOT INVOLVED WITH BLIND DOG RESCUE ALLIANCE (BDRA) in 2011, my original intent was to foster huskies since they were my breed of choice. However, my first BDRA foster was Seth, a sweet little blind and deaf Australian shepherd. Seth was somewhere around fourteen and had been tossed aside by his owners because of his age. Ultimately, Seth ended up being adopted by a wonderful couple in Illinois who gave him a great life.

After Seth, I continued fostering constantly for BDRA. The majority of the dogs were blind—until someone contacted me about a six-month-old double merle Aussie they saw on Craigslist who was partially blind and deaf. The woman who listed her said she bought the dog from a breeder near Pittsburgh, but she was going back to work and no longer had the time to devote to the dog. The dog, named Oopsie Daisy, had one good eye but the other eye was underdeveloped due to bad breeding. BDRA pulled her and I agreed to foster her.

The instant I saw Oopsie Daisy, I fell in love. Apparently she felt pretty comfortable too because she walked into my house, climbed onto my kitchen table, and laid down. I couldn't stop laughing. I never had a dog get up on my kitchen table before and thought it was absolutely hysterical.

Oopsie Daisy quickly became my first foster failure. I couldn't be happier because she continues to be a source of real joy in my life. She is a tornado of energy, always happy, extremely smart, and learns commands quickly.

My next foster was a six-year-old Siberian husky named Tasha whose owner was moving into an assisted living home and couldn't take Tasha with her. I drove to the owner's home in York, Pennsylvania, to pick her up. As I put Tasha in my car, the woman turned and walked back into her house. She couldn't watch because she was completely heartbroken.

Tasha had juvenile cataracts. Her eyes were drying up and shrinking and she was blind. Over time, we learned she also had diabetes insipidus, a form of non-insulin-dependent diabetes. I ultimately decided to adopt Tasha, but after only a year and a half, she passed from cancer. Tasha truly was the calmest, sweetest, gentlest soul I ever met.

Lincoln, my next foster, was an Aussie–Newfoundland mix who was blind in one eye. Lincoln came from down South and was the perfect Southern gentleman in every sense of the word. After passing the Canine Good Citizen test, Lincoln began visiting nursing homes and everyone loves his gentle, mellow soul. A coworker of mine adopted Lincoln, so fortunately I still get to see him all the time.

Two years ago, I got an email about a five-week-old blind pit bull on Craigslist. Knowing people look for special needs dog to use as bait dogs, I was concerned and immediately sent the dog's information to BDRA. They agreed to pull the dog and it was decided I would take her first and then Barb, another BDRA volunteer, would take her.

BDRA's owner surrender team reached out to the owners but they said someone else wanted her. A week later they called back and said the person decided not to take her so I told them I would come get the puppy. They told me there were eleven puppies in the litter but one had been stillborn. When I asked if I could meet the parents and the other puppies when

I arrived or see photos of them, they refused. I began to get a funny feeling they didn't want me to come to their house or see their other dogs, which was confirmed when they made arrangements to meet me in a parking lot in Maryland.

When I saw the puppy, I fell instantly in love, just like with Seth. She was eight weeks

Quinn

old, four pounds, and a beautiful cream color. By the time we got back on the road, it was dark, horribly windy, and rainy, so the drive home was dreadfully slow. As soon as we got home, I gave her a bath since she was covered with fleas—and named her Quinn.

I never had a pit bull before and had no idea what pit bull puppies were supposed to look like, but it seemed like Quinn's head was extremely domed. She also seemed lethargic and wobbly. Whenever I tried to feed her, she licked the food, so I began making her a mush-type food, and she devoured it. Once she began eating on a regular basis, Quinn started to perk up.

At her first vet visit, it was determined that Quinn had a severe case of hydrocephalus, which literally means water on the brain. Hydrocephalus is a buildup of fluid inside the skull that puts pressure on the brain and results in an enlarged, dome-shaped head and blindness, among other things.

Quinn wasn't expected to live past twelve weeks, but she continued to perk up. She needed an MRI to determine exactly what was going on in her brain. I knew BDRA couldn't afford it, but I also knew I couldn't give up on her so I took her to the neurologist and paid for it myself.

The MRI showed that Quinn only had 10 percent of her brain. It was believed she could see some shadows, which would explain why she didn't run into things, but she was almost completely blind. The neurologist suggested we wait to see how she did.

Barb and I discussed the results and decided I would continue to see how Quinn did because neither of us wanted to give up on her.

Quinn continued to thrive, and one week later, Barb took Quinn to her home, and just like I did, fell instantly in love with her.

With hydrocephalus, the symptoms are dependent on what areas of the brain are affected. Since so much of Quinn's brain had been affected, she had problems with vision and mobility as well as with learning how

Barb and Quinn

to eat. She couldn't chew and only knew how to lick.

Another symptom of hydrocephalus is that their eyes will often go outwards and down so Barb started sitting in front of Quinn and talking to her to get Quinn to concentrate on her voice. Now, if you look at Quinn, her eyes no longer go outwards.

Barb also started doing exercises to teach Quinn how to use her legs and build muscle, as well as giving her regular massages. We realize there are some things she may never learn or be able to do, but Quinn just keeps thriving.

Quinn lives with Barb, but I am known as Quinn's Mommy Two since I originally had her. If Barb and her family go on vacation, Quinn stays with me. Barb always brings Quinn's special spoon since she is very fussy about her food. The first time I watched her, I used a scoop from one of the other bags and Quinn turned up her nose and refused to eat. When I redid her food using her spoon, she ate it all. Her sense of smell is off the charts.

We recently celebrated Quinn's second birthday on August 10 with a huge party complete with balloons and cupcakes. So many people came—including some from far away—and we had a great time. Everyone was amazed at how well Quinn is doing because she wasn't supposed to live this long. She is a miracle.

The main lesson Quinn—or any of our dogs—teach us is that it is important to not feel sorry for visually impaired dogs and to treat them like any other dog. They are as full of life, love to play, and just as happy as other dogs so it's important to treat and love them like you would any other dog.

BARB

After speaking with Debbie for a while, she smiled and said, "And here they come now." I watched as a woman and her dog calmly and slowly walked through the gently falling rain toward us. Person after person came over to greet them. Once inside the tent, the woman helped the dog settle onto the dog bed next to Debbie's chair before introducing herself and the dog. "I'm Barb," she said, "and this is Quinn."

MY DOG STORY BEGINS, IRONICALLY, WITH A PAIR OF LUCKY THIR-teens. Thirteen years ago, I walked into a shelter and saw a thirteen-year-old Chihuahua mix who was nothing but skin and bones. Appropriately named Boney, he had been abandoned at the shelter because of his age. No one was even looking at Boney, which unfortunately is quite common for older dogs, but Boney kept looking at me. He didn't bark; he just kept looking at me. It broke my heart so I took Boney home.

For the next four years, Boney was constantly at my side. If I went somewhere in the house, Boney was with me. When I went to visit my in-laws in Michigan, Boney went with me and was the hit at their community center. I never needed a leash for Boney because he never wandered away from my side.

When Boney passed from pancreatic cancer, I was extremely depressed and decided to help the dogs that nobody else wanted.

As fate would have it, that weekend a woman I knew was doing a transport for Blind Dog Rescue Alliance. I wasn't ready to foster or get another dog but had considered doing transport, so I decided to ride along. After that transport, something shifted in me and I went home, filled out the BDRA application, and began fostering.

My first foster was a blind nine-year-old terrier mix named Abe. He was the perfect dog to introduce me to

Boney

the world of blind dogs, because in addition to being incredibly easy to work with, he was a total love bug and slept in my daughter's room every night

Deb was the first person I talked with from BDRA. They have a wonderful network of volunteers and trainers, but she is still the first person I reach out to for advice or help with a dog. Deb told me to place different things around my home to allow Abe to learn where things were and to make it easier for him to navigate his way around our home.

Since Abe was an older dog, we were concerned he wouldn't get adopted, but a couple from Erie, Pennsylvania, actually put in a request for him. I drove Abe to his new home. They were a wonderful couple and I was happy for Abe because I knew they would give him a really wonderful life.

That doesn't mean leaving him was easy. Pulling out of their driveway, I only made it halfway down their street before I started crying— and I cried all the way home. Waiting for me was an email from BDRA saying they had another foster for me: Joey, a nine-week-old Catahoula. Joey had an application and was scheduled for transport the following weekend, so he only needed a home for one week. I dried my tears and thought, "This is great! I drop one dog off and immediately get another one!"

The following weekend, Joey was scheduled to head to his new home, but it was ultimately determined it wasn't the right fit for him or the couple so Joey stayed with me.

Shortly before he turned one, another couple was interested in Joey, so I drove him to their home. When we arrived, Joey was fine with the woman, but the minute her boyfriend came around the corner, Joey's demeanor and behavior changed. It was obvious Joey didn't like men. The woman asked if I would leave Joey to see if they could work with him, so I went home to celebrate Thanksgiving with my family.

The day after Thanksgiving, the woman called to tell me it wasn't working out between Joey and her boyfriend and she needed to re-

Joey

turn him. I picked Joey up, and the entire drive back to my house, I kept looking at him. By the time we pulled into my driveway, I decided I never wanted him to go through that again so Joey became my first foster failure.

I knew from the outset that Joey had limited vision, but his eyes got worse the older he got. He is now two and is the best thing that ever happened to me because he taught me how to teach and work with other blind dogs.

When Joey first came to my house, he absolutely refused to go up steps. I tried everything and nothing worked—until I saw him trying to take the lid off a big bucket of animal crackers I had for my grandchildren. When I realized he loved animal crackers, I started using them as my teaching tool—beginning with the stairs.

I put an animal cracker on every second step, and since Joey was so focused on the crackers, he forgot he was on the steps and went straight up.

Next, I put two crackers to teach him where the couch was, one cracker for the recliner, and three for the loveseat. By doing that, Joey learned where everything was and mapped my house out in his mind. If you walked into my house today you wouldn't be able to tell which dogs are blind and which ones can see.

Just as Joey was getting settled in, Deb called to tell me she had a little pit bull named Quinn that needed to be fostered. She explained the dog had medical issues and the doctors didn't think she would live very long. I really didn't want to do it. My concern was that when and if something happened to the dog, I was going to be too sad. After thinking about it and promising myself I wouldn't get attached, I agreed to foster Quinn and Deb brought her over.

She was so tiny. Her head was always leaning to one side and she didn't walk. For the first two weeks, her inability to walk wasn't a problem because everyone carried her, but I ultimately wanted her to walk as much as possible so I took her to the vet.

The vet explained that mentally Quinn was on the same level as a child with Down syndrome. I researched how to teach a child with Down syndrome and started doing the same things with Quinn—only at a slower pace.

For one exercise, I put Quinn on a ball and rolled her back and forth so she had to put pressure on her back legs. In another, I picked up Quinn's front legs and made her look me in the eyes while I juggled her back and forth between her back legs. She hated it because she couldn't feel her front legs touching the ground, but over time she got used to it. As we continued doing the exercises, Quinn was starting to walk straighter and was doing things normal dogs are able to do.

I also learned massage techniques that are helpful for dogs with mobility issues, so every night I massaged Quinn—and every night I got bit. Quinn didn't like being touched anywhere on her body, but eventually she either got used to it or simply decided I wasn't going to stop and just let me do it.

When Quinn was six months old, I got my next foster dog, a twelve-week-old German shepherd–Pyrenees mix named Elsa. When other fosters came to the house, they didn't really do anything the first few days— but not Elsa. She headed straight for Quinn's toy basket and pulled all the toys out.

Initially Quinn didn't react, but then one day I saw Quinn going in and out of her ex-pen over and over. I kept hearing the sound of the giggle ball Deb had bought her. Quinn hated that ball and never played with it, so at first I just thought she was simply having a moment. Finally I realized Quinn was taking every single one of her toys and hiding them under her bed so Elsa couldn't play with them.

I have no idea how, at six months old, she knew to hide everything under her bed but she did. To this day, if anybody goes into her space, she has to be there, and if you take anything of hers, she head butts you on the leg as if to say, "Don't take that! It's mine!"

Another speed bump was teaching Quinn how to chew. We tried rawhide and a number of other treats but she wasn't interested in anything—until I bought her a pig's ear. At first she didn't seem interested, but then I heard her chewing, and when I looked over, she was sound asleep with a half-eaten pig's ear lying next to her. I started giving her a pig's ear every night, and after about fifteen minutes of chewing, she would be sound asleep.

One night, I forgot to give her one but still heard her chewing. The next night I purposely didn't give her one and again heard her chewing—which is when I realized Quinn was taking her half-eaten pig's ears and hiding them under her bed so she had a stash.

Quinn is extremely particular about her food. If I put anything new in her food, she won't eat it. If I stir her food with the same spoon I used to mix someone else's food, she won't eat it. If her dishes aren't placed in the same exact spot, she won't eat.

I get up every morning at 4:30 to get ready for work. One morning I was running late and hurried through preparing everyone's food. I put Quinn's dishes in her trays and she immediately took her paw and started slamming her food bowl.

I looked at her and her dishes. Everything seemed fine but she kept slamming her food dish. Finally, she slammed it so hard that the food flew out.

"Seriously, Quinn?" I said, clearly upset. "Now I'm going to be late for work!"

She walked over and got in my face with a look that said, "It's not me, it's you. You have a brain but you're just not using it."

I looked back at her dishes and instantly realized the problem. Quinn has to have her food bowl on the right and her water bowl on the left, but I had reversed them. I immediately made her more food, put the food dishes in their proper places, and apologized to her. Quinn looked up at me as if to say, "That's okay," and finally ate.

When I started fostering Quinn, my husband, Mike, and I decided we wouldn't adopt her. Mike felt we had enough dogs. Even though I agreed, I was concerned no one would be interested in Quinn. When a lady finally reached out to say she wanted Quinn, my initial thought was, "Great!" Then, sitting at my desk at work, the realization that Quinn was leaving hit me. I called Deb. The instant she answered, I said, "I can't do it, Deb. I can't let her go. Help me figure out a way to keep Quinn without upsetting my husband."

We decided I would be Quinn's forever foster—and that neither of us would tell Mike. A few weeks later, I was in the kitchen doing dishes while Mike played with Quinn. I heard Mike say, "Quinn, you have to go. I'm getting too attached." I smiled to myself, thinking, "Yes! I got him!"

A few days later at an adoption event, a woman asked about Quinn. Without realizing that Mike was standing nearby, Deb said, "Oh, Barb is Quinn's forever foster."

Mike's head whipped around. "What did you just say?"

I immediately piped up and said, "Quinn is never leaving."

Mike never said a word but I think he was relieved, because by then he was as attached to Quinn as I was. They have a special toy they play with together, and every night Mike tells her, "Go get your toy," and she searches the house until she finds it.

My husband and I have always had a dog, and one of our first was a German shepherd–Border collie puppy. My father saw a man beating puppies, stopped the beating, and took the puppies. When he got them home he called us and said, "Just come see them."

At the time, I really didn't want a dog but I took one look at a four-month-old puppy and I knew she was mine. I named her Tess and brought her home, which is when I realized she had no idea what dog food was and didn't want anyone to touch her. For weeks, I sat on the floor and read the newspaper, a book, or even my shopping list out loud in a calm, quiet voice. Other times, I just sat there. If I reached out to touch her, she would run and hide under the table, so for weeks, I just sat there and waited for her to come to me. Slowly, Tess started getting closer and closer.

One day, after a really bad day at work, I came home, collapsed on the couch, and started crying. As I sat there, Tess came over and lay

her head on my lap. Without realizing what either of us were doing, I instinctively started petting her and she didn't move. From that day on, there was never a problem with me petting her, although it was another year before Mike was able to touch Tess.

Tess was such a good dog and became my protector. If anyone got too close, she walked in between us to let them know they needed to step back or move. When she was sixteen, she got cancer and was the first dog we ever had to put down.

Six months later, my daughter's friend had a litter of German shepherd–Border collie puppies and we went to see them when they were eight weeks old. I

Oz

was drawn to a big fluffy furball, but Mike immediately pointed to another puppy and said, "I want that one."

I saw a puppy sitting in the corner looking at us with the saddest eyes that said, "I know you don't want me."

We told the man, "That's the one we want." We brought Oz home, and in so many ways, he is exactly like Tess. He is very gentle with people yet very protective of my grandchildren and Quinn.

One evening I was sitting in the living room watching a movie. Quinn was next to me and Oz was on the recliner when suddenly Oz lifted his head, looked at Quinn, and then at me. He did it several times, and a few minutes later, Quinn started to shake and have a seizure.

Initially I thought it was a coincidence, but a few days later, Oz alerted me again right before Quinn had a seizure—and this time it was a really bad one. Quinn bit her tongue and was having trouble coming out of the seizure so Oz continued to follow Quinn around and head-butt her in the side. When Quinn was by her water dish, her head was hanging so low that her nose was actually in the water, so Oz bumped her again to knock her out of the water and the seizure.

Even if they are small seizures, Oz somehow senses them in advance and will hover around Quinn and alert me. Any other time, Oz doesn't bother with Quinn because she doesn't run and play like the other dogs. Oz's buddy is Joey, but even if they are playing, if Oz senses something is going to happen with Quinn, he stops playing to hover around her and alert me. Knowing Oz does this makes me feel more secure and safe.

I love all my dogs but Boney and Quinn will always have a special place in my heart. I also know each of my dogs has been—or is still here—for a purpose.

Boney was the dog who changed my focus and dedication to helping dogs who didn't have a home or someone to love and care for them.

Joey was meant to be with me because as much as I taught him, he taught me even more about working with a blind dog.

Oz is here, among other things, to help me with Quinn.

We have a min-pin named Daisy who is my stress reliever. If I'm having a bad day, Daisy snuggles with me and lets me know everything is going to be okay.

Bubby, our Chihuahua, is my five-year-old rebel. I think every pack needs a little bit of bad to help keep the balance, and Bubby definitely brings that.

And then there's Quinn. Quinn is the result of two merle dogs being bred. Two merle dogs should never be bred because it can result in a dog who is blind, deaf, and any number of other related health issues. Many times people don't know or don't care because they can get more money if they produce a dog of a different color. That's what happened to Quinn.

In the beginning, there were people who asked me what quality of life Quinn had, but it's easy to see if you look at her. This is a dog that wasn't expected to live past twelve weeks, but she just turned two. We celebrated Quinn's first birthday, we celebrated her second birthday, and I want to celebrate every birthday because it's another year she wasn't supposed to be here.

Quinn has come such a long way. Five minutes before Mike walks in the door from work, Quinn always sits at the end of her ex-pen and stares at the door. Every day she amazes me with the stuff she can do—and sometimes I swear her brain is growing back. Quinn has shown me that any dog with a disability can learn if we have the patience and take the time to work with them. Quinn has also become an ambassador for blind dogs, disabled dogs, and pit bulls.

Quinn came into my life at a time when my children were grown up and leaving home. I was going through that mom thing where you're crying because your children are leaving and moving out, but having Quinn helped me get through that.

In the beginning there were people who wanted to give up on Quinn—including me. There were times when I thought I couldn't do it. Over and over, I promised myself I wouldn't get attached to her, but then I started seeing the progress she was making and now there is no way I could ever let her go.

Quinn has shown me that regardless of how hard life is, it's important to never give up, take it one day at a time, and enjoy each day.

CARLA

Before leaving that day, Debbie and Barb suggested I speak with two other women, Carla and Colleen, to round out my understanding of blind dogs and BDRA. I began with a phone call to Carla.

AS A CHILD, I RESCUED ANIMALS, AND THE LOCAL VETERINARIAN allowed me to come in and clean cages. Eventually he hired me, and since then every job I ever had has revolved around animals in some capacity. Whether working as a veterinary technician to Director of Humane Education for the Pennsylvania SPCA to breeding and showing Akitas and volunteering with rescues, I have worked with and been around animals my entire life.

Although I grew up with German shepherds, Akitas have been my breed of choice for over thirty-five years. Back in 2008, while volunteering for an Akita rescue, we got a call about two six-week-old blind Akitas. It was suspected a backyard breeder dumped them at the shelter since they were blind and couldn't be sold.

I drove to Western New York to pick them up after being forewarned that both puppies, named Odie and Pawlee, were in bad shape. Pawlee appeared to have an injured back leg.

When I arrived, Pawlee was in worse shape than I ever imagined. He had mange, ringworm, and kennel cough. His back leg wasn't injured, it was a congenital defect that resulted in one leg being shorter than the other. In addition, there was a bone sticking out the back of the leg, the toe bones were disconnected from the rest of his foot, and he didn't have any paw pads on that foot.

Since Odie was just blind, he was adopted relatively quickly. I have to laugh at how nonchalantly I say "just blind" now, because before I had blind dogs, I would have said it was a big deal. As a vet tech, I had been around blind dogs, but because I never was responsible for one, I imagined it would be extremely difficult.

My initial concern and nervousness dissipated fairly quickly after I started fostering them because I realized they were puppies first and blind second. The following year, BDRA came into existence. Thanks in large part to Odie, Pawlee, and BDRA, I understand that a dog being blind is not that big of a deal.

After caring for Pawlee for many months, I eventually adopted him. The truth is Pawlee stole my heart the moment I first saw him at the shelter. Pawlee was born blind so it was never an issue for him or me. He got acupuncture, massage, and chiropractic treatments his entire life for his other health issues, so being blind was the least of our concerns.

Pawlee
Photo courtesy of Douglas James Photography

Pawlee had a fabulous temperament and ultimately became a certified therapy dog and reading assistance dog, regularly visiting hospitals, nursing homes, schools, and libraries. Pawlee loved working as a therapy dog and it was absolutely what he was put on this Earth to do. Thanks to Pawlee, I was led to what I am meant to do: fostering special needs puppies and dogs.

Every foster has a special place in your heart but there are some who really stick out in your mind. In the summer of 2013, BDRA sent me a photo and email about a tiny puppy that had been found sleeping on a paper plate in an alley in Baltimore. The puppy, whom BDRA had named Radar, looked absolutely horrific and was scheduled to be euthanized.

I immediately agreed to foster Radar. Word spread on social media, and we were able to rally the troops really quickly. A volunteer picked him up from the shelter and drove him from Baltimore to Wilmington to meet me. Radar was this teeny tiny, smelly, almost dead tan puppy. I didn't think he would survive the trip back to my home.

The next morning, I took Radar to the veterinarian. He weighed in at one-and-a-half pounds, and was dehydrated, emaciated, had sarcoptic mange, and both of his eyes appeared ruptured. Still unsure if he was going to make it, the vet gave Radar fluids and we came up with a short-term game plan.

Radar in the early days

Knowing smaller breed dogs are prone to hypoglycemia, I stayed up all night with Radar and gave him tiny tastes of baby food every half hour. I wanted to start getting some regular sustenance into him and also wanted to regulate his blood sugar levels.

The next morning, Radar and I headed back to the vet. He still looked pitiful, possibly a little better, but he was still here. The vet gave him more fluids and told me to give it a couple of days and see how he did.

I continued to feed him around the clock, and every day Radar was eating a little more and getting a little stronger.

We began treating him for the sarcoptic mange. Since it is contagious to humans and other dogs, I took as many precautions as possible to avoid any possibility of cross-contamination. I isolated Radar, and my veterinarian applied a topical flea and tick product to my other dogs to help prevent them from contracting mange.

It typically takes six weeks to get rid of sarcoptic mange, but Radar had an extreme case so it took over two months. I knew human interaction was important for Radar during that time. He was a puppy who needed to be socialized and cuddled and still needed to play, so I took Radar outside in the warmth and sunshine. While his eyes still looked awful, he loved playing and being outside. I never played or handled him without being completely covered or wearing a pair of rubber gloves and made sure to put everything straight into the wash. My diligence paid off because I and all of my other animals remained free of mange.

Both of Radar's eyes had horrible infections, and we still believed they were ruptured. The only solution for ruptures is enucleation (surgical removal) of the eyes. But Radar was in such bad physical condition and we knew he would never survive the surgery, so we continued to keep him comfortable and used eye drops for the infections.

Over time we determined that only one of Radar's eye was ruptured, and once he was clear of mange, it was enucleated. The other eye simply had a horrible infection. We continued to treat it with medicated drops and were able to save the vision in that eye.

Once he was feeling better, Radar's personality came out. Based on his very wiry hair, we believed Radar was some kind of terrier. I believe it was all his terrier feistiness that pulled him through everything. He was a tough little rascal. I'm not sure how many other dogs would have had the inner fight Radar had to overcome all the obstacles he faced.

A friend who had recently lost her Jack Russell mix fell in love with Radar and decided to adopt him. She renamed him Jolly Roger—or Roger to all of his friends. He is now a therapy and reading assistance dog, trains in both agility and rally, competes in nose work, and goes kayaking regularly with his adopter. Roger is an awesome dog who went from an uncertain future to being loved by amazing owners and living a full life.

BDRA is a remarkable organization and working with them has changed me, but it was Pawlee who ultimately set me on this path. Pawlee broadened my horizons and opened me up to fostering and helping special needs dogs. It has been an incredible experience. Over time, I became known for fostering special needs puppies and other rescues started reaching out to me for advice or to foster their blind or special needs dogs since they were unsure how to handle, train, or ultimately find them homes.

Jolly Roger
Photo courtesy of Sue Wales Bulza

When people or rescues contact me for help or advice, I

tell them the first—and most important—thing is to remember they are dogs first and special needs second. Obviously safety is a concern, but beyond that, it is important to let them be dogs and live full, active lives. The biggest handicap for any dog with special needs is an owner who babies them and treats them like they have a handicap. We treated Pawlee like we would any other puppy. He went to obedience classes and puppy socials. He learned to walk up and down steps and everything else he needed to navigate his way through life. Oftentimes, when people meet him, they ask if he is really blind because he navigates through life as well as a sighted dog.

The second piece of advice is to think with your head rather than your heart. Don't fall in love with a dog simply because they have special needs. Make sure the dog is a good fit for your life, your household, and your finances. Some special needs dogs require a lifetime of expensive medical care: chiropractic, rehabilitation, physical therapy, hydrotherapy, prosthetic devices. If you are sure the dog is a good fit and that you can handle it financially and emotionally, don't hesitate to adopt a blind or special needs dog because they make awesome pets. You can have a lot of good, long, active years together to make memories and, like happened to me, they may change your life.

COLLEEN

Finally, I spoke with Colleen by phone. She's one of the founders of BDRA and provided additional information and history about BDRA and blind dogs.

FOR ME, THIS ALL STARTED AFTER I RESCUED A LITTLE BLIND BEAgle named Potter from a shelter in Yarmouth, Nova Scotia. I joined a blind dog list on Yahoo that essentially served as a support group for people with blind dogs.

Over time people began posting about blind dogs in shelters that needed help. The people monitoring the list were having problems balancing support posts with rescue posts and initially tried to discourage rescue posts.

I had been helping moderate the list along with another woman, Karen, who had a blind rescue dog named Ray Charles. We recognized shelter dogs also needed help, so we asked the list what they thought about starting another list devoted strictly to rescue. The response was extremely positive.

We began with a small group and also began working on our 501(c)(3) status. By the time we were approved for nonprofit status, we had approximately thirty members in the group.

The first month we took in our first rescue, a six-year-old pointer mix named Tex who was blind in one eye. Tex was at a shelter in Georgia and scheduled to be euthanized at nine o'clock Monday morning. We

Adam

saw his last chance post early Monday morning, contacted our foster homes, found a foster, and five minutes before the deadline, faxed in the request and got Tex out of there.

We renamed him Adam and our volunteers transported him from Georgia to Wisconsin where he was fostered and eventually adopted. All of our dogs receive numbered tags and Adam was tag #1. He was the one who started it all and is still happy and doing well with his family in Wisconsin.

We initially anticipated rescuing around a dozen dogs a year, but after Adam, it became real to people what we were doing and things began to happen pretty quickly. We rescued Adam in August 2009 and by early 2018 had rescued almost 550 dogs.

Since we are a foster-based rescue with foster homes spread out in different parts of the country, transport is an important piece of the puzzle. When we request a dog, we immediately find our nearest volunteer so the new dog has a temporary home while transport is set up and initial vetting is done.

We have approximately one hundred wonderful volunteers who make everything possible. It is not imperative that a volunteer have a blind dog or experience with one because once we know their area of interest (perhaps transport, foster, or fundraising), we will connect them with a team who trains them.

The majority of our dogs come from the eastern states, although we have taken dogs from many central and southern states as well as from Canada, Mexico, and one from Iran! Our volunteers also tend to be on the East Coast but we also have volunteers in the Midwest, on the West Coast, in several Canadian provinces, and one in New Zealand. Like any rescue, we could always use more volunteers but we are very grateful for the volunteers we already have.

One of the major misconceptions people have about blind dogs is that they don't get along as well as a sighted dog. Sometimes owners do not even realize initially that a dog is blind because they get along so well. That is due in large part to the fact that sight is not the primary sense for a dog.

I get emails all the time from people asking what kind of training they should do with their blind dog. People need to consider what kind of training would be best for their dog's breed, personality, and temperament.

Clicker training works really well for a blind dog. I had two blind dogs, both Siberian huskies, that did great with clicker training. One of the dogs was supposedly deaf and was scheduled to be euthanized, so I contacted the shelter and pulled him the same day he was to be euthanized. I decided to try clicker training and it turned out he wasn't deaf at all. He just didn't want to listen.

There are several concessions you have to make if your dog is blind. For instance, if I am walking my dog and we come to a step, I'll tap my foot and say "step" or "step up," but beyond that, they get the same training as a hearing or sighted dog.

Karen's dog, Ray Charles, was born blind and had no eyes, but if you

Poppy

watched him navigate the world and his surroundings, you would have thought he was sighted. The same is true of my dog, Poppy.

Poppy was born with one tiny, underdeveloped eye and she needed to have the other eye surgically removed. The day of her surgery, when I picked her up, Poppy came prancing out as if nothing had happened and headed straight for the treat jar in the vet's waiting room.

Poppy did really well—as most dogs do, especially if they are young. The younger a dog is, the quicker they adapt. With a senior dog, because they have spent so long being sighted, they may have more trouble adapting.

It all comes down to looking at the dog rather than the fact that they are blind. Above all, don't coddle them so you can help build their self-confidence. Once they are confident, other than a very few limitations, a blind dog can do just about anything a sighted dog can do.

Chapter Fourteen
LET'S PAWS: TIPS FOR LIVING WITH A BLIND DOG

A DOG'S PRIMARY SENSE IS SMELL, FOLLOWED BY HEARING, THEN vision. They also possess a skill called cognitive mapping, which is the same instinct that allows them to find an object they buried weeks ago and what enables a blind dog to "map" a house or yard. Their senses and natural instincts and abilities, along with the following suggestions, will help your blind dog live a normal, happy life.

- ✦ Try not to move furniture around or leave obstacles on the floor.
- ✦ Ask people to let your dog smell their hand before they pet or touch them to avoid startling the dog.
- ✦ Be creative with different scents to mark specific areas for your blind dog. Scented candles in the living room, a drop of vanilla extract in the kitchen, or a drop of lavender essential oil on their sleeping spot can help them identify key areas.
- ✦ Use textured materials to mark areas. Throw rugs or carpet sample squares in doorways makes it easier for them to find door openings. Wind chimes near the back door or dog door along with mats at outside door entrances can also be helpful to your dog.
- ✦ Putting bells or jingling tags on your other dogs will not only help your blind dog find and follow them but will also help him avoid being startled. You can also use bells on your shoes to help the dog find you.
- ✦ Don't be afraid to walk with a heavy foot when approaching them since blind and/or deaf dogs can still feel vibrations.
- ✦ Training is vitally important for blind dogs. Instead of "heel," "sit,"

and "stay," owners need to add commands like "step up," "step down," "slow down," and "stop" to help the dog find you, navigate places, and avoid obstacles.

✦ Consider using a basic tabletop fountain with a large bowl as your dog's water bowl. The sound of running water helps a blind dog find their water bowl and also orients them as to where they are in your home.

✦ If your dog uses a crate, try turning it on its side so the door opens upwards. Bungee the door in place to eliminate any worry for your dog that the door may only be partially open.

✦ Hearing your voice is soothing so talk to your blind dog frequently. Let them know when you are walking out of a room. Even some silly chatter is enjoyable for them. Remember to speak to your dog when you are approaching (especially if they are sleeping) to prevent startling them.

✦ Switch from a collar to a harness to give you more control of your dog and to reduce the stress on their neck and eyes. It's important to avoid strain on the eyes, particularly with glaucoma.

✦ Use a baby gate to block stairs until your dog has mastered them.

✦ If you are boarding your dog or leaving them at the vet or groomer, make a special sign to add to their kennel that reads "I'm blind" to make sure all caregivers are aware.

✦ Socialize your blind dog. Don't coddle them by picking them up to get to their food and water or to go outside. Treat them as a regular dog and let them figure it out.

✦ Be patient. Dogs can sense when you are frustrated or upset.

✦ Above all, remember, blind dogs can live happy, healthy lives.

This information was provided courtesy of Blind Dog Rescue Alliance.

Chapter Fifteen
JOE

The weekend after the pet fair, I had a book signing at a pet store in northern New Jersey. The event was also a fundraiser for Daniel's Dream, a rescue started by a local man in honor of his dog, Daniel.

As I set up, I noticed a man walking toward me with a shy beagle at his side. He introduced himself as Joe, then looked down at the beagle and said, "And this is Daniel." As Daniel relaxed nearby, Joe began to share their story. As I listened, I knew this wasn't just a random meeting. The dogs had connected us and it was a story I wanted to share in this book.

WHEN I WAS AROUND THREE YEARS OLD, MY PARENTS AND I LIVED in an apartment. I still have a very clear and wonderful memory of running to the front window of our apartment every day to look for a dog. I simply called it "black dog" and most mornings it was outside alone. Some days my mother allowed me to go out to see, hug, and kiss the dog, and those were, without a doubt, some of the happiest memories of my childhood.

Looking back, I realize the dog was probably homeless. Back then it didn't matter because that dog was my only friend. In addition to being an only child, my growing-up years were difficult, in large part because of a skin condition. I had the worst case of psoriasis the doctors had ever seen. It was incredibly embarrassing and also resulted in a complete lack of self-confidence and my being horribly bullied.

I constantly begged my parents for a dog, but every doctor, allergist, and dermatologist agreed that any kind of animal hair would further inflame and worsen my condition. I questioned how much worse it could get since I was already completely covered head to toe, but finally one day, it all changed.

When I was eleven, a dermatologist said I could get a dog provided it didn't shed or have any dander. My parents took me to the local pet store where I picked out a short-haired mini-dachshund. This was in

1971. Back then we didn't know anything about puppy mill dogs and pet stores but that is exactly where Fritz came from. He was probably only about four months old when we got him, but he had a lot of issues, including epilepsy and a bit of aggression from being a puppy mill dog. None of that bothered me because Fritz was my best friend, constant companion, and the brother I always wanted.

Fritz passed when he was sixteen. I was twenty-seven, completely distraught, and dealt with my grief by vacillating between two destructive behaviors: working obsessively and drinking obsessively.

I was fortunate to eventually be led to two things that helped me deal with my grief. The first was joining a martial arts school. Martial arts allowed me to physically release some of my rage and sadness over the loss of Fritz and also gave me the discipline I desperately needed. However, I was still struggling mentally with the loss.

One evening I was online and found the second thing that helped me: an organization called the Association for Pet Loss and Bereavement (APLB). After joining an online chat room, I sent a message asking for advice on how to deal with the grief that had such an intense grip on my heart, life, and soul. Several days later, I got a call from Dr. Wallace Sife, the gentleman who started the APLB. We talked at length, and I credit Dr. Sife with putting me on the road to dealing with my grief in a healthy way. At that time, I had no idea the role Dr. Sife and the APLB would ultimately have in my life.

When it comes to pet loss, there is no right answer. It is a personal journey. Some people never get another dog, some get one a few days later, and others do everything in between. For me, while I continued to volunteer walking dogs at the local shelter, I could not think about getting another dog because I compared every dog to Fritz. Instead, I stayed busy with martial arts, work, and taking an online course in grief with the APLB.

I had become extremely focused on my career and was making my way up the corporate ladder, yet despite all of my success, I was still left without any sense of fulfillment. The only thing that made me feel good was going to the shelter to walk dogs. Finally, ten years after Fritz passed, dogs began to find their way into my life once again.

The first two were dachshunds, Rommel and Greta, who I got from

Spartacus

a breeder. They had been bred for temperament and were wonderful dogs.

I continued going to the shelter before work to walk dogs. Seeing how happy Rommel and Greta were, I wanted the dogs in the shelter to know some of that same happiness, so I began going to the shelter after work, too. The more I volunteered, the more I saw and learned, and the more I wanted to do something to make an impact. That something turned out to be adopting my first rescue dog, Spartacus.

Spartacus was a beagle–basset hound mix who had spent his days tied up outside being both physically and emotionally abused before being brought to a shelter in Pennsylvania. When I found out about him, he was one day away from being euthanized. A rescue pulled him and I adopted him. Spartacus was wonderful one-on-one with people but crowds were not his thing.

At the time, I was working in a very stressful job. I found that spending time with my three dogs and the dogs at the Bloomfield Shelter was therapeutic and often the best part of my day. That was where I met a one-year-old pit bull who had been found by a police officer tied to a fence at a Shell gas station.

The shelter named her Shelby after the Shell station. There was no way to know how long Shelby had been tied to that fence, but by the time she was brought to the shelter, she was malnourished, had bite marks all over her body, and was unable to walk on her back legs.

Nancy, the woman at the shelter who took Shelby in, said it was heartbreaking to see her because she cowered, shook, and was petrified of other dogs and humans.

I began visiting Shelby at the shelter several times a week. My focus was on winning Shelby's trust because initially she was refusing to eat. As she began to warm up to me, she started taking food from my hand and walking short distances with me. Ever so slowly, she started to come out of her shell, but a few months later, everything started to change. Whenever anyone walked through the shelter, Shelby went to the back of her cage and stayed there. Many people had walked through the shelter in the months since her arrival, and it seemed like she knew that she wasn't going to be adopted. She grew depressed and began to shut down. Despite all the progress we had made, Shelby stopped walking and started taking less and less food from me. I tried to get her to come out of her cage and sit next to me on the bench but she refused to move. I knew if I didn't bring her home, she wouldn't make it. Thankfully, it was easy to convince my wife and Shelby came home with me.

The next step was arranging for TPLO surgery on both of Shelby's back legs. TPLO is an orthopedic surgery performed on dogs that have torn their cranial cruciate ligament, often referred to as the dog's ACL. In the twenty years since the surgery had been around, it had proven to be an extremely effective long-term solution for dogs with the type of injuries Shelby had.

I knew it was going to be expensive for us and difficult for her, but it had to be done.

Our plan with the veterinarian was to operate on one leg and allow it to fully heal and rehab before doing the other leg.

The day I took Shelby to Animal Emergency and Referral Associates in Fairfield for her surgery, I was a mess. They are some of the finest doctors and specialists around but I was hysterical. I probably would have waited in their office all day for the surgery to be over but my wife drove us. She dropped me off at work where I told my assistant not to bother me unless it was a call from the doctor, locked myself in my office, and waited.

When the doctor called, he said the surgery went well but from that point forward, Shelby's survival and recovery depended on me. He explained rehab was going to be intense and would take months, and I followed his instructions to the letter. We used a sling to carry Shelby up and down stairs and only permitted her to put weight on the leg five minutes a day. Gradually we were able to walk up and down the block and eventually around the block. There were also leg extension exercises that I knew were painful but necessary for her complete recovery.

It took one year for Shelby to completely heal and rehab her leg. During that time, I saw how kind and gentle she was with people and realized she would be a good therapy dog. Between surgeries, Shelby tested for and passed her therapy dog certification and we began visiting senior citizen homes, Alzheimer's facilities, and schools for children with special needs. She was also asked to go to a funeral home to comfort people who were grieving.

Shelby's toughest assignment was visiting an oncology ward once a week. If you or I visit a dying person, we can put up a guard to protect ourselves from emotional overload, but Shelby did not know how to do that. She was all in at every visit, so when we came home she was exhausted and would instantly fall asleep. Seeing the toll it was having on her, we slowly backed her out of those visits.

Three years after Shelby came into our lives, I was in Fort Worth, Texas, doing a presentation for the APLB on pet loss. On the morning of October 3, I turned on the news in my hotel room, and the first story was about a beagle mix who had survived the gas chamber in Florence, Alabama. I stood there glued to the television and heard that Eleventh Hour Rescue, a rescue I was volunteering for at the time, was bringing the dog to New Jersey.

In the South, beagles are frequently bred for hunting. In the first four to six months of their lives, they are taken out and tested to see how they do. If they don't make it as a hunting dog, they are often set loose or abandoned. Since this dog had been found wandering, people assumed that was what happened to him.

The details of how he came to the shelter are still not clear, but once he got there, he was given three days to be claimed. In some shelters a dog is only given twenty-four hours, and some breeds (like pit bulls) are sometimes automatically euthanized.

At the end of the three-day hold when no one came to claim him, the dog, along with seventeen other dogs, was taken to the gas chamber. After thirty minutes of carbon monoxide, the attendant opened the chamber and there he stood, slightly wobbly, but still standing and wagging his tail. That had never happened before at the shelter and I have been told the chances of it happening at all are extremely rare. If the gas hadn't been strong enough, other dogs would have made it through, but he was the only one. Other people suggested he may have buried himself under other dogs, but once I got to know him I realized that was not in his nature. To this day it is still a miracle that he survived—and what happened next was also a miracle.

The Animal Control officer's job was to put the dog back in the chamber, but instead he wrapped him in a blanket and handed him to the woman in charge of the shelter. She named him Daniel—after the biblical Daniel in the lion's den—and the next morning Karen from Schnauzer Savers Rescue picked him up and made arrangements to fly him to New Jersey. Thanks to great veterinary care, Daniel arrived in New Jersey healthy and hopeful.

Eleventh Hour Rescue had already set criteria for Daniel's adoption, which included a home with other dogs, a fenced-in yard, and no children. While Daniel had never shown any aggression with children, they did not know enough about him and wanted to err on the side of caution.

Linda, the president of Eleventh Hour, had phoned me earlier that day. She said it looked like a home was already waiting for Daniel. Since she was making a public appearance later that day, she asked me for some public speaking tips. I immediately suggested she bring Daniel with her. Afterwards, she called to thank me for the tips and advice—and to tell me that Daniel's adoption had fallen through. When I jokingly told Linda that Daniel would make a nice fifth dog, she immediately asked if I meant it.

I assured her I absolutely did *not* mean it. She told me to think about it and I assured her the answer was still no. Absolutely not. First, I explained, my wife would never agree to it because we already had four dogs, and in addition, while Spartacus tolerated Shelby, I was fairly certain that bringing another male dog into our home was probably not a wise thing to do.

Linda asked if I wanted to meet Daniel. Since his foster lived near us, I invited them over. Daniel walked in and it took approximately thirty seconds before I realized I wanted to keep him. When Spartacus saw him, he let out a little warning growl in true Spartacus fashion. Still unsure if the two would get along, I encouraged the foster to keep checking out all of the other applications. Eleventh Hour had received hundreds of applications—including several high-money offers that, to their credit, they never considered.

A week later, the foster brought Daniel back to our home for a visit.

This time, he and Spartacus got along really well, so I officially adopted Daniel on November 10.

Requests from reporters and the media had been coming in. I told Eleventh Hour that if Daniel did not like or was scared by meeting people and reporters with microphones, I would shut them down. My feeling was that more than anything, Daniel deserved to enjoy his life as a dog.

I could not have been more wrong about Daniel's reaction to the press, media, and attention.

Daniel and Joe

He not only loved it, he excelled at it! Requests poured in from Beverly Hills, the Anderson Cooper 360° Show, and the Rose Bowl Parade. Daniel was in high demand, but I still kept a close eye on his schedule because his life as a dog will always come first.

Daniel and I immediately became advocates for banning the gas chamber. A few days after adopting him, Daniel and I attended a rally in Pennsylvania. Senator Dinniman had introduced a bill banning the gas chamber in Pennsylvania so we went to offer our support and the bill passed.

Next, we went to Michigan to try and get a similar bill passed there. My daughter came along since it was Daniel's first plane ride, and he did great. The Michigan bill also passed, and following its passage, we did a press conference with Daniel on the steps of the State House.

Alabama, the state with the shelter where Daniel originally came from, has since banned the gas chamber. A few years ago, the shelter where Daniel had been contacted me to let me know they had completely renovated the shelter, and the gas chamber room had been converted into a room for dogs who require extra care.

A few years ago, I started my own foster-based rescue: Daniel's Dream. We are a small rescue doing what we can for the dogs we can. We typically get dogs the shelter cannot adopt: pit bulls and sick or senior dogs. We rescue dogs that are on death row in shelters. We vet them, put them with a foster family, and ultimately find them a new home.

I have also begun doing more speaking and training, including developing a program for middle and high school students where I inspire them by sharing Shelby's and Daniel's stories.

With Shelby, I remind them that we all have difficulties in life by discussing what she went through. She was abused, and to this day, faces profiling and discrimination due to her breed. Where others would curl up and admit defeat, Shelby instead turned it around and became a caregiver for people.

Shelby will soon be ten years old and she remains attached to my hip. I believe that, like most dogs, she will never forget the person who saved her.

Shelby does everything with an open heart, a quiet calm, and dignity and is a living example of unbelievable compassion, forgiveness, truly respecting everyone, and serving others.

And then there is Daniel's story. When I talk about the gas chamber, you can hear a pin drop. I explain that, like Daniel, they are going to face toxins in their life—emotional, mental, and physical toxins—but just like Daniel repelled the toxins he faced, they can do the same.

I remind the students of everything they just learned from two dogs who had been given up for dead. I tell them about Daniel's Dream and explain that while we are a small rescue and what we do may seem like a drop in the bucket, at least it's a drop. We are proud of every dog we save. Finally, I remind them that they are the future and invite them to help me save the other dogs out there.

I have been getting more involved with the APLB since Dr. Sife has asked me to take over the helm as the President. It's an incredible organization and his are very big shoes to fill but I am honored. Dr. Sife and the APLB were there for me when I needed it the most. I did not know what to do to get over the loss of Fritz until the APLB and Dr. Sife came into my life. I am immensely thankful to be able to pay that forward now and help others.

In addition to helping individuals through the loss of their pet, there are many individuals and groups who deal with the loss of an animal every day, such as pet sitters and veterinary hospitals. The APLB is moving toward reaching out to those groups.

Another huge concern for those working in the animal field—especially in rescue—is compassion fatigue. Day after day, they see dogs that did not get rescued, adopted, or fostered. It hurts, and oftentimes they need additional support and guidance, so we begin by acknowledging the loss and helping them through it. In turn, they go out and help others, which ultimately helps the rescue efforts. When that happens, it comes full circle.

Daniel and Shelby

So much of what we do with dogs and in animal rescue is about bringing things full circle. A dog that needs rescuing finds their person and that connection heals parts of that person they may not have been aware needed healing. In so many ways, dogs have been the great healer in my life—and the lives of many others I know or have met—simply by their presence and their love.

Chapter Sixteen
KAREN AND ROGER

Joe mentioned two rescues that had been integral in Daniel's journey: Schnauzer Savers Rescue and Eleventh Hour Rescue. I reached out to both of them and began by talking to Karen from Schnauzer Savers, which got Daniel out of the shelter in Georgia.

KAREN

I ALWAYS SAID THAT GOD CALLED ME TO RESCUE EVEN THOUGH I am allergic to anything that sheds—which proves that God has a sense of humor. I ended up founding Schnauzer Savers Rescue, which strives to rescue schnauzers and other small non-shedding hypoallergenic breeds. We are a small rescue, but over the past ten years, we have been blessed to rescue over 4,250 dogs—more than 2,100 of them schnauzers.

Over the years, we had pulled over 1,000 dogs from the shelter in Florence, Alabama. One day, Debbie, the rescue coordinator at that shelter, called to tell me they had a beagle who had survived the gas chamber. When the Animal Control officer opened the door to the chamber and saw the dog standing there, he was scared to death. He wrapped the dog in a blanket, handed it to Debbie, and told her to "get him out of the building." Debbie asked if we could come get him.

Early the next morning, we made the two-hour drive from Tennessee to Alabama. When we arrived, Debbie took us into the kitchen area and there, lying on a bed wrapped in his blanket, was the beagle. Debbie had named him after Daniel in the Bible who survived the lions' den. As soon as Daniel saw us, he immediately got up, came over, and greeted us with kisses and a wagging tail.

We brought Daniel home and I immediately took him to our veterinarian for a thorough exam. The vet listened to his heart and did a chest

X-ray and told me there was absolutely no evidence in his lungs or any-where that Daniel had breathed in any carbon monoxide.

Everyone involved in his rescue was convinced that angels had plucked Daniel out of that gas chamber and put him back in there after the chamber was turned off. How else could he be standing at the door wagging his tail when the officer opened the door? How else could he not have any sign of carbon monoxide in his lungs or body? How else could he have survived?

Next I contacted Scott, a beagle lover and Pilots N Paws volunteer pilot, to see if he could help me find a beagle rescue for Daniel. When Eleventh Hour Rescue agreed to take Daniel, we made plans for his trip to New Jersey.

Eleventh Hour Rescue got so many applications for Daniel that they had to remove him from their site. When they finally decided, I was thrilled because it was such a wonderful fit. Joe is a motivational speaker as well as a huge animal advocate. He and Daniel have travelled the country and done so much good banning gas chambers in other places.

Six years after Joe adopted Daniel, my husband and I travelled to New Jersey to visit them. Even though it had been so many years since Daniel had seen us, he remembered us instantly and kissed all the tears and makeup off my face.

Daniel is one of my favorite and most memorable rescue boys. He is, without a doubt, the happiest dog I have ever met. Daniel greeted any-one who came to our home with his signature kiss and smile and all he ever wanted to do was love, kiss, and play with everyone—humans or dogs. It was as if he knew that God spared him for a much greater pur-pose.

ROGER

I reached out to Eleventh Hour Rescue and they put me in touch with Roger, one of their volunteers, who shared his experience with Daniel, Eleventh Hour, and dogs.

ELEVENTH HOUR RESCUE IS BASED IN MORRIS COUNTY, NEW JER-sey. We are primarily a volunteer-based rescue whose focus is on saving animals on death row in high-kill shelters. We maintain relationships with overcrowded shelters around the country and act as a safety net for them to pull dogs before they are euthanized.

I began volunteering with Eleventh Hour Rescue in July 2009, shortly after our golden retriever, Honey, passed. Honey was the most wonderful dog, and since I was not ready to get another dog, I decided to volunteer and foster and see how that went.

The communication system among rescues and shelters throughout the country has been greatly enhanced by the internet. Through that network, Eleventh Hour first heard Daniel's story.

For a dog, death in a gas chamber is brutal. It is not peaceful or pain-free, but since it is economical, a lot of overcrowded shelters still use it. Many states had banned the use of gas chambers, but Alabama still had not.

We knew we had the resources and were a good organization to take Daniel. We made arrangements to vet him and make sure he was healthy before his flight. Once he was cleared to travel, Daniel flew to New Jersey with Pilots N Paws.

The person who arranged the flight went out of their way to ensure there were eighteen dogs on that flight. Just like there were seventeen other dogs in the gas chamber with Daniel, on his flight from Alabama to New Jersey, Daniel was surrounded by seventeen other dogs. That was done purposefully, and by design, for Daniel.

Eleventh Hour volunteers and the media were waiting at the airport when Daniel arrived. As the plane taxied towards us, I noticed the Pilots N Paws plane had a beagle painted on the tail rudder. How prophetic.

We started getting the dogs off the plane and I began to help Daniel—who was now known as the Miracle Beagle. You could tell right away there was something different, something special, about him. I have volunteered and seen enough dogs that when you touch certain dogs, you get a certain feeling, and that is how it felt with Daniel. He was super friendly and you could tell he was happy to be alive.

Jill, a very experienced foster for Eleventh Hour, had been designated to foster Daniel as we went through the process of finding the right adopter for this amazing dog.

After the *Star Ledger*, a local newspaper, posted a video of Daniel arriving at the airport, other news stations began to pick up on it. Suddenly we were flooded with calls from people wanting to adopt Daniel.

We could tell when the story hit different time zones in the United States—and when it broke internationally—because as soon as it hit in an area we would start getting calls from that location. We got calls from Japan, Australia, and every time zone around the world. We were absolutely inundated with calls and a lot of passionate people wanted to be part of his story.

We wanted to take our time to identify the right person to fulfill what we thought was Daniel's special purpose: to help promote the end to gas chambers throughout the country.

We weeded through applications and requests, and hit a home run with Joe and his wife, Geralynn. He is a fabulous guy and they are a wonderful couple who embraced our vision of Daniel being the face of ending gas chambers.

Shortly after getting Daniel, Joe brought him to a rally in Bucks County, Pennsylvania, where Senator Dinniman had introduced legislation to ban the use of gas chambers in Pennsylvania. Shortly after the rally, the law passed and became known as Daniel's Law. The hope is that Daniel's Law will continue to spread to other states that still utilize this inhumane form of euthanasia.

It is unfortunate that we even have to discuss dogs being euthanized or that organizations like Eleventh Hour Rescue have to exist—but we do. The overpopulation of animals around the country is overwhelming. While statistics vary, the number most widely accepted is that 5,500 dogs are euthanized in the United States *every day*. That is an enormous number to wrap your mind around. There is an artist who has taken it upon himself to create 5,500 paintings of dogs so that people have a visual of what that number looks like.

Some dogs end up at the shelter as owner surrenders. These happen for a number of reasons: some are crappy and some are understandable. People get sick, move into nursing homes, get divorced, or have economic hardships. Life happens, and when it does, they need to know there is someone who will take care of their dog and get it into a good home so they can get their life back on track. In many cases, Eleventh Hour is that someone.

Beyond owner surrender, much of the problem is due to spay and neuter—or lack thereof. It is about educating and getting the general population to buy into the importance of spay and neuter so dogs are not allowed to make more puppies. It would be great if we never had to have another discussion about gas chambers. It would be great if rescues were able to go out of business and were no longer needed, but until all the cages are empty, we cannot stop.

Many years ago, I got our golden retreiver, Honey, from a breeder. He wasn't even reputable; he was a backyard breeder, but I knew nothing about rescue back then. I didn't realize how bad the situation was until I got into rescue. Much of the population today doesn't realize how bad the situation is so it comes down to education and awareness.

Rescues like Eleventh Hour are on the right side of the problem. We deal with Animal Control officers and high-kill shelters around the country and will swoop into an overcrowded shelter to save a dog in the eleventh hour, hence our name. If there is a dog in North Carolina and the eleventh hour arrives for them, we tag them for rescue and get them to a local situation until we can transport them to New Jersey.

Being a volunteer and foster for Eleventh Hour led my wife and I to the two dogs we have now. The first, Charlie Bones, is an eleven-year-old shepherd mix who was heartworm positive. Heartworm is fairly common for rescue dogs, but his was so advanced his body was beginning to shut down. The foster coordinator contacted me and explained the dog was at the emergency vet and estimated to have maybe two weeks remaining. Knowing our last foster had just been adopted, she wanted to know if we would bring him to our home, provide hospice care, and love him for whatever time he had left.

I was determined to make sure he was comfortable in his final days and agreed. I immediately got a big crate along with a super soft mattress and cushion and went to pick him up at the vet. He was so weak that I had to carry him to my car. The cardiologist explained they had gone through his carotid artery to manually extract as many worms as possible, but there was still a fist-sized infestation around his heart. He instructed me to make him comfortable and if he was alive in two weeks to come back and we would talk.

He was skin and bones—thus the name Charlie Bones—and petting him felt like touching a skeleton, but he loved being touched so we hugged, petted, and nurtured him. I followed the doctor's instructions, and two weeks later, he was alive, moving around on his own, getting stronger, and starting to put on a few pounds. The vet was stunned.

Thirty days later, we started him on heartworm treatment. That was five years and forty pounds ago. When we got him, he was only forty-five pounds, but he is now a healthy eighty-five pounds.

Charlie Bones

Charlie Bones was a dog who picked me during his recovery process, and I have never been loved by an animal the way Charlie Bones loves me.

Our other dog, Gracie, came to us in a much different fashion. Gracie was a purebred English cream golden retriever who was giving birth and needed an emergency C-section. The breeder took her to the vet, who determined she needed a blood transfusion. With mounting medical costs, the dog was now a financial liability rather than an income-producing asset, so the breeder gave her away.

The person who got Gracie put her in their car and started driving home. Gracie was still drugged up and not fully conscious, so when the woman stopped and opened the back hatch of her car, Gracie bolted. It was the end of January in New Jersey. It was cold. For weeks, Gracie was spotted running through unfamiliar suburban territory.

When a volunteer for Eleventh Hour heard the story, she tracked down the woman Gracie had gotten away from. When the woman said she no longer wanted the dog, she signed her over to us. We immediately got trackers, cages, and cameras. My wife, Terry, and I began putting up fliers and stalked the camera all day and late into the night.

Temperatures began to plummet and snow began to fall, but Gracie was trap-savvy, meaning she was afraid of the traps and enclosures we had set up and refused to go in them. We continued posting and handing out fliers until one day someone spotted Gracie napping along the tree line in their backyard and called the number on the flier. The professional trapper was nearby and was able to sneak up on Gracie and capture her.

Gracie had been outside for twenty-six days, so she was rushed to a local emergency vet. Terry was home at the time Gracie was captured so she immediately met everyone at the vet. Terry had already fallen in love

Gracie

with Gracie just from her photos and seeing her on the trail cameras. However, the instant Terry and Gracie met, they bonded and we adopted her on the spot.

She was put on antibiotics as a precaution and was severely underweight, so we fed her slowly to bring her weight back up. She also had a damaged paw so we had surgery done shortly after adopting her to repair her paw.

To give back for all the help we got capturing Gracie, Terry has embraced an unofficial role of helping other dog owners recover their lost dog. She helps search, puts up trail cameras, posts fliers, and sets traps—and has been successful a number of times.

From the moment they met, Gracie and Charlie Bones got along; however, Gracie was afraid of everything else. We took it slowly but also decided to put her on medication for a few months to help her acclimate to normal life with less fear and anxiety. Gracie is now off all medication and her confidence and personality have emerged. She is absolutely wonderful. Even more importantly, Gracie is safe and Gracie is home.

Chapter Seventeen
AN ACT OF DOG

Roger had mentioned an artist who was painting 5,500 paintings to represent every dog that is euthanized each day in America in order to provide a visual for people to understand the enormity and impact of that number. I did some research and learned that the project was called An Act of Dog and spoke with Mark and Marina, the project's creators and visionaries, about the project and dogs.

Mark: Early one morning, I was walking to church to drop something off and passed an abandoned building. Outside the building was a little puppy who looked to be only about seven months old. When I started to walk toward it, it yelped like I was beating it. Not wanting to frighten it even more, I kept walking.

As I started to walk home, I decided to retrace my steps. The puppy was still outside the abandoned building. It was January in Kentucky and it was cold. The temperatures were already in the low twenties, and I knew it would get even colder when night came. I reached out my hand, and this time the puppy came up to me and started to follow me.

She followed me all the way home and up the steps to the front porch. She sniffed her way around the side of the house and after several minutes came back and lay down on the welcome mat by the front door. I opened the door but she didn't move. She

Santina

stayed there for the next six hours, but with evening fast approaching, I opened the door one more time and she finally came in. I named her Santina.

Shortly after I got Santina, my tools started disappearing. One day the tools were there and the next day they disappeared. I looked everywhere and couldn't imagine where they were. Then one day I went to change the mat in Santina's kennel and discovered she had been taking my tools and hiding them under her mat. In her own way, Santina was a bit of a hoarder.

The first time I took Santina to the veterinarian, he told me he believed she had been beaten. I was shocked but then he told me something that set me back again. He warned me that if anyone ever came up to me claiming she was their dog to deny it and not give her back. That thought had never crossed my mind and I wasn't sure exactly what he meant, but I promised Santina I would keep her safe and that she would never ever go through anything like that again.

One day, Santina and I were out for a walk when two teenagers approached us and told me Santina looked like their dog. I said that was impossible because I had brought her back from Wisconsin. They glared at me, insistent that she was their dog. Recalling what the veterinarian had told me, I looked them square in the eye and said that before I got her she had been beaten. As soon as I said that, they changed their story, said she wasn't their dog, and walked away.

Kentucky is a hellhole for animals. If you are a dog, it is not a state

Rudy

you want to live in. People regularly dumped dogs at the Red Cross knowing that the constant stream of people going in and out to give blood or volunteer meant a good possibility someone would see the dog and either keep it or find it a home—which is exactly how I got Rudy.

I was pulling into the Red Cross when I saw a little

black ball. Approaching it, I realized it was a puppy that had been dumped, so I picked her up, brought her home, and named her Rudy.

Rudy and Santina became best friends. Since Rudy watched and copied everything Santina did, it made training Rudy extremely easy.

They were both unique and wonderful in their own way: Santina was mellow and easy to get along with while Rudy was a tad more mischievous and very curious. Whenever I was out in the garden, Santina sat in the window and watched me. If I looked up and Santina put her head down, that was my signal that Rudy was up to no good. I would run into the house, and every single time, just as Santina had warned me, Rudy would be getting into some sort of mischief!

One night, over eighteen years ago, I found myself sitting in a nearly empty home. Fresh from getting divorced, my ex had taken everything other than a sofa and my dogs. I had hit one of the lowest points in my life, and as I got off the sofa to get another drink, I looked over at Santina and Rudy. All I wanted to keep from the divorce were my dogs, and seeing them staring up at me, I realized if I didn't stop drinking I wouldn't be able to take care of them. In that instant, I knew what I had to do. I got up, poured all of the alcohol down the sink, went to bed with my dogs by my side, and the next morning went to my first twelve-step meeting.

Rudy was with me sixteen years before passing of cancer. Shortly before she turned twenty-two, Santina died. She had been doing really well until the last six weeks of her life when the wheels starting falling off pretty quickly.

One night, Santina wanted to go out, but when we did, she stumbled in a hole outside of our apartment and couldn't get back up. It was the middle of the night so we took her to the emergency vet and a decision was made to put her down. For the next four or five weeks, I was incredibly depressed.

Fortunately, in the interim, I had begun a new relationship with a woman named Marina. Marina was a woman of substance, an amazing friend, the love of my life, and a huge support through that phase of my life—and beyond.

We were living in St. Louis where I was doing consulting work for a company in Evansville. After Santina passed, I didn't want to do that any longer. I also didn't want to stay in that house because there were simply too many memories of Santina.

Marina and I talked and she had a couple of other options for us. The first was Louisville, Kentucky, but we had gotten Santina in Kentucky so I did not want to move back there. The other option was Santa Fe, so we packed up and moved to New Mexico.

Even though we were in a new home and a new location, it was still hard and I was still depressed. I'd had Santina half of my life. She had been with me through my darkest days and had helped me find my own redemption. Losing Santina was a huge loss for me.

The little casita we were renting was directly across from a dog park. Every day, Marina encouraged me to go over there, thinking it would be therapeutic. Finally, after some initial hesitation, I went and met some really nice people who have since become good friends.

Marina felt it was time for us to think about getting another dog. I wasn't ready, but Marina started looking online for dogs to adopt. As she got further into her search, she learned what was happening in shelters around the country and her focus began to shift as she saw the chilling statistics of the number of animals being euthanized and gassed on a daily basis. She told me about it and showed me graphic videos and pictures.

I was still grieving and didn't want to think about another dog—and I especially didn't want to see pictures of dogs being gassed—but Marina remained steadfast. She kept telling me that thousands of dogs were dying every day and kept asking me what we could do. I finally told her to get me the exact number of dogs.

Marina: I started by contacting some of the larger well-known animal organizations: ASPCA, HSUS, and PETA to ask how were they arriving at their numbers. All three said it was a best guess. Since shelters are not required to report their numbers, it is next to impossible to get a true count.

Next I reached out to Best Friends Animal Society, who estimated the number to be over two million dogs and three million cats annually. I knew that ethically and morally there was something wrong with that reality.

That was six years ago when the no-kill movement was just starting to bubble up and have some success. People were beginning to use the compassion method rather than the old paradigm of dump and kill.

I researched how many states still had gas chambers, and sent graphic videos and articles to Mark so he could see what was going on. It was very hard for him to look at because the truth is that nobody wants to see it, but once he did, he agreed that something needed to be done.

In that moment, we had a choice. We could turn away and do nothing or we could try and do something. But once you know, how can you in good conscience do nothing and simply carry on with your life?

Since Mark is an artist, he decided to illustrate what was happening in just one day in America. Knowing the enormity of the numbers, he had to pick one animal—so he chose the dog.

Mark: Two million dogs a year equates to 5,500 dogs per day but you need to realize that number doesn't include owner surrenders. Many owners don't realize that when they surrender their dog at a shelter they are signing away their rights to that animal, and in many cases, their dog is immediately killed or destroyed. The shelters see it as a case of the owner in essence asking them to euthanize the animal. As a result, those dogs are not included in the overall number, but because we needed to start somewhere, we used that number knowing, in reality, it was a lowball number.

People ask why I didn't include cats. We have two cats and love them but to add three million cats to the two millions dogs would come out to over 8,000 animals per day, many more years of painting, and an additional cost of over $300,000. Taking all of that into consideration, I decided to focus strictly on dogs.

Studio space in Santa Fe was outrageously expensive, so we wrote to thirty-two cities around the country asking for a subsidized space to paint the 5,500 paintings. Thirty responded with possibilities for us. Ironically, we found ourselves back in Kentucky once again because a local philanthropist gave us free studio space.

The next step was for me to cash in all of my retirement savings. That was really hard for me to do, not only because it was really hard for me to save that money in the first place but also because I am not a man of means. But I knew I could not turn away so I cashed it in and began painting.

Marina: We reached out to rescues and shelters around the country, and a few of their volunteers created a Facebook page where shelters would post pictures of dogs every night that they were not able to save. Mark took those photos and began painting those dogs so they would forever be memorialized in a positive way.

We knew 5,500 was a just a number. We wanted to put a face on that number so people could see what it looked like. As we say, we wanted them to "Face it, feel it, fix it" because that's how change happens.

Additionally, Mark painted eight-foot-square paintings to represent the various issues dogs faced, including animal fighting, testing, abuse, breed-specific and other legislation, puppy mills, killing for space or food bowl aggression, domestic violence, and other issues people needed to be educated about in order to change the future for dogs.

Mark: It took me four years to paint the 5,500 paintings. When I began the project, Marina and I had only been dating for about a year and neither of us had anticipated taking on a burden of this magnitude. It put enormous stress on our relationship, but as Marina said, we learned early on that our life together was no longer just about us.

Marina: The evening Mark completed the final painting, it started to snow on his way home and it continued to snow throughout the night. The next morning, he frantically called me from the studio. Snow had seeped in through a leaking roof and damaged 1,000 paintings, which he now needed to repaint.

Mark: Sometime during the process of painting the 5,500, documentary filmmakers and PBS connected with us and wanted to tell our story. Marina had taken photos and filmed the entire process before they ever came on the scene. They used that early footage and, for the next four years, followed the progress of the painting and the struggles we faced.

Marina: The documentary premiered in Kentucky in November 2017 before rolling out to PBS stations nationwide, as well as making the national and international film festival circuit. As our project is covered around the world, we have gathered a lot of international support.

Mark: As a result of this project, we also created a charity and use the artwork to raise funds for shelters and rescue groups. I also work with

Mark painting three eight-foot-square paintings

schools and universities to show the students how they can use their art and creativity to make a difference and be a voice for social change.

This entire project began because of my love for my best friends, Rudy and Santina. They became the spiritual anchor in my life. Without Santina and Rudy, I never would have gotten—or stayed—sober. Each daily walk with them was like a walking meditation. Rudy and Santina played a vital role in my healing and redemption and were ultimately the catalyst for my charity, An Act of Dog.

Without knowing their love, I would not have cared enough to help voiceless shelter animals. No human has ever given me the unconditional love I experienced from my two best buddies, Rudy and Santina. An Act of Dog is my way of honoring them and being of service to all the shelter animals whose lives are decimated every day. I hope to be the voice that creates a village of compassionate advocates that changes the fate for these animals and gives them a second chance at a beautiful life. Today, I give them my all because Rudy and Santina gave me their all—including giving me back my life.

Chapter Eighteen
CAROL

In the first Magical Dogs *book, I wrote about reconnecting with my first love, Robb. Robb's daughter, Phaedra, had mentioned a woman named Carol to me over the years. When I began working on this book, Phaedra connected us and Carol agreed to share her story of dogs and witches.*

GROWING UP, I RESCUED DOGS. WHILE I LOVED EVERY SINGLE ONE, they were dogs, just dogs—until Dakota. Dakota Aspen Lang was the dog that changed the way I think about animals and molded me into the person I am today. Dakota remains the inspiration behind all I do to help animals.

When my son was ten, he wanted a dog, so we reached out to our neighbor who raised black Labs. He never sold them but rather gave them to friends he knew would give a dog a great home and a lot of love.

We asked to be placed on his list for the next litter and learned we were thirteenth on the list. Thinking there was no way Belle would have thirteen puppies, we asked to be put on the list for her next litter, but he said this was very likely going to be Belle's last litter. We decided to wait and see what happened.

Dakota

Belle went into labor and birthed thirteen healthy, happy puppies. My son got his puppy, who he named Dakota. Another neighbor got a puppy for their son, and those two dogs and two boys were together nonstop, literally growing up together.

After my son went away to college, Dakota and I got extremely close. We went through therapy dog training, and after being certified, we started visiting nursing homes and a children's hospital. Everywhere we went, Dakota was so giving and made people smile. When I saw the impact Dakota was having on others, I decided it was time for me to do something to give back too, so in 2005, I started the Ballston Spa Witch Walk.

The Witch Walk is an annual pub crawl held on the Friday before Halloween in Ballston Spa, New York. The witches, dressed in their finest garb and witch hats, travel to local establishments. Every participant pays a registration fee, with half of the money going to animal organizations and the other half going toward food and prizes. The first year we had thirty witches, but we now average 200 witches every year. It has become the biggest night for bars and restaurants in Ballston Spa. More importantly, the witches have raised thousands of dollars for local animal organizations.

The Witch Walk is a wonderful event because everyone comes together to raise money for animals. We have helped the Estherville Animal Shelter, a no-kill shelter in Greenfield, New York, that relies solely on donations. We have partnered with the Adirondack Veterinary Clinic to help seniors receive discounted rates and assistance with veterinary bills. We have donated to Veterans Moving Forward to support veterans who need dogs to help with their lives as well as Paws Across America and Hope for Paws. Animals make a difference in people's lives and oftentimes nobody speaks up for them, so I am thankful for all I and my friends have been able to do to help them.

For years, I also organized the Busy Bones 500, an annual walk for the Saratoga County Animal Shelter (SCAS). The monies raised from the walk helped SCAS build their new shelter and pay for expenses the county did not cover. It also helped pay for outside pens for meet-and-greets and to allow the dogs to play outside.

For two years, Dakota was the mascot of the dog walk, but the second year she developed bone cancer. We kept her going, but when she was thirteen-and-a-half, she fell and broke her leg. My husband, son, and I were with Dakota when she went.

The next year we did the walk in memory of Dakota, but I stopped doing it because the Witch Walk was growing and taking up more of my time.

Dakota and I were so close and it was like losing my best friend. I

Gracie

cried for eight weeks. My husband tried everything to pull me out of my grief but I just kept telling him I would get over it in my own time and my own way. We lost Dakota in February, and that November, the shelter called about Gracie Mae, a six-year-old, 104-pound, Lab–Rottweiler mix that had been picked up as a stray by Animal Control. Despite placing ads in all the area newspapers, no one ever claimed Gracie.

Gracie was animal-aggressive and the shelter was going to put her down. Even though I still wasn't ready for another dog, I also couldn't have a dog put down, so we brought Gracie home. It turned out that the shelter was right. Gracie was wonderful with people but not with other dogs. She had a favorite tree in our yard that she loved to lie under, but we could never leave her off leash because she would go after other dogs or animals.

Gracie taught me a lot. She showed me the other side of an animal, because as good as Dakota was, Gracie was that bad. I worked with an animal behaviorist, but the bottom line and my biggest lesson was that Gracie was simply being Gracie. It's who she was. I don't know what happened before we got her, but based on some of her actions and reactions, I think Gracie may have lived where she was tormented by dogs on the other side of a chain-link fence.

When Gracie was found, she was wearing a collar and had just had her toenails done, so I know someone cared for her. I don't know if they got tired of her always trying to get out and finally just told her if she wanted to go then to just go. Initially, we weren't able to touch Gracie's tail or feet, but over time she turned out to be a real snuggler. We had Gracie for over six years and we loved her every single day until she passed.

Then SCAS called about three purebred black Lab puppies who were being brought in by a man who had gone to a breeder. When he saw the puppies' living conditions, he was so upset and concerned for them that he bought all three puppies. He did his best but was ultimately overwhelmed by the amount of time and work required to care for them, so when they were six months old, he asked SCAS to help him find them homes. The puppies were named Timber, Cedar, and Spruce. We chose Timber, and a few days later, Cedar and Spruce also went to wonderful homes.

When we first saw Timber at the shelter, he was so forlorn. He constantly stared down at the floor and wouldn't make eye contact with anyone. Now Timber is vibrant and happy. He loves to jump off the dock and swim. Timber gets along with everybody, listens, never gets in trouble, and has been a godsend.

Timber's best friend is my grandchild, Pinecone, who happens to be a guinea pig. My son and daughter-in-law have chosen not to have children and instead to focus on animals. My daughter-in-law is like my best friend. She is my heart and has the same mission as I have: helping animals. I am so glad my son found her and so is Timber, because now he can eat and sleep with Pinecone. They are so cute together.

While time has helped heal the loss of Dakota, it is still difficult for me to talk about her. She has a piece of my heart and always will. I had her cremated and her ashes sit on my dresser. I talk to her and ask her to watch out for the animals. I still feel like she's a part of my life.

I also credit my girlfriends for helping me through everything—especially the loss of Dakota. They stood behind and

Timber and Pinecone

beside me, and their support helped me get through it and enabled me to do all that I do now to help animals.

Sometimes healing and blessings come in small and unexpected packages. Another person who helped me was a friend's daughter, a little girl who just turned seven, who I call Ms. Gregory. On the fourth Christmas after losing Dakota, Ms. Gregory gave me a puzzle. The picture on the puzzle was of all of my dogs who had passed, and when I saw it, I burst into tears. She immediately started to apologize for making me sad but I assured her they were happy tears. It truly was the best present I ever received.

I know there will be special dogs again in my life, but none will ever be as special as Dakota. She totally engrained herself in me. All of the work I do is because of Dakota, and she truly made me the person I am today.

Chapter Nineteen
WALTER

The first time I met Walter, I was drawn in by his sense of humor, incredible wit, and amazing stories from his years spent working in the music business. I loved hanging out with Walter and his dog, Bear, and wanted to share their story in my first Magical Dogs *book but the timing wasn't right. Thankfully, the timing was right for this book because I can now introduce you to my friend Walter and a dog named Bear.*

WHEN I WAS ABOUT TEN, MY PARENTS AND I DROVE TO HOWELL Township in search of a dog. There was an AKC breeder who had pure-bred poodles and schnauzers. While I did not want a schnauzer and wasn't too thrilled about a poodle either, the bottom line was that it wasn't my money so it wasn't my choice.

When we arrived, the woman had three separate litters of poodle puppies. She opened the door to one room and five puppies ran out. After she got them all back in, she opened the next door and six little puppies ran out—with the exception of one. That one puppy ran over to my father and jumped up on him. She couldn't have been more excited so my father immediately asked about her. The breeder explained she was not for sale and that she was actually going to have her put down because her coloring was not perfect.

My father looked at the woman and said, "Let me understand this. You're going to kill this puppy because her color isn't perfect?" When the breeder said she had to in order to protect the pedigree bloodline, my father said, "Then that's the dog we want. I don't care what color you put on the papers. We want her."

The woman filled out the papers and we left with our puppy. Driving home, I realized my father had just saved this puppy's life. That had a huge impact on me. As I looked back at the puppy sitting on the rear deck of the car, she looked back at me—and proceeded to throw up all over me.

She was a parti poodle, which are dogs that have a white base and large irregular patches of another color. She was predominately white with patches of grey and a touch of apricot. She was a miniature poodle, but being the runt of the litter, she only ever grew to be the size of a toy poodle. After learning from her papers that the sire was from West Virginia and named Prince Sapphire Star of Sassafras, we named her Sapphire.

A couple of years later, we were all watching "The Tonight Show" when Doris Day came on with her three poodles. She started telling Johnny Carson about her dogs and explained that one was named Sassafras and another was named Star after their father: Prince Sapphire Star of Sassafras from West Virginia. From that point on, we told everyone that Sapphire was a half-sister to Doris Day's dogs. Sapphire was a great dog who died in her sleep when she was seventeen.

In the early '70s, I was attending Livingston College, a division of Rutgers University, and worked at the campus radio station. One weekend, Andie, who also worked at the station, brought in her bearded collie, Heather. Heather was one of the funniest, smartest dogs I ever met and I instantly fell in love with her.

The radio station fired Andie's boyfriend that same weekend, and he walked out, leaving Andie and Heather stranded. I drove them home and went back to school, but Andie and I eventually started dating, got engaged, and married.

We were married less than two years when I came home one day and realized Andie's curling iron and Heather were missing. Knowing she never went anywhere without Heather or her curling iron, I knew she was gone and the marriage was over.

Even though I always wanted a dog, after college I was working in the music business. When I wasn't on tour with bands or travelling to radio stations around the country, I was working in New York City. In 1984, I started my own artist management company, and after more years of traveling, I started dividing my time between California and the East Coast. Between being so busy and constantly travelling, I knew the time wasn't right to get a dog.

By 1999, I had sold my California office and was spending most of my time back in New York. I was living in Hunterdon County, New Jersey, and started volunteering and serving on the board for two New

Jersey rescues: St. Hubert's Animal Welfare Center and Rawhide Rescue. The more involved I got in the world of animal rescue, the more I started thinking about getting a dog. My parents lived only an hour away and I knew they would watch my dog if I had to travel. I had also met great dog walkers and pet sitters and soon realized I had a system in place that would allow me to get a dog.

Bear

One of the first dogs I saw on Petfinder was the saddest excuse for a Border collie I had ever seen—and I fell in love. He was with Sweet Border Collie Rescue, which was part of Glen Highland Farm in New York State. I inquired about him and learned he was with a foster family in Connecticut, so I drove three hours to meet him.

The foster mom told me his name was Bear, although his original family called him Schmooky Bear. When she figured out that Schmooky Bear was their attempt to say Smokey the Bear with their thick Eastern European accent, she shortened his name to Bear.

As I walked up their driveway, she said, "He won't come to you but for the heck of it, call him and let's see what happens."

I called his name. Bear looked up, ran to me, and started jumping all over me. We hung around the house talking, and the entire time, Bear stayed by my side.

Prior to my visit, I had completed all of the Glen Highland Farm paperwork, so when the foster saw the connection we had, she called Lillie, one of the owners and founders of Glen Highland Farm. Lillie said I could take him home. Before leaving, the foster warned me that Bear was not thrilled about riding in cars. Once again, she suggested I call him to get him into the car and see what happened.

I walked to my car, opened the door, turned to Bear, and said, "Bear, do you want to go for a ride?" Bear ran, jumped into my car, and made himself at home. I had never seen a dog more excited to go for a car ride.

My Jeep had two bucket seats with a console in between. Bear sat in the passenger seat but kept jumping up on the console, grabbing my arm, and holding it up to his chest. He would look out the window, look at me, and then kiss me. He couldn't have been happier or more at home.

I got Bear home and everything went great. During the week while I was at work, I had great pet walkers who came in and walked him around the state park across from where I lived. The rest of the time, Bear stayed in my game room and was content looking out over my four acres of land at the deer, squirrels, and birds.

On the weekends, he loved being together and would run in circles around the pool chasing the pool cleaner. He loved living in the country—we both did—and everything went fine for the first few weeks.

Then one day, we were walking down the stairs and I foolishly still had him on a leash. The leash wrapped around my legs and I fell down the stairs and broke my leg. It was the first time I had ever broken anything in my life. I was in serious pain but managed to crawl to my phone and call an ambulance. When I came home later that day, Bear kept coming over and kissing me. You could tell he felt bad about what happened but I kept reassuring him that everything was fine.

Since I owned my company, Concrete Management, I decided to start taking Bear with me to work. He loved being in the car and loved the commute from New Jersey to SoHo every day, barking with his tail wagging the entire drive. The women in the office loved him and he would either lie under my desk or theirs or sit next to a window where he could look out at the city. Whenever there was a siren, which happens a lot in New York City, he howled, but thankfully that was the only time he ever howled.

Our office was located on the corner of Broome Street and West Broadway. Every day, Bear and I took a break and went for a walk around the block. At the end of our walk, before going back into the office, we sat together on the front stoop and relaxed. We regularly passed a woman and her dogs, and over time, we began to stop and talk while our dogs played. She introduced herself as Carolyn.

One day, I saw Carolyn and her dogs walking toward me with a tall dark-haired guy at her side. As they got closer, I realized the guy was John F. Kennedy Jr.

As our dogs began to play, Carolyn turned to him and said, "John, this is the dog and the guy I was telling you about."

He introduced himself, we shook hands, and we talked while he knelt down to pet Bear. It turned out I had been talking to Carolyn Bessette-Kennedy, the wife of John F. Kennedy Jr. Tragically, a few weeks later they both died in a plane crash.

In 2003, I closed my office in New York, retired from the music business, and went back to Rutgers University to finish my degree in journalism. I began writing for a local newspaper, and anytime I was on assignment, Bear came along. He met the local police, emergency squads, mayors, and people in the small towns near where I lived. Bear was a really popular dog and everybody knew and loved him.

Bear had a great sense of humor and was incredibly smart, calm, affectionate, and well-behaved—and also redefined the term "party animal." Anytime I had parties or visitors at my house, Bear started at one end of the room and walked over and touched someone on the knee with his paw. He would stand there and wait for them to pet him; when he got tired of them, he walked to the next person and repeated the entire process. Bear literally worked the entire room until everyone had either petted him or scratched him behind the ears.

The only time Bear ever acted out was when a motorcycle or truck passed us—then he went absolutely nuclear. He would get upset, start shaking, and bounce from window to window.

All I knew about Bear's past was that he was kept unleashed in a yard and constantly ran into the street to chase motorcycles and trucks. The police were constantly catching him and returning him home and finally told Bear's owners that they needed to keep him on a leash. They also told them that if they found him running loose one more time, they were going to take him to the shelter. Sure enough, one more time happened and the police brought Bear to the shelter. The shelter, in turn, called Glen Highland Farm.

A few years after Bear came into my life, we went to a reunion at Glen Highland Farm. We had such a great time meeting other dogs and owners, and with acres of fenced-in property, Bear could just run and play with the other dogs. Even when he was off running and playing, if Bear turned and saw me, he would come back and sit next to me before running off again to play. We had such a great time.

Lillie and I were talking that weekend when we heard some really loud half-menacing barks. We turned and two dogs were in a scuffle. Bear got up, ran over, and banged into them. The dogs were stunned and immediately stopped and broke apart. Bear stood between them, barking and staring at one before turning to bark and stare at the other. Both dogs stood and silently stared at Bear. As he started to walk back toward Lillie and me, Bear turned one final time and barked at them as if to say, "Break it up and knock it off!" Then he ran back to me, his tail wagging, satisfied that he got the last word.

He did the same thing at the dog park. If he saw a dog getting too rough, Bear would go over and stop things before it got out of control, restoring and ensuring peace before coming back to me, tail wagging.

In 2009, I was in a bad front-end car accident. Luckily, Bear was in the back cargo area. I immediately called out to Bear. While I knew he must have gotten bounced around, he seemed okay. I was coherent enough and able to pick up my cell phone with a broken arm so I called a friend who lived down the road to come get Bear. My concern was that someone would accidentally open the back door and Bear would jump out and run onto the highway.

When my friend arrived, the highway had been shut down and there were ambulances, police cars, and fire trucks everywhere. The road was closed for hours.

I spent the next three weeks in the hospital going through several surgeries. When it became obvious that I was not going to be returning home for months, my mom and dad moved from their house into my house and brought Bear back home. For the next four months, they came to the nursing home twice a day and brought Bear along so I could see him.

At first, when Bear saw me lying there unable to stand or get out of bed, he was confused. He would look at me then walk into the corner of the room and stare as if he was trying to process what he was seeing. I believe that, in his own way, Bear was trying to figure out where I had been, what I was doing there, and why I couldn't get up and walk out with him.

After visiting me for about a week, Bear finally came over and put his head on the bed. It seemed that on some level, he was finally starting to accept and understand what was happening.

Eventually, Bear started enjoying the visits and people definitely enjoyed Bear. He would come to see me first, then he would walk down the hall to see the other patients. He entered each room, put his head on their bed and let them pet him, then went to the next person and did the same thing. He was doing the same thing at the nursing home that he always did at my parties!

Anytime Bear was at the nursing home, word spread like wildfire. Before

Bear

long you heard people yelling, "Send Bear in!" He made his rounds and everybody loved him. He was like a therapy dog without the credentials.

Unfortunately, when he was sixteen, Bear started having trouble walking and began to lose control of his bladder and bowel functions. He struggled to walk or stand. When he began falling down, I used a cradle to support him, but finally, he couldn't do it anymore. You could see in his eyes that he was near the end, and the vet confirmed it was time.

I was with him, lying on the floor petting him, and will never forget when she gave him the final shot. You could see Bear quieting down, then she said, "He's gone." My parents were there and we were all crying. It was terrible. It was torture.

My grandmother died when I was thirty-three, but the loss of Bear, while it may sound silly, was the first major loss in my life—and it's a loss I don't think you ever get over.

My dad passed away recently from Parkinson's disease and my mom and I have been talking about getting another dog. Since I don't have a big backyard like I did with Bear, it would have to be a smaller, calmer dog—perhaps a senior dog. It hasn't happened yet but we could be close. There will never be another Bear but I would love to bring another rescue dog home.

Chapter Twenty

LET'S PAWS: PET LOSS AND BEREAVEMENT

Carol, Walter, and so many others shared the impact the passing of a beloved dog had on them. Kristian called it a "come-back-down-to-earth moment." It is a common denominator for everyone who has loved and lost a beloved pet, yet everyone's response to it is unique and different.

On the day I met Joe and Daniel, he asked what brought me to write Magical Dogs. I explained it was a response and a way to heal after my dog Brooke passed. Even though it had been several years, I cried as I told him.

Joe invited me to be his guest at the Association for Pet Loss and Bereavement (APLB) Eighth International Conference the following week in Atlantic City, New Jersey.

The conference offered seminars on a wide range of topics ranging from compassion fatigue and anticipatory grief to pet hospice and pets and the elderly. I found it to be an incredibly healing and inspirational day on many levels. I was grateful when Joe introduced me to Dr. Wallace Sife, the CEO and founder of the APLB, and was incredibly honored when Dr. Sife took the time a few weeks later to speak with me for this piece.

IN 1987, MY BELOVED SEVEN-YEAR-OLD MINIATURE DACHSHUND, Edel Meister, died suddenly and unexpectedly due to congestive heart failure. I am a psychologist with extensive training in thanatology, the scientific study of death, yet I could not find any practical insights to help me through my intense and inconsolable grief over Edel Meister's death. It was two weeks before I could even begin to make the slightest pretense at functioning normally.

At the time, pet bereavement was little understood or respected.

There were only three books available but none of them addressed the emotional issues that I felt really needed to be taken into consideration. Much of what was being published was simply to support the belief that pet bereavement was real and valid. Nothing was being written to help the person who was grieving or offer them any immediate help.

Edel Meister

I painfully crawled through my own grief until I was able to finally gain some perspective on what was happening. After much time, many tears, and intense research, I resolved to write the book I would have wanted for myself after Edel died.

The Loss of a Pet: A Guide to Coping with the Grieving Process When a Pet Dies is a loving and healing memorial to Edel and to all the other beloved pets who have passed through this world.

At the urging of many of my readers, I founded the APLB in October 1997. Our initial meetings were held in private homes and in the basement of a library in Long Island, New York. In June 1998, we created a website. Today, we have loyal members across the globe. In order to connect them, we offer bimonthly sessions both online and via teleconference. We also have online chat rooms where people can receive support from my trained assistants.

All living things die, but the purpose of my book and the APLB is to help you connect with others and to draw upon the love you shared with your pet to minimize your grief and pain. In many ways, bereavement is the start of permanently celebrating the life and love you shared with your pet.

It is important for people to understand they are not alone and that the anguish they are feeling has been felt by millions of others. The shock of losing a beloved pet is one of the most profound emotional traumas one can experience. You are mourning the loss of your dearest friend and soul mate, as well as a member of your immediate family. Mourning this unique kind of loss is painful and can seem unending, but understanding how to deal with it helps make some of the anguish more bearable.

While intellectually we might understand the death of a beloved pet, emotionally it is hard to accept. The grief and heartbreak may seem out of proportion. While the exceptional feelings and irrational periods are common symptoms, some people are stunned and left questioning their own sanity and stability.

One of the questions I am often asked is, "How long will this terrible pain go on?" There is no easy answer to that question because there are too many different and personal factors involved in the healing process. However, there are several things you can do to assist you as you heal.

Reading and learning about grief and what you are going through can be helpful because it is like having a roadmap when traveling through unknown and frightening territory.

It may also be helpful to keep in mind that humans are creatures of habit and structure. Life with a beloved pet often means that we adapted our home and life around them, so changing or modifying daily routines—or creating new patterns and routines—can help the healing process.

Too many physical reminders and associations of the pet in our life and around our home can be upsetting, at least initially, so it may be helpful to remove or reduce them for a while.

Regardless of the pet's age, we can never be truly prepared for the loss of the pet. The resultant shock and unavoidable psychological reaction cannot and should not be easily dismissed or glossed over.

It is absolutely essential to give yourself permission to heal, to allow yourself time, and to be patient with yourself. Bereavement is a slow process and happens in stages.

It is also helpful and important to allow ourselves opportunities to both speak about the loss and grieve freely and openly. In doing so, we are able to release some of the pain to make room for healing. The result is a shorter and more constructive mourning period.

There are people who will tell you it was "just a dog," but many of those people have never known the unique love of a pet and are unqualified to judge us or our grief. Other well-intentioned people will try to cheer you up, not understanding that tears and going through a deeply personal period of mourning is a necessary step to healing.

While what others do or say may be upsetting or aggravating, it is important not to overreact to a person or situation. Remember that you are in a vulnerable state. It is wise to keep your own best interests in mind, which usually means waiting before making any impulsive decisions or comments.

Finally, surround yourself with others who understand or have experienced what you are going through. The APLB was started to create a community of individuals who understand what you are feeling, as well as to support you in your journey of healing and to ultimately celebrate the life and love you shared with your beloved pet.

Chapter Twenty-One
CHRISSY

Looking back, it's obvious that long before I ever thought about writing this book, the dogs already knew I would. My proof of that lies in the fact that shortly after the release of Magical Dogs, *I went to Florida on a book tour. While there, I made connections between dogs and stories for this book, although at the time I wasn't aware of them happening.*

The first connection occurred while having dinner at a beautiful ocean-side restaurant in Ormond Beach with my friend Trish. Trish and Great Dawg Rescue appeared in Magical Dogs. *Over dinner, Trish casually mentioned a woman we had worked with years before back in New Jersey, saying, "If you ever write another book, reach out to Chrissy. She has a story to tell."*

After this book started coming together, I remembered what Trish said and connected with Chrissy. She definitely had a story to tell.

FOR THE FIRST FIVE YEARS OF MY LIFE, THE ONLY DOG I WAS EVER around was my uncle's Chihuahua, Charlie. When I was six, my aunt's collie had puppies. She gave me a puppy and I named her what I thought was the only logical (and best) name: Collie. We all loved Collie and she had a wonderful life with my family until she passed at thirteen. We then went years without getting or even talking about another dog.

One afternoon, my mother and I were walking around Cook Forest State Park in western Pennsylvania and saw a Keeshond puppy. My mother instantly fell in love, and a few months later, we drove to Ohio so she could adopt one. She named her Misty, and soon after she adopted another Keeshond she named Samantha.

Misty and Samantha were totally loved, completely spoiled, and had wonderful, long, happy lives, both eventually dying of old age.

My husband, Dave, and I got married in October 1985. I don't think the ink was even dry on our marriage license before I started telling Dave that I wanted a dog. Dave didn't want the responsibility and constantly told me, "Absolutely not. Nope. No dogs."

As Christmas approached, I reminded Dave that a dog would make a really wonderful Christmas present. Dave's response didn't change. "Absolutely not. Nope. No dogs."

Christmas came and went without a dog, so on New Year's Eve, I took matters into my own hands. After seeing an ad for golden retriever puppies, Dave's mother and I hopped in my car and drove to Pittsburgh to see them. The instant we pulled up to the curb in front of the house, we realized we weren't in the best part of town. We decided to get in and out as quickly as possible. I stuffed the money deep into my pocket, and we locked arms as we walked up to the front door and knocked. We heard shuffling inside followed by the sound of someone sliding and unlocking a succession of chains and bolts. Our concern and fear mounted, but I was determined to get a puppy.

The door finally opened a crack and a man peered out at us from amidst a maze of chains that still remained locked. "What do you want?"

"I'm here about the puppy," I said.

"Hold on." Closing the door, we heard him removing the rest of the chains. He finally opened the door, and without any introduction, he led us through the living room toward the basement door. Pointing down the steep basement stairs, he said, "The puppies are down there."

My mother-in-law looked at me. We both knew she was physically unable to navigate the steps. Keeping a tight grip on my money, I followed him down the stairs while my mother-in-law stood at the top and watched. There in the dark, dusty basement were eight adorable golden retriever puppies in a pen. I noticed they were constantly distracted and upset by a loud noise. Since it was distracting me too, I asked what it was.

"Don't worry. It's nothing. It's the ice machine." I looked around. There was no ice machine.

I had always been told to let a pet pick you, so I sat down on the dusty, dirty basement floor with the puppies. Slowly, one by one, they came over to meet and sniff me—and then one came back and curled up in my lap.

Realizing my puppy had found me, I knew I should get out as quickly as possible. I picked the puppy up, followed the man upstairs, and handed him the money. My mother-in-law and I turned to leave, but he put his hand on my arm and said, "Slow down. I want to get to know you."

We talked with him for several minutes before finally convincing him that we needed to get back on the road. He walked us out, and once we and the puppy were settled in my car, the man leaned his head in the window and quietly said, "Lock your doors and get out of here! Whatever you do, don't stop for anything or anybody. Just go! Get out of here!"

We did exactly as he instructed: we locked the doors and drove, without stopping, to my mother-in-law's house. I called Dave to tell him we would be home soon. There was an awkward silence before Dave said, "We?" Without answering, I hung up.

I drove home, put the puppy in the basement, and went upstairs. Dave took one look at me and said, "So, where's the dog?"

I pointed downstairs so Dave went down to see her. Although he tried to be upset with me, he took one look at her and it was love at first sight. Nikki was home.

The first week, Nikki was erratic and unpredictable. Her behavior was unlike any dog or puppy I had ever been around. Weeks later, my mother-in-law heard there had been a drug raid on the house where we got Nikki. I wondered if Nikki's behavior in those early days was because she had drugs in her system.

Since Nikki's mother and her pups had never been out of the basement, Nikki didn't know what grass was or how to walk on it. With the exception of Dave, she didn't like men, so we began working with her to overcome her fears by introducing her to new experiences and people. She became such a sweet dog and the three of us had such a good time together.

One night, while Dave was at work, someone tried to break into our house. Nikki and I were home alone but she immediately bolted off the bed, hit the door full throttle, and scared away whoever was on the other side of the door. Nikki sat at the door without moving the rest of the night to make sure I was safe. In many ways, Nikki was always my protector. Sometimes I wondered if it was her way of thanking me for getting her out of that house.

When Dave and I decided to move to New Jersey, many of our discussions revolved around Nikki. We were concerned how the move would impact her. She loved wide-open spaces but we were moving into a tiny apartment. We discussed our concerns with our veterinarian and he immediately offered to take Nikki and let her live on his farm. It was heart-wrenching to leave Nikki, but we knew it was the right decision because it allowed her to live the best life she could.

We moved to New Jersey and two years later started building a house in Pennsylvania. I wanted another dog but Dave kept reminding me we were busy building a house. We finished our home and moved in on the first of December. Once again, I started telling Dave a dog would make a wonderful Christmas present. Dave kept telling me, "Chrissy, we just finished building a house. Give it time."

Undeterred, the week after Christmas, I once again took matters into my own hands and brought home a black Lab puppy. Once again, Dave loved the puppy. We began tossing names around but nothing seemed to fit. That night, I took her outside. It was a beautiful night and the full moon lit up our yard. As we walked around the yard, the moonlight cast her shadow onto the lawn and she started growling and barking at it. We named her Shadow.

Shadow loved everyone. The first weekend we had her, she ran over into our neighbor's yard to meet him. The neighbor took one look at Shadow, turned to me, and said, "If I find her in my yard again, I'm going to give her antifreeze."

I looked at him, confused, and said, "But that would kill her."

He looked me square in the eyes and said, "My point exactly."

Shocked, I immediately picked Shadow up and went home. That is one of the meanest things anyone has ever said to me or my dog, and from that day forward, I always made sure Shadow was never off leash when we were outside. I never wanted to take the chance she could wander over to my neighbor's yard.

The remainder of our first weekend together was wonderful—then Monday rolled around. Dave had already left for work, so when I left, I decided to let Shadow have the house to herself. After all, how much trouble could a puppy get into? I said goodbye, hopped in my car, and went to work.

Dave got home first. As soon as I pulled into the driveway, he stepped out onto the porch. I immediately knew something was wrong. In an even, calm voice, he said, "Come on in and see what your dog did."

We had only been in the house a little over a month, and one of the last things we did was have brand-new carpeting installed throughout the house. Shadow had apparently gotten hold of a loose carpet thread on the stairs and ran with it. By the time Dave got home, she had managed to unravel two entire steps of carpeting, leaving a long string spread throughout the house.

We built a pen to keep Shadow and our house safe. It worked great until the day she got out of the pen and into our recycling. She chewed up several Pepsi cans, and we spent an anxious forty-eight hours watching her until we were sure she was going to be fine.

My dad came over and built a partition in the basement, which worked great until the day I accidentally left my coat down there and she chewed the zipper off. Shadow wasn't a bad dog. She simply didn't want to be alone or confined, so two years later, I adopted a husky. Most huskies have silver coats but this one was the color of hot chocolate so I named her KoKo.

Initially, KoKo and Shadow merely tolerated one another, but ultimately they became best friends. As KoKo grew, she learned and taught Shadow how to climb over the partition, so my dad came back and built the partition a little higher. Since the partition was too high for them to get over, KoKo changed tactics and opted instead to start chewing the plywood in an attempt to get out. We now had two dogs who didn't like being confined, but over time, they both calmed down and stopped chewing things.

While Dave always started out being upset, it never lasted. He always fell in love with the dogs and realized they were good for us. Ultimately, the dogs also ended up saving my life.

It was a cold, windy Saturday in February. Dave was at work, and since my parents were scheduled to arrive on Monday for a visit, I woke up early to clean the house. When I finished cleaning, the dogs and I sat down in front of the woodstove for an afternoon nap.

Shortly after three-thirty, Shadow and KoKo started barking and nipping at the back of my leg. Thinking they had to go out, I walked over and opened the door. They refused to go out, instead looking up at me then out the door. They wouldn't budge and just kept barking.

Finally I looked in the direction they were barking and saw flames shooting out of the side of the house around the chimney. Opening the

KoKo and Shadow

sliding glass door, I told Shadow and KoKo to go to the truck and ran to grab the phone to call 911. When the operator answered, I gave her our address and screamed, "There's a fire. I have two dogs here and I need to get out of the house. Please hurry!"

I remember running out of the house, closing the sliding glass door, and looking over to see Shadow and KoKo sitting next to the truck. They didn't have their leashes on but they did exactly as I had instructed. The three of us sat in the truck and watched the fire company come and start to fight the blaze. We watched as the fire billowed up into the attic and came back down the other side of the house. We watched as the wind whipped and the fire turned into a blazing inferno.

When Dave got there, the four of us walked over and sat under a tree in a neighbor's yard. Holding one another, we watched the roof cave in on the exact spot where I had been sitting and sleeping just a short time before. We watched as our bedroom went up in flames. We watched until the only thing left in our bedroom were the springs to our mattress.

We lost our house and everything in it. We still had our memories but the pictures that captured those memories were gone. Yet I still had what was most important: my husband and my dogs who had been my angels and saved my life.

Neighbors we barely knew immediately offered to let the four of us stay with them that night. They continued to open their home to us as one night turned into one month. We are forever grateful for the kindness and generosity they showered on us and our dogs as we started to put the pieces of our life back together.

A recovery company finally brought a small trailer for us to live in on our property right behind where our house had been. Even though it was horrible to look out at the charred remains of our house, it was still wonderful to have a place of our own.

KoKo and Shadow weren't so thrilled about living in the trailer. In fact, KoKo disliked it so much that she actually dug a hole in the floor trying to escape. It didn't help that the trailer came complete with mice, because every night we heard them scurrying around and the dogs went crazy digging at the vent in an attempt to get to them.

We lived in the trailer as we began building a new home. We completely redesigned our home because I was afraid if we built the same house, it would happen again. It was ultimately determined that the fire was due to builder neglect. The chimney had been improperly constructed and it was suspected the fire had probably been smoldering in the wall for hours that day before finally igniting.

Knowing the problem with our first house was a construction error that should have been found, I constantly checked the new house to make sure everything was being done the right way. I checked every wall and every stud. I checked everything going in and out of the house in the hopes we would never have to go through anything like that again.

When the house was finished and we moved in, I was concerned how the dogs would react, but they walked in, immediately found a space to call their own, and were fine.

Shortly after moving into the house, I was outside with Shadow and KoKo. It was a beautiful cool night, and when I called for them, they ran up the deck steps followed by a little grey dog. I opened the door and they ran in. The little grey dog followed them, ran in, and immediately lay down on a dog bed.

The dogs looked at me as if to say, "You're bringing something else into the house?" but Dave's reaction was a tad more serious. "Chrissy, get it out!"

"No," I said. "It's a puppy and it found us."

"It's not a puppy, Chrissy. It's a wolf!"

What I thought was a tiny grey husky was, in fact, a wolf.

"Its mama is probably right outside," Dave said.

I looked out onto the deck and didn't see anything, so I opened the door and tried to lure the baby wolf outside, but it just lay there staring at me. I put another dog bed outside and it finally went out and lay down on it. The next morning, the bed had been pulled to the edge of the deck and the baby wolf was gone. Just as Dave predicted, the baby wolf's mama must have come and gotten him.

Dave, Shadow, KoKo, and I had a great life together in our new home. KoKo passed from liver disease at fifteen and Shadow passed at seventeen from old age. I will forever be thankful for the life and love we shared. They will always be my angels.

After KoKo and Shadow passed, a Westie named Spike came into our lives. At the time, my parents were going through some health issues. My dad was a ten-year cancer survivor, but in the twelfth year, the cancer came back full force. My dad loved Spike, so I would put Spike in my bag and sneak him into the hospital to see my dad. We kept it up until the staff discovered us and asked us to leave. While my dad was in the hospital, we shared Spike with my mom so he could keep her company.

My dad's cancer was really aggressive and he didn't live very long. By the time he passed, my mom was in a nursing home but I was allowed to bring Spike to visit her. As soon as we were in the lobby, I unhooked Spike and he ran over to the elevator and scratched at the door. He would calmly ride in the elevator, but as soon as the door opened on my mother's floor, Spike ran straight into her room and jumped onto her bed. Spike brought life and happiness into my mother's life. There wasn't anything seriously wrong with my mother other than a broken heart, but exactly five weeks—almost to the hour—after my father passed, my mom passed.

After my mother passed, we got another Westie that Dave named Pinkie. Very quickly, Pinkie began to rule the roost—including Spike, Dave, and me.

The following year, I decided to visit Road Trip Rescues in Mount Bethel, Pennsylvania. I told Dave I was going to just "look around." Before I left, Dave looked at me and said, "I only have one question. How many are you going to get?"

How *many* was I going to get? This was awesome!

I immediately decided to adopt an eight-week-old black Lab–

Rottweiler mix—until I saw the little brown puppy who refused to leave his side. Every time I picked up the black puppy, the little brown one barked. If I put the black puppy down, the brown puppy stopped barking. I learned they were brothers who had been brought up together from Tennessee. They both had a white star on their chest in the same exact place. Once I saw that, I knew I couldn't leave the brown one behind. We named the black puppy Dozer and the brown puppy Diesel because my husband works on heavy equipment.

Even though all of the dogs loved one another, sometimes Pinkie and Spike wanted their own space. Not Diesel and Dozer. There was an extra-special connection between them. Other than at night, they always wanted to be around and touching each other.

A few months ago, Diesel crossed the Rainbow Bridge. He hadn't been himself for a few days, and initially I thought he just missed Dave, who was out of town for his brother's funeral. When it continued, I took him to our veterinarian. She drew blood and walked back into the room somberly and told me Diesel was very sick. He had advanced diabetes that had been wreaking havoc on his organs for a while. I was shocked because he never once showed any signs of illness or distress. He was always happy and just wanted to be close and get hugs and kisses.

Dozer, Spike, Pinkie, Diesel
(clockwise from top left)

When I was finally able to wrap my mind around what the vet was telling me, I understood my desire to have Diesel live a little longer would mean him suffering a little longer. I made the heartbreaking decision to let him go because I wanted Diesel to have peace. I know with certainty that the day I pass, Diesel will be there to greet me.

I always wondered

if animals grieve and now, because of Dozer, I know they do. Dozer looks for his brother. He hits his collar, which still hangs by the door. All of our dogs have their own dog bed, but Diesel was the only one who ever actually slept in his bed. Dozer now sleeps on Diesel's bed every night and Pinkie brings Diesel's favorite toy to bed with him.

Even though Shadow chewed the zipper off my coat and Koko chewed the partition and plywood, in the end it was just stuff. It could all be replaced. The most important thing Dave and I learned after the fire was that anything is replaceable except those you love—and for us, then and now, it is one another and our dogs.

Chapter Twenty-Two
KERRY

The dogs made another connection on my Florida book tour while I was staying in Key Largo at the home of my friend Captain Jim, his girlfriend, Barbie, and their magical American Eskimo dog, Astro. One morning, Jim said that if I ever wrote another dog book, I needed to talk to Mush because "Mush has stories to tell." It was almost word-for-word what Trish had said about Chrissy.

Jim connected us on Facebook, where I learned her name was actually Kerry. Shortly after I began working on this book, I followed Jim's advice and reached out to her. She invited me over for a visit. While her two little dogs intermittently sniffed and lay by me, Kerry told me about them and other dogs that had impacted her life and journey.

WHEN I WAS FIVE, MY FATHER BROUGHT HOME A BULLDOG NAMED Maggie. Maggie was my first dog and I loved spending time with her but suddenly one morning, I woke up and Maggie wasn't there. My mother said Maggie was giving birth. I was too young to understand or ask what that meant, but Maggie never came home; she just mysteriously disappeared. To this day, I have no idea what happened to her.

After Maggie, we got another bulldog named Happy. Just like Maggie, one day Happy was gone. This time my mother said Happy went to live on a farm, and again I was too young to question or understand. Looking back, I believe my mother may have struggled with having animals, but regardless of the cause, we did not have any more animals.

It wasn't until after I graduated from college that another dog came into my life. I was visiting my friend Jim in Key Largo when one morning he said, "Mush, I have the best dog for you." He told me the dog's owners had let her loose, she had wandered onto U.S. Highway 1, and was hit by a car. The people didn't want the dog back so she was taken to the shelter. "Her name is Heidi," Jim said. "She really is the sweetest dog. You should go visit her."

While I wanted a dog, I wasn't sure I had the time or energy to devote to one. I was working with horses, which often meant long hours and extensive travelling. I also wasn't convinced Heidi was the right dog for me, but based on everything Jim told me, I went to the shelter anyway.

Walking in, I saw a beautiful mixed-breed pup standing there with her tail wagging. It was Heidi. Every time she tried to walk toward me, she fell down. They explained this was due to a broken hip from being hit by the car. Seeing her in that condition broke my heart and I knew there was no way I could walk out and leave her there. Heidi came home with me that day.

I scheduled surgery for Heidi's hip, and Jim offered to let her recuperate at his home while I travelled for work. It was perfect because Heidi was well cared for and every day she swam with Jim, which further enhanced her recovery.

After she was completely healed, Heidi and I started travelling around the country. She stayed right next to me while I braided horses, and we went everywhere together. Heidi and I loved and enjoyed being together. She was with me through so many life events, including my marriage and the birth of my son. Then life took a few unexpected turns, starting with my divorce.

The divorce began a downward spiral and difficult period for Heidi and me. We had to move into a small apartment. That was followed by my getting a regular job, which meant I no longer had the ability to bring Heidi to work with me. Gone was our constant time together along with the wide-open spaces for Heidi to run. Before long, she began eating through doors anytime I left her alone and started to get increasingly aggressive and destructive.

When a friend offered to take Heidi and keep her on their farm, I faced a heart-wrenching decision. For years, Heidi had been my constant companion. I loved her, but coming home from work every day and seeing her like that absolutely broke my heart. I knew she was acting out because she wanted to get out of the house and be in the fresh air. I knew the right thing to do was allow Heidi to go live on the farm. She lived a long, happy life on the farm, but I was absolutely heartbroken.

For years, I didn't want to get another dog. Then one day while waiting for my son to finish his tae kwon do class, a woman walked past me with two beautiful Cavalier King Charles spaniels. I commented on how adorable her dogs were and she said they weren't hers. They had been found in the Everglades, somewhere between Naples and Marcos Island. She had been unable to locate their owners and was now looking for a home for them. When she asked if I was interested, I told her I was.

I posted ads and called shelters, rescues, and animal hospitals, both in New Jersey and Florida, but when no one ever came forward, I named them Marcos and Naples.

All I knew about them was that they were a male and a female and both under ten pounds. They had the most precious personalities, but several years later, history repeated itself. While going through another extremely difficult time in my life, I found myself once again searching for a new home for myself as well as for Marcos and Naples. While I found them a wonderful home, once again I was heartbroken and promised myself I would never do that again to a dog—or myself. I stayed focused on my work with horses, and for many years, I did not get a dog. But as we all know, sometimes a dog finds its way into your life—and that's what happened with Georgia.

With years of experience grooming horses and dogs, I applied for a job as a dog groomer. The day of the interview, I walked into a room filled with adorable little dogs. The woman explained that she bred Shih Tzus and that I would be her private groomer.

During the interview, one little dog came over to me and put her paw on my leg. I instinctively picked her up and looked in her big brown eyes. "Her name is Georgia," the woman said. "I am looking for a home for her."

I was shocked. "Why would you give this little dog up?"

The woman explained she was "done with her." In other words, Georgia was a breed dog who, at four years old, was no longer useful to this woman.

I looked at Georgia and her message to me was clear: "Please take me out of here."

The next day, I arrived for work. Once again, Georgia immediately came over and wanted me to pick her up. As I held her, the woman came in and began pointing at dogs. "Can you get that dog, that dog, that dog, and Georgia ready?"

I realized when she pointed at Georgia that she was getting ready to find someone to adopt her. Without realizing it, my feelings must have been written all over my face because the woman asked, "Are you all right?" When I failed to answer, she said, "Do you want Georgia?"

I instantly blurted out, "Yes!" I hadn't been thinking of getting a dog, but there was something about Georgia. There was also an unbelievable and undeniable connection between

Georgia

us, so I left my first day on the job with dog toys, beds, food, treats—and a dog.

I had loved other dogs and animals before, but when Georgia entered my life, something shifted and my life completely changed. She was a remarkable dog. She never had an accident in the house and never made a mess. She loved to be close and snuggle, and every night she slept by my head. Regardless of where we were—horse shows, a hotel, a friend's house—Georgia never barked. Being so well-behaved and quiet made it easy for me to take her places. As a result, Georgia and I went everywhere together.

Georgia was incredibly intuitive and knew if you were a good person. If she liked you, she was all over you, but if she felt you weren't a good person, she went behind the couch and refused to come out.

The only time Georgia wasn't happy was when I was at work. I knew she was grateful I had taken her out of there but we were still going back there every day and it was obvious something had happened there that made her not want to be there. I knew I came into her life for a reason and that she came into mine for a reason, too. Knowing how Georgia felt when we were there, I quit and went back to working strictly at horse shows.

Georgia loved springtime. She never played with toys, but every spring when the ladybugs came out, she turned into a little puppy. She was completely enamored with ladybugs and incessantly searched for and tried to play with them.

Every winter, my work with horses brought us to Florida, and one year we visited Jim in Key Largo. Jim loved Georgia and called her "his girl." Our first night there, Jim and I talked for hours while Georgia relaxed nearby. When Georgia and I went to our room, she hopped into bed, curled up next to me, and immediately fell asleep. I started to read, and a short time later, Georgia's breathing turned into a snore—which got louder . . . and louder. I giggled, knowing the snore showed just how relaxed and happy she was.

The next morning, Jim handed me a cup of coffee and said, "Geez, Mush, you sure did snore last night!"

I laughed and told Jim it was Georgia. He laughed and said I shouldn't blame my snoring on "his girl."

Later that afternoon, Jim and I were sitting outside. He was reading while I was sat with my eyes closed, enjoying the breeze and the sound of the palms. Georgia was quietly sleeping next to Jim when once again she began to snore louder . . . and louder. Jim looked at Georgia and then at me, smiling. "Well, I'll be darned."

Since the grounds at horse shows are so large and spread out, I bought a golf cart so Georgia and I could ride around. Everyone waved to her because everyone on the horse circuit knew and loved her. The extent of that love became apparent early one summer morning as Georgia and I headed to a horse show.

Shortly after five-thirty that morning, an off-duty police officer ran a red light and hit us going sixty miles per hour. The steering wheel went into my chest and the windshield was at my face. I broke my left arm in four places, broke my left hip, broke off the balljoint on my left leg, and fractured my neck.

I still remember being in the car that morning. I was not worried for myself; my only concern was for Georgia. Where was she? Was she okay? As police and emergency personnel tried to get me out of the car, I asked them to call my son so he would come get Georgia. When my son arrived, I was in the process of being cut out of the car and airlifted to a hospital.

Miraculously, Georgia wasn't injured. Her favorite spot in my car was on her bed behind my seat and it ultimately saved her life that day.

Word of the accident spread like wildfire and everyone's major concern was Georgia. It was heartwarming that everyone was so worried about her and reaffirmed what I already knew: everyone loved Georgia.

Two months later, I came home. Without the use of my left arm or leg, I needed a walker to get around, so my son carried Georgia out to see me. The instant she heard my voice, she ran over to me, and from that moment on, she never left my side. She became very protective and did not want to go anywhere without me ever again, so I made sure she never had to.

It took a year before I was able to walk comfortably and another year for me to regain my balance. To this day, I still suffer from nerve damage in my left leg, and problems with my spine have recently emerged. It's been a rough road.

Even though Georgia wasn't physically injured, she and I both suffered from PTSD as a result of the accident. For a long time it was difficult for me to get into a car but it was even worse for Georgia. She would shake uncontrollably anytime we were in or near the car. She no longer liked going to horse shows and was frightened of loud noises.

One night I was braiding when a grooming box fell off the wall. It frightened Georgia and she ran off. I panicked. There were twenty tents on the grounds and I had no idea which direction she went so I hopped on the golf cart and started driving around yelling her name. One of the night watchmen said he saw her run through Tent 14, so I headed in that direction, still calling her name. Georgia heard me, ran out, and jumped up next to me on the golf cart.

Georgia continued to struggle whenever I worked. She was afraid to be near me while I braided and initially only wanted to be in the car. Eventually, I bought a canvas chair for her, and over time she started to curl up in it while I worked. Apparently, her dislike of being near the horses was outweighed by her desire to be close to me.

A couple of years ago, I found a lump on Georgia's chest. Knowing we would be travelling for several months, I took her to the vet to have it checked. The vet was not overly concerned and said to check in with him when we got back home in April. At the beginning of March, the lump felt bigger. The vet on the road said she would be fine, but within three weeks, I noticed other lumps popping up. I immediately took her to a wonderful clinic in West Palm Beach where she ended up having a major mastectomy. Seven of her nipples were removed, and while the original lump was determined to be cancerous, they assured me they got all of the cancer.

While Georgia recovered physically, she began acting differently, and instinctively I knew something wasn't right. The vet said she had an infection and kept her on round after round of antibiotics while they continued searching for the source of her problem.

In May, as I began to prepare for a big annual horse show called the Garden State, I still knew something was not right with Georgia so we went back to the vet.

After checking her thoroughly, he said, "I have good news and bad news. The good news is I found out what is wrong. The bad news is it's her spleen and we need to do something immediately because it could rupture."

Georgia was taken into surgery, and she was lethargic and unable to walk properly when she came home. Initially I thought it was a reaction to the anesthesia, but then she started shaking—something she had never done before the operation. The shaking stopped then it started up again a few months later. One minute Georgia acted like she could not function, then she would rally and be fine.

As summer turned into fall, the vet found more infection and Georgia was having difficulty holding her head straight, could not eat, and was losing weight. She was on antibiotics and other medications and I was desperate to get it under control.

Georgia always did this little hop when she walked, and one day she began hopping. My first thought was, "Oh my God, I got my dog back!" She had rallied so many times and I thought she was rallying again. We headed to work, but once we were there, she did not want to go anywhere. She lay down on the bench and seemed really out of it so I lay down and held her.

On our way home, a deer ran into the front of my car. While neither of us were injured, the front end of my car wasn't so lucky. It was completely smashed in, which made it impossible for us to go to work the next day. Looking back, I thank my Higher Power, I thank God, because the next day Georgia was not doing well.

My veterinarian was on vacation. Before he left, Georgia had been fine so neither of us were concerned, but now I faced a very different situation. The vet on call couldn't fit her into his schedule, so when Georgia started to pant and act strangely, I took her to a nearby emergency hospital.

The veterinarian there told me I might have to think about putting her to sleep. I wasn't ready to hear that and told him, "She'll rally; she'll be fine. I'll talk to my vet when he gets back. Can you just please give me something for the pain?"

He gave her a sedative, which completely zonked her out. I brought her home and put her in bed next to me. Around four o'clock in the morning something woke me up. Georgia's hind legs were stiff and she was panting and absolutely petrified. I knew something was terribly wrong.

We went back to the emergency vet. As I held Georgia, the vet explained, "You can keep her like this or . . ."

I knew what the "or" was but was still not prepared to face it. It was the fourth of September. One month before, on August 4, I had posted on Facebook that it was the six-year anniversary of "the horrific car accident that changed my life." So much had transpired since then. I had been changed and blessed in so many ways over those six years—and without a doubt, one of my biggest blessings was Georgia.

Now, as I sat holding Georgia, all I could think about was that our time together was coming to an end. Georgia looked at me with those eyes and I could tell she was scared. I held her, comforted her, and told her how much I loved her—and then my little sweetheart was gone. I had gotten her when she was four, believing with absolute certainty that I would have her until she was eighteen, but she was only thirteen the day she passed.

I was devastated, destroyed, and completely fell apart. Driving home, all I could do was cry. People kept asking about Georgia, so one week later, I wrote on Facebook: "I am completely heartbroken and grief stricken to let everyone know that last Sunday morning, I had to suddenly put my sweet Georgia to rest. This past week has been so very hard and I've been trying to accept that she is no longer with me. She was a huge part of my life and my constant companion for the past nine years. She was one of the kindest and most loving little souls I have ever known. She entered my life and healed me and gave me joy. She made a bad day good and a good day even better. All she wanted was to simply love me and to be loved back . . . and we did that for each other. She made my life better, and a piece of me went with her. In time it will get better but right now I am lost and miss her so very badly."

I shut my computer and phone off—and shut the world out. I ignored email and social media. I would not talk to anyone. At work, I would start sobbing and leave because Georgia was not with me. Other people began handling my accounts. To do things without Georgia by my side was horrendous. It was like my left arm was gone.

People told me I needed to snap out of it; others suggested I get another dog. I did not want to hear any of it.

Weeks later, a longtime friend named Bill called. I decided to answer, and the first thing Bill said was, "Check your Facebook page. There are hundreds of people sending you a lot of love." I looked and quickly read the messages before shutting my computer off and retreating back into my world of pain and grief.

My ex-husband and I are still close friends, so one day I called him. When he answered, all I could do was cry about Georgia. Finally, he said, "Kerry, you have such a big heart and so much love to give. How could you deprive another dog of the same good life you gave Georgia?"

I told him I wasn't sure I could ever love another dog like that again but he remained steadfast, saying, "You have so much love, Kerry. You can give a dog a beautiful home."

Georgia was my love and there was a part of me that felt like I could never even consider another dog. At his suggestion, I looked on Petfinder for another Shih Tzu but did not see anything.

Several nights later, I looked again, and on the very last page saw a grey and white Shih Tzu named Queenie. It said her owners were moving and could no longer keep her. I inquired about her and got an immediate response saying if I was interested I needed to come right away since they were taking her to an adoption event that weekend.

I got in my car and drove two hours to the shelter. When I arrived, it was obvious that I wasn't in the best neighborhood—which was confirmed when I knocked on the door and an armed guard came out. I told him I was there to meet Queenie so he let me in. The sound of dogs barking was overwhelming but the odor was even worse. It was completely overpowering, and as much as I wanted to leave, my immediate thought was that if I was scared, I could not imagine what the dogs were going through.

The guard came back out holding a dog who was shaking violently. Her hair was hanging down in front of her face, so I gently moved the hair away from her eyes, half-expecting (and hoping) to see Georgia's face or eyes. Instead, I saw her eyes and gasped: they appeared almost humanlike.

Knowing I had to take Queenie outside to get even a small glimpse of who she was and how she would be outside that environment, I took her into the parking area and tried to walk her, but she had no idea how to walk on a leash. She smelled horrible and continued to shake uncontrollably.

When we went back in, they showed me papers that indicated Queenie was spayed. They said a Haitian couple had bought her online as a puppy for $1,000 but could no longer afford her—a very different story from the one on their website.

I didn't feel any connection with Queenie but I knew I could not leave her there, so I adopted her on the spot and headed home. On the way, we stopped at my best friend's house. As I picked her up, she clung to me. My first thought was, "What a sweet dog!"

When we got home, she was stressed and kept panting. I tried to take her outside but she looked at the grass like it was something strange. She had no idea how to walk on a leash and pulled me everywhere. She didn't know how to go up or down stairs, was not housebroken, and, quite literally, didn't know anything.

I decided to give her a bath, and when I lifted her up, I was shocked. Her entire backside was fiery red and inflamed, and she clearly had an infection. A visit to the vet determined she was almost three years old and was not spayed.

She didn't respond to the name Queenie. When the name Chloe popped into my mind, I said it out loud and she immediately responded, so I changed her name to Chloe.

One day, while putting Chloe in her crate, she bit me. The first month she bit me five times. The next month, she bit me a few more times. Pretty soon, it was a good day if Chloe didn't bite me. I never had a dog bite me before and began to question whether or not I could do this.

I prayed, realizing I had two options. The first was to return her, knowing she would probably be euthanized. The other option, and the one I chose, was to start working with her. I taught her to navigate stairs and how to walk on a leash. Over the next few months, through a combination of kindness, love, understanding, and positive reinforcement, Chloe began to change—and so did I.

When Chloe came into my life, I was still depressed and missed Georgia. Chloe was the complete opposite of Georgia, and there were times I would look at her and think, "Why did I get you? I don't even like you." I think Chloe sensed I did not like her, but what I didn't realize is that Chloe was pulling me out of my deep depression. Now, every day, I had to walk and train her, and in the process, she was forcing me out of my house and back into the world.

A few months later, I got a part-time job. Every day, as I got ready to leave for work, Chloe would start to shake. I thought maybe another dog as a companion might help, but this time I decided to go another route.

The horse world is a close-knit community and there were two men I knew from the horse circuit: Danny and Ron. I knew they started a rescue after Hurricane Katrina called, appropriately, Danny & Ron's Rescue. They would arrive at horse shows in a bus full of dogs and later would ride around in an oversized, elongated golf cart with all the dogs. Every single one of the dogs had been rescued and was available for adoption.

I knew that most of the money for their rescue came out of their own pockets because they never charged for an animal but simply asked for a donation. I had been supporting them in whatever way I could—by spreading the word about their rescue, buying their annual calendar, and helping video or photograph the dogs or events. The kindness and love these two men had for the dogs was so apparent. I truly believed they and their rescue were the greatest.

I'd also heard remarkable stories about the extreme lengths they had gone to in order to save dogs. I knew they did whatever was needed to get a dog healthy, safe, and into a loving home and that they took the time to make sure they found the perfect match between a dog and a human. I decided that perhaps Danny & Ron's Rescue might be able to help Chloe and me find our perfect match.

I checked the available dogs on their website but nothing really struck me so I decided to wait and see what happened. Every day as I

braided horses, Chloe would lie in Georgia's chair and wait for me to finish. Looking at her, I wondered if I really needed another dog. Maybe the
two of us were enough.

Then one night, while braiding, something told me to log onto
Danny & Ron's Rescue page. I stopped what I was doing, checked their
page, and the first thing I saw was a photo of a little five-and-a-half
pound Shih Tzu–Pomeranian mix named Yager. I filled out an application, sent a text to Kim, and went back to braiding.

Danny and Ron had brought Kim onboard to work with their rescue.
She was incredibly organized and a huge advocate for dogs. She also went
to extraordinary lengths to rescue a dog and connect it with the right
home, so I knew if it was meant to be I would hear back from her.

I didn't hear back from Kim that night so I thought the dog was already adopted. The next morning, I turned my phone back on and there
was a text from Kim asking if I was in Florida. I texted back that I
wasn't. Kim said there was a lot of interest in the dog but he was mine—
the only problem was he was in Florida.

I immediately contacted a few friends and one said she would help
but would have to call me back later because she was on her way to look
at a dog. An hour later, she called and said, "Darn you, Kerry! That was
the dog I wanted. I'll bring him home for you." Before we hung up, she
said, "Kerry, he is absolutely precious."

As I sat back and waited for him to arrive, I decided to change his
name to Jagger. The minute Jagger arrived in New Jersey, I hopped in
my car to go meet him. When my friend handed him to me, I couldn't
believe how tiny he was—and how cute.

She gave me a bag filled with food, treats, a cuddler, his tags, and lots
of other goodies Kim had packed for him and away we went. Jagger immediately made himself at home. Chloe stood there watching as Jagger
started jumping and running around. She gave me a look that clearly
said, "I don't know what you did or where you just went but this is *not*
going to work."

Immediately I thought, "Oh no, what have I done?"

Jagger kept stealing Chloe's toys and Chloe was getting angry, so I
packed them both in the car and off we went to the dog store. Since it was
the middle of winter and Jagger had just come from Florida, I bought
him coats, sweaters, and a big basket of new toys and treats.

The first week, Jagger constantly tried to play with Chloe, but she was clearly not interested. She wouldn't even look at him. I decided to leave them alone to figure it out, and before long, they were running around the house playing.

They also learned from and influenced one another. When I first got Jagger, he ran around the house nonstop, but thanks to Chloe, he has mellowed and learned how to play and be with another dog.

Chloe had never barked or made any attempt to communicate with me in any way, but Jagger was a different story. Before long, Chloe started barking and trying to communicate with me, thanks to Jagger's influence. She now felt free to be a dog, to love her life, to bark and run around, and just be happy.

Chloe and Jagger are loyal and loving and bring me so much joy—just like Georgia. On the other hand, Chloe and Jagger are both different from Georgia, which has been good for me. It has allowed me to release old hurts and to become more active and more involved. I have begun to take them with me when I braid and they are doing great.

When Jagger went to his first horse show, the two of them slept on top of one another in Georgia's chair. We have our routine, and just like Georgia, they want to go with me and be with me.

Our journey together is still new, but I am learning from both of them and it has been extremely healing. When I lost Georgia, many people did not understand what I went through. She was so loyal and loving that I felt like I lost a part of me. In some ways, I did.

They are both starting to teach me that if I sit quietly and listen for guidance, it will allow me to be more attentive to them and to what they need. Chloe and Jagger give me purpose, and I truly believe they came into my life for the next level of my own spiritual journey.

Chloe, Jagger and Kerry

Chapter Twenty-Three
BETH

Beth and I met while working at a local natural foods market. I loved Beth's unique funk, flair, and wicked sense of humor. She was also a huge animal lover. I wanted to share her story in the first Magical Dogs book but roadblocks appeared. With this book, the dogs reconnected us, the roadblocks disappeared, and on a sunny May afternoon, we sat down to talk while her dogs ran and played in the yard at her ex-husband Joe's house.

GROWING UP, WE HAD CATS. I WAS NINETEEN WHEN I ADOPTED my first dog: a five-year-old Boston terrier whose owners surrendered her because they said she kept getting out of their yard. In all the time we were together, I never saw any of that behavior and often wondered if they surrendered her because they just had a baby girl and the dog had become something of an afterthought.

They named her Gus because they wanted a boy but I changed her name to GussieLou. I adored her. Shortly before she turned four, GussieLou developed Cushing's disease. I tried every treatment available but nothing worked or helped her, and eventually I had to put Gussie down.

It was awful. I was in my early twenties, and GussieLou was my first dog. But the truth is it's never easy. It doesn't matter how old you are or how old the dog is. If a dog is fourteen, people say, "You were so lucky. You had all those years with them," and while that's true, you've also had all those years to connect and create memories with your dog. No matter when it happens, it's always difficult.

Years later, after moving to Salt Lake City, Utah, I finally convinced my husband, Joe, that we had to have a dog. The next morning, as I backed out of the driveway to head to the local kill shelter, Joe ran out of the house motioning for me to stop. I rolled down the window and Joe held up his pointer finger. "One," he said. "One dog. That's it." I smiled and drove off.

There was a dog at the shelter named Jack, who was part Chow Chow and part something else—perhaps Lab, maybe Rhodesian ridgeback, no one knew for sure—but Jack had this wonderful purple tongue that looked like he had just eaten a grape popsicle.

Joe got home from work, took one look at Jack, said, "He's a lot bigger than I imagined," and that was that. We let Jack walk around the house to get acclimated while we sat down to eat when we suddenly heard a horrible sound. It sounded like someone dropped a water balloon from a second-floor window so we ran into the next room afraid of what we were going to find. Jack stood there, looking sheepish and apologetic, having just had explosive diarrhea. Thankfully, it was just a reaction to the stress, recent changes, and moves in his life and was nothing more serious.

A few nights later, we were lying in bed reading. Jack was sound asleep on the bed between us when a bug began buzzing around the overhead light. It was annoying me so I rolled up the magazine I was reading and threw it at the light. The magazine missed the light, boomeranged, and came back and hit Jack on the head. He instantly jumped up out of a sound sleep and was so skittish and afraid something else might fall out of the sky onto his head that for the next two weeks, he slept in the bathtub. Poor dog.

We all settled into a comfortable routine, but six months later, we decided to move to New Jersey. We put Jack between us in the front seat of our big Ryder rental truck, and for the next five days, drove cross-country. Every mile of that trip, Jack was a real trooper.

We moved into our home in Lambertville and loved it, but every day we came home from work to the sound of water running. While neither of us remembered doing it, we figured one of us was leaving the water on when we left for work. Then we finally realized Jack had figured out how to turn on the bathtub faucet and shower to get a drink—he just never figured out how to turn the water off.

Jack was Joe's first dog and they both loved the outdoors. They went on regular climbing trips together and were extremely close. On one of their climbing trips, they were with a group of people, including a young kid and his dog, Porter, a chunky white hound–pit bull mix. This kid had no business having Porter because the way he treated him bordered on neglect, abuse, or both. The one saving grace was that Jack loved Porter and they played together all day.

A few months later, we heard through the grapevine that the kid had moved. He didn't want Porter and neither did his parents so the kid apparently felt the logical thing to do was leave Porter in his parents' garage and drive away.

When we found out, Joe and his friend Carl drove over to get Porter. The parents handed Porter over without any questions or a second thought. It was summer and they had the car windows rolled down on the way home. Joe warned Carl to keep an eye on Porter. Carl laughed, saying, "No way is he going to jump out the window," but the words were barely out of his mouth before three-fourths of Porter's body went out the window. Thankfully, Joe was able to grab him.

Porter was really sweet, but shortly after coming to live with us, we realized he had separation anxiety. He barked at a seizure-inducing frequency all day long and our neighbors began to complain. We tried everything, including a citronella bark collar, but the day we put it on, we came home from work to the sound of barking. We thought the collar had malfunctioned but apparently Porter had once again barked all day long and emptied the canister.

It broke our hearts. We knew Porter's previous circumstances weren't great and that the only person he had ever known abandoned him. We continued to love him, and over time, Porter got used to our routine and came to trust that we always came home. Over time, he settled in and felt safe.

It helped that we had Jack because Porter instantly loved him. Jack liked him too, but after two days he looked at Porter then at us with a look that said, "Okay, that was fun. He can go now."

Porter transferred some of his clinginess and neediness onto Jack. Luckily, Jack was a good big brother and so patient because, at times, Porter was a bit much. Every night, Porter left his bed to lay on Jack—not lay on Jack's bed but on Jack himself. Porter didn't just love Jack; he was actually obsessed with him—and that never changed.

The other thing Porter never got over was eating everything and anything, including devouring an entire can of dog food. We only gave our dogs wet food on special occasions, but Porter had been to the vet and they had given us a few cans of prescription wet dog food, which he loved. One day, without thinking, we left an unopened can on the counter. When we came home, the can was on the kitchen floor, empty. Somehow he had punctured the can and eaten all the food without cutting himself. I never saw anything like it in my life.

Our next madcap adventure with Porter's desire to devour anything began early one morning while we were all in the backyard. Joe noticed a piece of tape hanging off Porter's bottom. On closer examination, he realized Porter had gone into his gym bag and eaten a roll of his climbing tape. I called the vet, who told us to avoid pulling the tape and to bring him in immediately. The vet very slowly began to pull the tape, but when it got stuck on the cardboard core, Porter headed into surgery.

Knowing Porter would be sedated and lethargic for the remainder of the day, we decided to let him rest and pick him up the next morning. A few hours later, the phone rang. It was the vet's office. "Porter's awake, barking nonstop, and is disrupting the entire office. Come get him."

Porter and Jack went everywhere with us because it honestly never occurred to us that we shouldn't or couldn't bring them along. Porter loved being in the car and slept the entire trip. Jack on the other hand turned green and drooled the entire trip.

One summer, we rented a cabin on a lake in the Adirondacks. Our plan was to take both dogs out in a boat, but we were concerned because Porter wasn't the best swimmer. He was more the type that, if you tried to help him out of the water, he suddenly panicked, began flailing, and in the process drowns himself—and you. We bought Porter a life vest at a sporting goods store on our way to the cabin, choosing one with a zipper up the entire back because it seemed like it would be easy to put on and take off.

We got to the cabin, quickly unpacked, and got ready to head out onto the lake. With quite a bit of difficulty, we finally got the life vest on Porter. He stood there motionless for several minutes then took one big deep breath, the zipper broke, and the vest fell off.

We decided to head out onto the lake anyway and to keep a close eye on Porter. Thankfully, both Porter and Jack were great in the boat and every day we took them to an uninhabited island where they tore around. They absolutely loved it.

Christmas morning, a friend called to alert us to the fact that there was a cat outside our front door. It was freezing out so we brought the cat in and named him Myles. For the first six months, Myles wanted no part of the dogs and stayed in the basement. After that, from time to time, Myles would come up and hang out for a bit before retreating to the basement.

Jack, on the other hand, loved Myles and wanted Myles to like him so badly in return. Anytime Myles came up out of the basement, Jack sat there looking at him hopefully with his tail wagging. Myles would sit quietly on the kitchen counter looking down at Jack, then, BAM! He would hit Jack on the top of his head with his paw and run back into the basement.

Then Rosie came into our lives. I was waitressing one night when a coworker who was involved with a rescue told me about a purebred Great Dane named Rosie that was going to be put down. We already had our hands full with Jack, Porter, and Myles, but I agreed to foster Rosie.

I went to pick up Rosie the next day and she trotted out to my car and hopped into the back seat like she owned it. When we got home, she walked into the house like she owned it. Rosie acted like she was the queen, but never in a mean way. She was simply confident and the other dogs, in turn, loved and respected her.

The only problem was the next day we were heading to the West Indies for a week for a friend's wedding. We had made arrangements for Porter and Jack to go to a friend's kennel, but we now had a six-month-old Great Dane, too. We called our friend to explain. He listened and finally said, "Oh, what the heck. Bring her." The next morning we dropped all three of them off and headed to the airport. The entire plane ride home, all we talked about was Rosie. "What are we going to do? We can't have three dogs—and we certainly can't have a Great Dane."

Ultimately we decided we *could* have a Great Dane, so we now had three dogs and a cat—unaware another cat would soon be living with us as well.

While visiting my favorite independent bookstore, the owner and I began talking about his cat, Folio, who was curled up and sleeping in a patch of sunlight by the front window. The owner's wife had been diagnosed with leukemia and could no longer have the cat in their home, so he had begun keeping Folio at the store. We talked for a while and finally decided I would bring Folio to our house.

Other than the fact that Folio thought she was a dog, she was extremely well adjusted and absolutely fearless. She slept next to Rosie and ate out of her dog bowl. It became commonplace to see Folio run through the kitchen with Rosie hot on her tail. Then you'd hear a crash and Rosie would come running back through the kitchen with Folio in hot pursuit. Even when she was fully grown, Folio was extremely tiny, almost like a dwarf cat, which made it even more ridiculous that her bestie was a Great Dane.

Then Joe and I separated. I took the dogs and Joe kept the cats. After Myles passed, Folio was sad being an only child, but when our friend recovered from leukemia, Folio went back to their home. It was a nice full-circle ending.

By that time Jack was ten or eleven years old and having respiratory problems. Jack, who loved being outdoors and active, now found it increasingly difficult to even walk up the block. When it became obvious he was in pain, we made the decision. I have known Joe over twenty years, and the only time I have ever seen him cry is the day we put Jack down.

That left Joe not only without Jack but without any animals living with him, so he decided to volunteer. He began driving dogs to meet-and-greets for Lulu's Rescue, a local foster-based rescue. One day, Fran (the woman who runs Lulu's Rescue) sent us an urgent email about a six-month-old Border collie mix named Louie whose foster parents had a change in circumstances and could no longer keep him. Fran wanted to know if we would consider fostering Louie so he wouldn't have to go to a shelter or kennel.

There's something you should know about Fran. She is the nicest person in the world, and if she needed a kidney, you would give her a kidney. We knew Lulu's had an exceptionally high and quick adoption rate so Joe and I talked and he decided to foster Louie. We were confident Joe wouldn't get attached to Louie since he would probably be adopted within a few weeks—but a few weeks turned into a couple of months and Louie still wasn't adopted.

Fran said whenever Joe brought Louie to meet-and-greets, Louie was calm and happy until Joe left. From that point on, and throughout the entire meet-and-greet, Louie was out of control—until Joe came back to pick him up. Fran said, "Louie isn't looking for his forever family because he thinks he already found it." Meaning Joe.

Joe wasn't convinced, so to increase his chances of finding his forever home, Joe started putting an "Adopt Me" vest on Louie and walking him around town. The day Joe came home from work to find that Louie had completely shredded the vest, he finally decided it was a sign and adopted him.

Louie and Porter got along immediately. Initially, Rosie couldn't stand Louie, but eventually everyone got along. Honestly, it never occurred to us that animals wouldn't get along—we just assumed they would and they did. Everyone fit right in.

A few years later, Rosie passed, and then I was diagnosed with a brain aneurysm. My doctors instructed me to remain calm and quiet, but my personal life and living situation had begun to spin out of control. I was in an extremely emotionally abusive relationship. The final straw came when he and I were arguing one day and he shoved me against the door as I tried to leave the room.

Joe and I still co-owned our house, which he lived in, so I packed up Porter, walked out of the house and relationship, and moved in with Joe and Louie.

The entire time I was dealing with the brain problems and waiting for surgery, Louie was incredibly empathic and an amazing companion. I was on a tremendous amount of blood thinners and anti-seizure medication and was home all day for four months, but Louie stayed by my side all day, every day.

In October 2012, as New Jersey began to prepare for Hurricane Sandy, Fran called to tell us there was a kennel trying to get their dogs into homes because they anticipated losing power for an unknown period of time. Fran wondered if we might be able to take in a dog named Finn.

Joe looked at me. "Five days," he said. "That's it. Five days." And that's how Finnie came into our lives. When Finnie and Louie met, it was an instant connection. I adopted Finnie and he and Louie became the best of friends.

Finn (left) with Louie

They are comparable in age and came from the same area in the South. Sometimes Fran, Joe, and I wonder if they might have known one another when they were younger and living in the South.

After recovering from surgery, my new boyfriend, Michael, his dog Button, Finn, and I moved into a beautiful third-floor apartment together. Louie was living with Joe while Finn and Porter jumped back and forth between our homes. Life was good and everyone was happy—until February 28, 2014, when everything changed.

Porter hadn't been doing well for a while. He was fourteen, covered with tumors, and along with other health problems, he was in obvious pain. Joe and I knew it was time so we began our morning by taking Porter for his final heartbreaking trip to the vet.

That evening around seven o'clock, Michael, Button, and I were watching a movie. I was sitting on the couch, crying about Porter, when there was a knock at the door. Michael answered the door and a few seconds later came back and calmly said, "Get dressed, get Button, and get out."

There were a total of nine apartments in the building. Our apartment took up the entire third floor and there was a grocery store and deli on the ground floor. A worker had left the grill on in the deli and a rag had caught fire.

When I think back to that night, it was weird. Michael was calm, I was calm, and we just jumped into action. Michael grabbed a fire extinguisher to try and put out the fire. I got dressed, got Button, and began going door to door to make sure everyone was out.

I knocked on one door and could hear a dog barking on the other side, but when no one came to the door, I started pounding on it. Finally, I tried the handle and the door opened. On the other side stood an Akita growling at me. Seeing smoke, I ran around him. The girl who lived there was listening to music with her headphones on and had no idea anything was happening. I screamed at her to get out of the house.

A special needs man and his brother lived in the next apartment. The man answered the door dressed in his Ninja Turtles pajamas and hesitated when I told him to get out, saying his brother was at work and wouldn't want him to go. Seeing smoke behind him, I grabbed his hand and said, "Trust me. Your brother would want you to come with me."

Walking outside, I saw smoke pouring out of the front of the building, and all our neighbors standing outside in the parking lot watching the fire. It was freezing out, below zero, and the firefighters' hose kept freezing. None of us were dressed for the weather—most of us were in our pajamas. I remember thinking, "I hope they put the fire out before there's too much smoke damage." By one o'clock in the morning, the entire building had burnt to the ground.

Fortunately, Louie and Finn were with Joe that night. Mike, Button, and I were fortunate as well because we all got out of the building safe and sound. All of our neighbors got out of the building safely but several cats were lost in the fire.

Mike and I were also fortunate that we had friends who were in Florida for the winter and allowed us to move into their house so we were never homeless. We stayed for a few months before moving into an apartment a few blocks from Joe.

Finnie became a permanent resident at Joe's house. Even though I adopted Finnie, he loves Louie and he also really connected with Joe's girlfriend, Liliana. She is a runner so Liliana and Finnie spend a lot of time running together.

Button is diabetic and blind but doing great. Dogs compensate and Button compensated, remaining really energetic. She's a little schnauzer

Finn and Louie modeling sweaters handmade
by Liliana's mother

mix and is head over heels in love with Louie—and Louie is absolutely terrified of her. I feel bad for Louie.

In our early days, maybe it was just youthful ignorance, exuberance, or foolishness, but we put everyone—dogs, cats, life, and the mayhem—together and it always worked out. Back then, it never occurred to us that it wouldn't work. We just expected the best from the dogs, cats, and everyone, and that's what we got in return: their best.

It's funny how when you look back on your life you gauge time by your dogs. You try to figure out when something occurred and it's always based on "Oh, that's when we had Porter," or "Jack was with us then." They become so pivotal in your life that they actually create a timeline for your life.

Liliana had been living in Scotland for two years, and when Joe went to see her, I took care of the dogs. Now Liliana is here pretty much all of the time and we only live a few blocks from one another. The dogs have always gone back and forth between our homes. It's different but it works—for all of us. We're all happy, and in the end, that's what matters.

Chapter Twenty-Four
YVONNE

As Beth and I walked through the kitchen at Joe's house, I noticed a unique ceramic switch plate. When I commented on it, Beth immediately said, "Yvonne! Oh my gosh! You need to talk to Yvonne!" Yvonne was the artist who made the switch plate. Trusting the dogs were continuing to make connections for me, I reached out to Yvonne, who was happy to tell me about her life and journey with dogs.

LOOKING BACK, MY FAMILY PROBABLY WEREN'T IDEAL DOG PEO-ple. We always had dogs, but anytime a dog misbehaved, my parents would tell us they "went to the farm." After a while, I stopped asking where the farm was and just accepted I would never see the dog again.

After my husband and I got married thirty-two years ago, we decided to get a toy poodle since they were one of my favorite dogs growing up. This was in the '80s, and back then the only way to find a rescue animal was through a typed list—assuming you were lucky enough to know where to find a list. Unable to find any rescue poodles, we ended up buying two toy poodles and a Doberman we named Jade.

After getting Jade, we became aware that certain dogs at certain times are considered "in style" or status symbols. In the '80s it was Dobermans, in the '90s it was Rottweilers, and more recently, it is pit bulls. Adopting a dog based on status rather than on what fits a person's life and lifestyle oftentimes results in a situation that does not work out and the dog ends up in a shelter. That knowledge sparked my interest in rescue and rescue dogs. Since Jade, we have had over thirteen rescue dogs.

While living in Philadelphia in the early '90s, I saw a Shar-Pei running loose on Roosevelt Boulevard, an extremely busy thirteen-lane highway. Afraid for the dog's safety, I pulled my car over but the dog was too far away. Since I lived nearby, I ran home, grabbed some cheese, and headed back in the direction the dog had been running. A man helped me find and get the dog.

I phoned the Philadelphia SPCA but no one had reported a missing dog fitting the description I gave them. I gave them my contact information and took her home. She had a terrible ear infection so I brought her to the vet the next day. When no one came forward to claim her, I named her Willy.

Two months later, the SPCA called and said they had found Willy's owner. When he came to my house to get her, I packed up Willy's ear medication along with her favorite toys, but as I handed him the bag, it was painfully obvious he didn't care. Since I had his phone number from the SPCA, a few days later I called him to see how Willy was doing. He said she was sitting there "like a lump of shit."

Shar-Peis can be very aloof and oftentimes don't like to play. I immediately told him if he ever decided he didn't want her to let me know and I would come pick her up, but I never heard back from him.

Right before Thanksgiving, my phone rang and a woman who could barely speak English said, "I have your dog."

I had bought a collar for Willy along with tags engraved with her name and my phone number. Willy's owner had apparently never taken the collar off, so the woman who found Willy running loose in North Philly called me to come get her. Willy was sitting at the woman's front door looking out when I arrived, and as soon as she saw me, she began scratching at the door. Willie ran out and hopped right into my car. When we got home, Willy ran into the family room and lay down on the sofa. Her "owner" never called me looking for her and Willy made it abundantly clear that she was happy to be home.

Willy came back into our lives at the holidays, and the song "Home for the Holidays" was constantly on the radio. I always sang along and when we reached the refrain that says, "There's no place like home for the holidays . . ." I would look at Willy, smile, and sing it directly to her. Willy wasn't the only one happy that she was home.

We moved from the city to the country. While Willy loved wandering around our property chasing squirrels, she was not a dog to be contained. She dug under the fence and always found a way out. Thankfully, she always came back.

Willy was with us for twelve years until one day she died in our yard with a dead squirrel two feet from her mouth. Willy went from being a city dog wandering along the highway to a country dog wandering in open fields. Even though we were sad when she died, Willy truly lived life her way being a wild beast, and she was happy every single day. Even now, all these years later, whenever I hear the song "Home for the Holidays," I think of Willy.

I started doing volunteer transports for Operation Scarlet, a Shar-Pei rescue, and on one transport there was a black Shar-Pei named Onyx. Onyx looked like a teddy bear and had been pulled from a shelter in Montgomery County, Pennsylvania, for biting someone. The rescue decided to give him a second chance, so my husband and I fostered him for the weekend before he was adopted out.

After a relatively short period of time, Onyx tried to bite his new owner, so my husband and I took him back. Onyx cornered anyone who came into our home, and since he had gotten into a fight with another dog, we immediately began working with a professional trainer.

He was doing really well but then he began having seizures, and two days before Christmas, we came home and Onyx was dead in our backyard.

It was horrible. I was devastated. The day after Christmas, I struggled to pull myself out of bed. Thinking writing might help, I started to write a note to my pen pal in Washington State and began by telling her about Onyx. Pouring my heart out, I wrote: "We are heartbroken. My heart is so heavy. I wish I could get some relief from the pain and know she is all right."

No sooner had I written those words than a butterfly appeared in my room. It was the twenty-sixth of December. It was only nineteen degrees outside and we were living in a poorly heated house yet, in that instant, there was a butterfly flying around the room. I held out my hand and the butterfly landed on me. It was big and black—just like Onyx. I took out my butterfly book and when I saw that it was a mourning cloak butterfly, I knew it was a sign from Onyx.

I typically don't share that story because I am afraid people will think I am weird, but I truly believe it was a gift from Onyx letting me know he was all right.

A short time later, I got a call about a pit bull named Timmy who had been at the rescue for a year without anyone even looking at him. After all we had heard about pit bulls, we took him with some trepidation because we believe every dog deserves a chance.

Timmy had been left in an abandoned house in Trenton. When he was found, he had a twelve-pound bowling ball, a tire, and a log with him. When Timmy moved into our home, he brought all of that with him.

Timmy truly was the pit bull ambassador. He loved people, our farm animals, other dogs—everyone and everything. I once found him licking a baby fox in our yard who had been abandoned. Timmy exuded happiness and loved (and licked) everyone. If you were wearing shorts, Timmy would lick your leg until your skin literally hurt. The pool man once left our gate open and Timmy escaped. A young man left us a voice mail and in between laughing told us he had our dog in his car and that Timmy wouldn't stop licking his face.

Timmy loved his twelve-pound bowling ball. He carried it with him and rolled it all day long. He rolled it to the point where he actually developed shoulder issues, but you could not take it away from him. Timmy kept that twelve-pound bowling ball with him every day of his life.

After we got Timmy, we learned about a black and white pit bull named Peety who had been found as a stray in Pittsburgh. We contacted Animal Protectors of Allegheny Valley, and one of their volunteers met us halfway on the Pennsylvania Turnpike so we could adopt Peety.

Timmy, a dog and his bowling ball

We gave him a week of quiet to decompress. He settled in perfectly, got along great with Timmy, and we never had any problem. Peety died two years ago after being with us for sixteen years. Even after all those years, you could never raise your voice around Peety or he would cower. The reality is that we usually have no idea how the dogs were treated before we get them. The only thing we know for certain is that we can give them love and a good home.

Since Timmy, we only rescue pit

bulls and have become ambassadors for the breed. Pit bulls are so often misunderstood and end up in the wrong hands, so we believe it is important to educate people about the breed as well as what it means to be a responsible pet owner.

Again, it goes back to what I said about people needing to choose a breed that fits into their life and lifestyle. While it is important for every dog owner to be responsible, those who choose a pit bull need to be even more so because other people oftentimes judge this breed. I've heard stories of fights between dogs where the pit bull was blamed due to their breed even though the fight was started by the other dog.

The smartest owners always slowly introduce dogs on neutral territory. When I brought Bella home, I had friends meet us halfway down the road. We walked together, very slowly, until we were able to allow the dogs to walk closer and closer.

One of our pit bulls was an old fellow named Ernie who needed a lot of medical care the shelter was simply unable to provide. We were told he would probably only live a month. We believe it is important for a dog to be in a home with a family when they pass so Ernie came home with us—and lived another thirteen months. Ernie has been gone since 2005 but our twenty-nine-year-old parrot still screams, "Ernie! Ernie!"

Clive was a brindle pit bull puppy we saw at the Center for Animal Health & Welfare in Easton, Pennsylvania. Since we already had five other dogs, we brought all of them to meet Clive. There has never been a problem.

For over a year, Clive had been passed by at the shelter, which was fortunate for us because he was the best and easiest dog we ever had. He never misbehaved and was always a perfect gentleman. From the day we brought him home, he never needed to be housetrained or leash trained. He could be loose outside of the fence and never leave the yard. He got along with every dog and even farm animals. It was like he had lived here before because there was absolutely no adjustment period. It was like he just settled back in.

Like Timmy, Clive was a licker, but his nickname became "The Masher" because he would sneak up on you and somehow always managed to kiss you on the mouth. Always. One year at the shelter's annual Blessing of the Animals, Clive even managed to mash the priest.

When Clive started to cough up blood, we took him to the vet thinking he just had a cold. This lovely young doctor took him in the back for an X-ray and walked back into the room looking like she saw a ghost. "He has lung cancer," she said, close to tears. "Both lungs are full of cancer." It was so unexpected, and everyone there was so kind and compassionate when Clive passed.

Our theory and practice had always been that when a dog died, we would go to a shelter to give another dog a home. It wasn't to forget or replace the dog we had just lost but because we knew there was a dog at a shelter that needed to get out. The problem this time was logistics. We had moved from our home in the country with acres of land to a smaller house in town with a small yard, so logistically, we needed to start cutting back on the number of dogs we could keep. If we had more space, we would have more dogs. At this point, two dogs is manageable so we now have Bella and Eddie.

Bella is a pit bull we found on the internet. She was at a shelter in Maryland and they said she got along with other dogs. That was important since we had five other dogs at the time. We drove to Maryland, brought Bella home, and shortly thereafter started taking her to obedience school. Bella not only graduated but was also named Most Improved! The only thing that still lingers from Bella's previous life is that if we raise our hand to do something as simple as swatting at a fly, she cowers. We try to be extra careful with our movements and make sure we never raise our voice because that upsets her as well. These twelve years with Bella have been wonderful for the simple reason that she is a sweet soul and a wonderful dog.

Eddie is a Lab–pit bull mix we got when we still lived in the country. Every day around the same time, Eddie would disappear, but since our yard was fenced, we assumed he was in the wooded back portion of our yard. One day we decided to go looking for him and he wasn't there. We began calling for him and one of our neighbors, who we had never met, called across the field, "I have Eddie."

We had no idea Eddie could jump the fence, and when we walked over to our neighbor, he laughed and said Eddie came over at the same time every day to have a snack with him and his little Yorkie, Lucy.

After that, we kept a close eye on Eddie and made sure we had a fence Eddie couldn't jump over. We knew Eddie would never cause a problem, but we knew people might react negatively to a pit bull running around loose. We also knew that Eddie might get himself into trouble. The year before, he had gotten into a trashcan and eaten six corncobs, some bird-feed, and who knows what else. The vet had to perform surgery and said he had never seen anything so grotesque. They were actually so impressed by all Eddie had eaten that they took a picture of it!

Eddie will beg anyone for food—including Ralph, our African Grey parrot. We don't lock Ralph's cage so he typically sits on top of it. Eddie will sit and beg Ralph for food, and if he doesn't get a response, he tries to put his head in Ralph's cage to get food. Like I said, we keep a close eye on Eddie.

We always loved to travel, but an essential part of planning any trip was ensuring our dogs were well cared for in our absence. Once, we made arrangements for our dogs to stay in a really nice kennel. Our dogs were used to going outside to pee and had never peed in a contained kennel so it took them several days to adjust. By the time we returned, three of our dogs had developed urinary tract infections and had to go to the vet. We now vacation separately. I go away by myself while my husband stays home with the dogs—and vice versa. Our dogs are part of our family and we don't see it as a burden because we prefer knowing they are home and safe.

Left to right: Ernie, Peety, Clive and Bella

I have always donated to several rescues but lately have begun to supplement those donations with my artwork. Last year, I made a Day of the Dead type mosaic of a skeleton pit bull that I donated to Hello Bully pit bull rescue in Pittsburgh, which brought in $800. This year I made two mosaic pieces that brought in $900. I have now begun to make smaller mosaic pieces that I sell and donate the proceeds to support shelters.

One of the wonderful things about living in a little town like Lambertville is that if anyone has a dog, I don't hesitate to talk to them. As a result, I have met a lot of really nice people. In truth I may not always remember the person's name, but I always remember their dog's name.

I value every single dog who has come into our life. I believe each one came for a reason and every one has changed me. They have taught me patience and unconditional love and have shown me that regardless of what their past life was like, love and kindness can make any soul shine.

Chapter Twenty-Five
SHARYN

Sharyn and I worked together many moons ago at a local newspaper: she was a photographer and I was the assistant editor. Even after leaving the newspaper, Sharyn and I stayed in contact, and in the ensuing years, our friendship grew stronger.

Sharyn had a dog, Simone, who had a huge impact on my life. I wanted to include their story in my first Magical Dogs *book but Simone had recently passed and it was too soon for Sharyn to talk. But now Sharyn was ready. On the day we got together, I thought we would talk about Simone. Instead she chose to talk about her new puppy, Finn, and the magical journey that brought them together.*

A FEW MONTHS AFTER SIMONE PASSED, I STARTED DREAMING about another dog that would be coming into my life. Initially, I did not think about it or do anything because Simone was still on my mind and in my heart. I wanted to keep sacred space around her not being there and I still wanted her energy around me. I also wanted to honor her by not bringing another dog into our lives.

The dream, however, was unlike any dream I ever had in my life. The details were extremely vivid and I could clearly see the dog was a full-size white male dog that in some ways resembled a wolf. He was outside in the woods surrounded by rocks. Standing above me on a boulder, he was staring down at me and made it known we were going to work together. He was also very specific about the type of work we were going to do: search and rescue.

After the dream, I began feeling the dog's energy and began having visions of him while in meditation. His face, his body, the details—everything was always the same and extremely vivid. Finally one morning I woke up and my first thought was: "It's time to start looking for another dog." It had been over a year since Simone passed and instinctively I knew it was time.

Since the dog in my dream and visions was a full-size mature dog, I thought perhaps he was out there waiting for me so I began searching online and with local rescues. I explained that I was looking for a German shepherd, a husky, or even a mixed breed but the dog had to be white. After several months of searching without any success, I let it go and decided perhaps it wasn't time or the dog wasn't ready. I knew, in time, the dog would find me.

While I discussed the dream several times with my husband, Rick, it never went beyond a casual conversation—until one Friday night while I sat watching television. Rick came into the living room and said, "Are you really serious about wanting to get a dog?" When I told him I was, he asked, "And you're serious about finding the white dog?" Again I told him I was.

Without another word, Rick walked out of the room only to come back ten minutes later and hand me a piece of paper, saying, "Here are three websites for English cream golden retrievers. They're white."

Together, we sat down at the computer and started looking through the pictures on the websites—and then a dog's picture came up on the screen and I gasped. It was a pure white golden retriever with the same face and stance as the dog in my dream—and he was standing by a boulder. I immediately told Rick, "We need to go here. That's the white dog from my dream."

Rick and I talked and put together our wish list, starting with wanting a male puppy. If possible, we also wanted to bring the puppy home around the holidays since our entire family would be there and we would all have an opportunity to bond.

We called the breeder the next day and were told they had two litters due the week of October 20, which is my birthday and our anniversary. It also meant we would bring the puppy home just in time for the holidays.

The first litter was already spoken for, so knowing it would depend on the second mother's litter, we began the wait.

And then the visions started again. Just like before, they were vivid and in such detail that I could actually feel and see the puppy being formed in the womb. I could see where he was in the womb; I knew when his paws were forming and exactly what was happening. I could feel his energy and that he had a connection to plants. It actually felt like I was bonding with him as he was being created, again unlike anything

I had ever felt or experienced in my life. This time I chose not to tell Rick because I knew it would be a little too out there for him.

When we got the call that the mother was going into labor, we waited. We decided that if we were blessed with a male puppy, we would name him Finley, Gaelic for "fair-haired hero," but we would call him Finn for short.

Finn

The next call informed us that seven healthy puppies had been born: six females and one pure white male. Our Finn was here.

Three weeks later, we drove to see Finn for the first time. Before meeting him, I asked if I could spend time with his mom. The breeder was surprised by my request but I sat down on the floor and waited.

When they brought Finn's mother in, she walked over, sat down in front of me, and looked into my eyes. She calmly listened as I told her, "You did such a great job delivering these babies. I know it was difficult so I wanted to thank you. I also wanted to introduce myself because, if it is all right with you, I am going to take your son." I wanted to honor Finn's mother and recognize all the hard work she had done bringing him and the other puppies into the world. I also wanted to know, with certainty, that she approved and accepted our decision to bring Finn into our home and family.

The breeder watched me give Finn's mother the respect she deserved. She said no one had ever done that before. When I was ready, she got Finn, and as soon as she placed him in my hands, his mother came over and the three of us sat together in silence. In that moment, it felt like we were all one, all connected, and one energy.

As soon as I handed Finn to Rick, he started nuzzling Rick, giving him kisses. He was so excited. Finn's mom walked over and laid her head on Rick's arm, watching as he and Finn got to know each other. Finally, she walked back and leaned toward me, communicating in a way only dogs can that she was happily giving us permission to take her son.

On the drive home, I couldn't get Finn's mom out of my mind. We had connected on such a deep level, and for the next few weeks, I wondered what was going to happen with her. When Finn was eight weeks old, Rick and I brought our son and daughter with us to pick him up, and I immediately asked the woman what was going to happen to Finn's mother.

She assured me that this had been her last litter and she was currently reviewing applications from people who were interested in adopting her. Because of our connection, I was thankful she would be going to a loving home.

As soon as we got Finn home, we brought him into the yard, where he instantly gravitated to my garden and began eating my chamomile, peppermint, and thyme. He ignored everything else and was completely focused on the herbs—then I remembered how, in my visions, I saw that the dog would have a connection and fascination with plants.

Over the next few months, I watched Finn's unbelievably strong and almost inexplicable affinity for scent work. I remembered the dog in my dream had said we would do search and rescue work together, so I started looking for classes.

Rick found an article in a local newspaper about our Community Emergency Response Team (CERT). As part of a CERT team, trained handlers and dogs go in to help emergency personnel and first responders in the event of a natural disaster, emergency, or catastrophe. When I learned a dog must be at least fifteen months old to begin CERT training, I trusted that when Finn was old enough and the time was right, we would begin training together. I shifted my focus to completing my portion of the training and Finn and I started obedience classes.

Finn is such a smart dog and did so well that if I dropped the leash, he would heel and follow every instruction I gave him. Hiking through the

Finn with Sharyn's herbs

snow or into the woods, Finn always wanted to be in the lead, yet he constantly stopped to put eyes on me. If he felt I was too far behind or laboring, he sat and waited until he was confident we could move forward. He was a puppy, yet his focus, attention, and ability to learn were amazing.

During our training sessions, I began having increased episodes of labored breathing and Finn was spending more and more time coming back to sit next to me. As my own health issues began to surface, I went through an intense period of healing, which meant taking time off from our training.

I am now healed and whole once again and Finn and I have resumed training with a woman on her land. It is astounding to watch Finn. He can be happily playing in the creek, but the minute I put my hand down and say, "Finn, touch," he stops playing, comes over, and touches my open palm with his nose.

I do energy work, and before I got Finn or even thought about getting another dog, I had researched healers in other cultures and was particularly drawn to the single-minded and fierce focus of many Russian healers. When I learned Finn's lineage goes back to Russia, so much of what I was seeing and experiencing with him made sense. He has that same fierce and single-minded focus. I believe he was born to be a healer and that together we will heal and help by doing search and rescue work. I look forward to what the future holds for me and Finn, the dog of my dreams.

HAPPY BIRTHDAY, SIMONE!

Before moving on, I'd like to pause and acknowledge Sharyn's dog, Simone, and the impact she had on me and my life. Without realizing it, the day I wrote this was September 15, Simone's birthday, making this my happy birthday gift to a very magical dog named Simone.

Simone,

I met you at a time in my life when I was still nervous and a tad fearful around dogs. Although there was no real basis for those fears, they still existed. It was you and your extraordinary patience with me that began to shift those feelings of fear into a feeling much stronger: love.

Your mother, Sharyn, sensed my fears, and while we never discussed it, she saw the change in me when I was around you. She witnessed the impact you had on me. In her infinite wisdom, she sealed the deal by asking me to help take care of you one weekend while they went out of town. I was flabbergasted, excited, and nervous. I was more nervous for you than for me because I wasn't sure what to do. Again, to your mom's credit, she invited me to your house and went over everything. On the day they left, I had her go over everything one final time. Assuring me everything would be fine, they hopped in the car, your mom smiled, waved, and they drove off.

We went outside and sat side by side on your front steps. I looked at you wondering how we would survive the weekend. As I began to pray that nothing I did (or didn't do) would cause you any harm in any way, you laid your head on my shoulder, and in that moment, I knew we would be fine. And we were.

For the next three days, we played ball and walked around your yard. We sat on the front steps and you nuzzled your face into mine. In those three days, you changed me, Simone. The more we connected, the more my heart was cracked open and the deeper my love and understanding of you—and of dogs—began to grow.

Every time I visited you and your family, you met me at the front door, greeting me with a big smile and a wagging tail. I loved petting you, burying my hands in your thick fur while I looked at your happy eyes and smiling face. I started bringing you a gift every year on the fifteenth of September for your birthday.

Several years later, you were diagnosed with cancer. Your mom researched and used every traditional and non-traditional path available to bring you relief—and a possible cure. For a long time, you thrived and were happy, but ultimately the cancer came back with a vengeance, and slowly your health and strength began to wane. While you struggled to get up when I visited, you still had that signature smile and wagging tail. I sat with you and you always placed your head in my lap while I buried my hands in your fur and looked into your happy eyes.

On the day you were scheduled to go to the vet for the last time, your mom invited me to come over and spend time with you. Having never said goodbye to a beloved animal before, I was afraid and nervous—just like I was that weekend we spent together. We sat together on the floor and you put your head in my lap one last time. Once again, you were kind, patient, and loving with me as I sat there thanking you for all the moments and memories. You listened while I thanked you for teaching me, on a very real and very deep level, about the love of and for a dog. And then it was time.

I walked with you and your family to the car. You had been struggling to walk, yet on that day, you jumped into the back seat. I gave you a kiss, told you I loved you, thanked you, and then you were gone. Driving home, I sobbed uncontrollably—and I sobbed for the rest of the day and for the next few weeks. I'm sobbing as I write this.

I think of you often, Simone, and every September 15, I still celebrate and honor you in some way. Therefore, it shouldn't have been any great surprise when I realized that today, the day I am writing this, is September 15. I didn't purposely plan this, and while I could say it just happened, I know better. I know it is you and your ongoing presence, love, and magical influence in my life. I also believe you are the reason behind everything that magically unfolded today.

For weeks, I had been struggling with the edits to your mom's story about Finn, but as soon as I opened my eyes this morning, I could see the edits with absolute clarity. I made the edits, ate breakfast, and then the doorbell rang. Opening my door, I found a woman standing there with a basket of bright, beautiful basil, garlic, and tomatoes. I invited her in.

She introduced herself, and I smiled. Her name was Simone. Fifteen months earlier, Cheri, a mutual friend of your mom and me, told me about Simone and her family who were working to build a farmstand on their farm, The Old Millpond Farm. I had made a small donation to support them. Now here in my home was Simone from The Old Millpond Farm holding a basket of goodies from their farm in gratitude for my donation.

She apologized that it had taken her so long to reach out and thank me. There had been a computer glitch and I had fallen through a cyber crack. I smiled knowing it wasn't a computer glitch; I knew it was you, Simone. The irony that she shares your name wasn't lost on me. The fact that I had made the donation so long ago yet here she was on this day, your birthday, to bring me these wonderful gifts from her garden was not lost on me.

In that moment, I knew I wanted to celebrate and honor you on your

Simone and me on the weekend
I helped care for her.

birthday this year, Simone, by sharing you with the world. I want everyone to see your happy face and know who you were and the impact you had on me and in my life. Thank you for being a sweet, kind, and loving soul. Thank you for being patient with me and for breaking my heart wide open in unforeseen and unimaginable ways. You were one of the original magical dogs who led me down this path of honoring the blessings and magic a dog brings into our lives. You will always be one of my very special, very magical dogs.

Happy, happy birthday, my dear sweet Simone!

Chapter Twenty-Six
LET'S PAWS: SEARCH AND RESCUE

Sharyn's story piqued my interest in search and rescue, so I reached out to the National Association for Search and Rescue (NASAR) and spoke with Christopher, their Executive Director. He provided me with additional information about their organization, the training, and the dogs.

NATIONAL ASSOCIATION FOR SEARCH AND RESCUE

THE NATIONAL ASSOCIATION FOR SEARCH AND RESCUE (NASAR) is an international nonprofit organization. Since 1973, we have provided education and certification for all types of search and rescue including ground searching, canine and mounted search units, and other resources.

In the United States, almost 90 percent of all search and rescue is done by volunteers. Individuals from all walks of life come to search and rescue (SAR) with a set of skills and are then trained by local teams using NASAR materials.

We use all kinds of dogs for search and rescue. Typically they are working, hunting, or herding breeds, but the only real requirements are that the dog be healthy and have an athletic body and a long nose. The athletic body is necessary because the dog will spend a great deal of time running and climbing up and over things during a search. A long nose enables them to do scent work, which is why we can't use pugs, bulldogs, Shih Tzus, or similar short-nosed breeds.

We start the selection process as early as seven weeks when we start puppy testing and looking for good SAR candidates. Candidates then begin training in obedience, agility, direction and control, and scent detection. We need the dog to be able to heel, stop, or go out and move around an area while still being directed at a distance by their handler using only a whistle or hand signal.

From there, the dog begins scent detection training in a discipline like live or human remains. SAR dogs typically specialize in a discipline for which the training is customized. The most difficult discipline is trailing, where the dog learns to find a specific person's scent, perhaps from their pillowcase or a piece of their clothing. Since scents can be blown around by the wind, a dog does not follow the exact route a person took, but they are able to follow their scent trail to their final location.

The final piece in the puzzle is alerting so a dog can alert their handler when they find something. Dogs alert in different ways. Some do a sit and bark alert while others may do a bringsel alert where they grab a tennis ball off their handler's belt to alert them.

It typically takes twelve to eighteen months to fully train and certify both the dog and handler to be deployed.

Search and rescue is handled differently in different parts of the country. In California, search and rescue is legislated and under the authority of the sheriff's department. As a result, every sheriff in the state of California has a search and rescue unit and there are a total of about 300 SAR canines throughout the state. California is the third-largest state in size and first in population, and they definitely are the most progressive when it comes to search and rescue.

By comparison, search and rescue in Texas, which is the second-largest state in the US in both size and population, is not legislated. Many SARs are community-based organizations who may or may not have a relationship with law enforcement and may or may not charge for their services. This isn't to imply that they aren't as skilled, but just that it is handled differently in different parts of the country.

After getting out of the Marine Corps, I started looking for a way to give back to the community. I happened to see a flier from the local sheriff's office that they were recruiting for their volunteer search and rescue teams.

At the time, I didn't have a dog, so my job as part of the team was to hide for people who were training their dogs. I noticed that people with dogs got out more, and since I wanted to go on more missions and deployments, I decided to get a dog.

One day, one of the instructors, Cindy, called and said, "Chris, I have the perfect dog for you. Come meet her."

I got in my car and drove to San Rafael to meet Blanche, an eight-month-old black Lab who had been undergoing training to be a guide dog for the blind. Blanche wasn't completely suited for working with a blind companion so they were looking for a career change for her. Blanche and I met and got along so I adopted her and renamed her Scout. We began training to become a human remains detection team and were certified by the State of California.

SAR canines are true athletes, working long hours in rough terrain and terrible weather. The length of a SAR canine's career can vary based on their health and athleticism. Once a canine retires, they typically stay with their handler's family as a pet. Scout and I worked together for seven years, and I had her until she passed from old age at sixteen.

After Scout, I became a reserve law enforcement officer for Contra Costa County in California as part of their search and rescue team. At the time, they were looking for trailing dogs to work criminal cases. I got a puppy from a family in the Redding–Chico area that bred bloodhounds for law enforcement and named her Guppy. I began training with her, but after working together for about a year and a half, it turned out Guppy had hip dysplasia, which is an abnormal formation of a dog's hip socket. She had such a severe case that they actually did triple pelvic osteotomy (TPO) surgery to try and correct it. While the surgery was a success, she

Guppy

ended up with such severe arthritis that I had to retire her before she could become certified. Guppy stayed with us until she passed.

After retiring from my full-time job as an emergency manager for the sheriff's department, I moved to Texas for the lower cost of living. I was looking for a job when a friend who was on the board of NASAR told me they were looking for an Executive Director. I applied, got the job, and have been the Executive Director now for five years. It has been a wonderful opportunity because I get to work with SAR responders from all over the world who are true stewards of their communities.

Every search and rescue story is important because every family, and every family member who is missing, is hugely important. When a detective reopens a twenty-year-old cold case and you are able to provide that family with answers simply by using a canine, it's a wonderful thing.

UTAH SEARCH DOGS, INC.

I asked Chris if there was someone I could talk with who had search and rescue experience. He connected me with Nancy from Utah Search Dogs, Inc. She shared more about her organization, her work with search and rescue, and what brought her to devote so much time and energy to this work.

I GREW UP HELPING MY FATHER TRAIN GERMAN SHORT-HAIRED pointers for hunting. He was a pilot in the Air Force and later became a pilot for the US Forest Service. In 1979, he was taking a group of smoke jumpers to a training camp in Montana when one of his engines overheated. He shut the engine down, but the other engine caught fire.

He knew the safest option was to put the plane down in the river, but on his approach, the left wing caught the tip of a tree and the plane nose-dived into the river. Only two people survived the crash; my father was not one of them. For thirty-three days, we waited as they searched for his body. Finally, on the thirty-third day, they pulled the wreckage from the river and found my father's body.

While on ski patrol, I saw a demonstration by a newly formed search dog group. As I watched, the training looked very similar to what my father did training hunting dogs, but the dogs were looking for people instead of birds. I decided to get involved in search and rescue and got my first dog, Aja, a German shepherd.

German shepherds are my dog of choice for search and rescue because you want a dog with a double coat to withstand the cold Utah weather as well as webbed feet that can handle the snowy terrain.

Aja and I began training together, and shortly after she turned one, we went on a search for a twelve-year-old boy who had gone missing down in the Canyonlands National Park area. His family was camping with other family members and he and a cousin had been up on the Joint Trail, so named because all these rock masses come together and there are little trails down in between them. The two boys were jumping from one mass to another when the cousin decided it was getting late and headed back to the campground. The other boy said he was going to find another way back down and that was the last time he was seen.

Aja and I were flown down that evening. We were the only ones that could make it out before bad weather hit. It was only our second search so we were still fairly green. They helicoptered us to the site where we paired up with a local Ranger and started up the trail. The Ranger was having radio difficulty, so while we waited for the Ranger to get radio contact Aja checked things out. Suddenly, the winds switched and Aja did a ninety-degree turn and headed toward a little trail. Within a half

Kallie and Aja

hour of our arriving, Aja found the boy's body. We think he tried to jump from one rock to another, didn't make it, fell about fifty feet down between two rock masses, and hit his head.

Aja and I worked for the next seven years until she ended up with knee injuries. I had her until she was eleven.

My second dog, Kallie, was one of Aja's offspring. One of our most rewarding finds was when we got a call about a two-year-old boy who had gone missing in the desert of Arizona.

The little boy's family lived on the outskirts of the desert. He had been outside playing hide-and-seek with his four-year-old brother while their mother kept watch through the kitchen window. When the older boy went into the house, she went out to look for the two-year-old and he was gone.

Arizona has a unique situation where they can pull resources from the whole state. There were local police, bloodhounds, and a number of different groups looking for this little boy. Our group opted to work at night since we had come from a snowstorm and our dogs were acclimated to the cold and would now be working in an area where it was over 100 degrees in the middle of the day.

Heat does things to the scent and air current. In the daytime, the heating of the earth causes the scent to rise straight up along with the heat. At night, the cooling of the earth allows the air current and scents to stay low. The cooling also rejuvenates the scents and the winds are also more consistent, so working at night was more conducive for the dogs.

I told everybody on the team to choose an area to search and we all headed out. They had found the boy's diaper about a half mile from where he went missing. Kallie was basically tracking along until we got to this wash. The wash was one of my boundaries so I would go away from the wash to cover more area, but Kallie kept taking me back there. She seemed to have tracking indications until the wash dissipated.

When they called us back in the first night, I could hear coyotes howling in the distance.

The next night, I hadn't finished my area so we went back. We were coming out of a deep wash, and after passing through a lot of cactus, I heard a cry, followed by silence, then another cry. Kallie and I started running in the direction of the cry. Kallie was on point at a palo verde tree, so I shone my flashlight underneath it and there at the base of the tree was the little boy. I climbed under the tree and began doing first aid. At first, he didn't respond, but as I continued to check him over, he opened his eyes. I carried him out to where I could get radio contact and a helicopter picked him up in the field and flew him directly to the hospital. It was determined at the hospital that on a scale of one to ten for dehydration, he was a ten-plus.

In the three and a half days he had been out there, the little boy had managed to wander three miles from his home.

I found him in the same area where the coyotes had been the night before. The coyotes had been circling, waiting for him to die.

The following year, I went to Arizona for a NASAR conference and got in touch with the little boy's mother and went down to see them. I still keep in contact with his mother, and that little boy will be turning thirty soon. His mother said he didn't seem to have any conscious memory of it, but any time they went back to that area he threw a fit, so the following year they moved to the Phoenix area. To this day, he doesn't really remember everything and only knows what other people have told him.

Before a team can be deployed to a national disaster they need to be FEMA-certified, which is a process that combines skills in agility, obedience, directability, bark alert, and rubble pile searching. One of my dogs, Ivey, was FEMA-certified. After 9/11, we went to New York City and worked for nine days, where Ivey found multiple bodies.

Situations like that can be extremely difficult so I need to constantly remember: It goes down the leash. In other words, if I'm depressed, upset, or whatever I'm feeling, it goes down the leash and the dog can sense it. In the aftermath of 9/11, dogs were getting depressed, which they were feeling from their handlers.

My philosophy is that I've trained my dogs to find people, alive or dead, and when they do, they get a reward. It doesn't mean I'm being disrespectful to the family or the deceased. People sometimes may not understand that when you train a dog and they do their job—even if it is the recovery of a body—you need to be upbeat and reward your dog to reinforce their behavior and for doing their job.

In 2003, we had a search in southern Utah for a seventy-year-old man who had gone fishing. He was supposed to meet up with others around three o'clock that afternoon but when he didn't show up, they called the local search and rescue. After the local search and rescue went over the area three times, Ivey and I were flown down. I gave Ivey the scent article and she started tracking him. She went back and forth over the creek and through thick brush in ninety-degree temperatures and found his body two hours later.

The man had had heart problems and had a bypass a few years earlier. When we found him, his fish were lying next to him, and it looked

Ivey

like he just sat down, went to sleep, and passed.

Ivey found another elderly man with Alzheimer's who had wandered from home. She tracked him to about a mile from his home where he had fallen into a canal.

Ivey was trained for live finds, yet all of her finds were bodies. Ivey was a professional and all she wanted to do was work.

The dogs are trained to do certain things to alert that they found something. When Ivey found the fisherman, her head immediately went up and there was a change in her behavior that indicated she'd found something. Some of a dog's alert is based on their natural behavior and some is based on the work the dog will be doing. For FEMA or disaster work, there are often piles of rubble and we don't want the dog going back and forth multiple times so they are trained to stay and bark so you can direct the resources to that area.

Some dogs do a recall/refind where if they find a person, they come back to their handler with an indication, such as touching their handler's hand or jumping up on their handler. Other dogs do a bringsel alert where they have a small stick, tab, or other device suspended from their collar. When the dog finds the object of the search, they put the bringsel in their mouth, bring it to their handler, then lead the handler back to the object.

Some dogs have a natural recall/refind and, in that case, that's what you use. I like the stay and bark since I do a lot of disaster work.

After working with a search and rescue organization for twenty-five years, several of us decided to leave and form our own group. In 2007, we formed Utah Search Dogs, Inc., and one year later, we were incorporated and had five members. We now have seventeen people, and we train people and their dogs to find people (alive or dead) in numerous scenarios: urban areas, in the wilderness, in water, after an avalanche, or in any disaster situation. There is never a charge for our services and we are part of NASAR since they have specific standards and a certification process.

Every search has an impact on you. Every one changes you in some way.

Back in the '80s, there was a sixteen-year-old boy who had gone hunting in an area known as Steed Canyon in Davis County. It's not a fun canyon and is actually quite difficult because of the terrain. People had dropped him off at the top of a mountain before it started to rain. When the rain turned to snow and the boy didn't return, they called us out.

My friend Stephanie and I went and I brought both Aja and Kallie with me since it was local. They told us the boy was supposed to come back down by a southern route, but our dogs kept going toward the north.

We were quite a ways up the mountain yelling his name when he started yelling back. We were on the south side, but he was clearly calling from the north side of the canyon. We could only hear him because we were at the same level on the mountain as him. We radioed to the county sheriff's search and rescue and they started up the canyon.

We yelled and asked him if he knew his location but he didn't so I told him, "Start whistling Dixie." He started whistling and we all basically converged on him at the same time.

He was wearing jeans, a vest, and tennis shoes. Since he had gotten wet, he was hypothermic. Stephanie and I had brought down sleeping bags with us, so he took his clothes off and we wrapped him in blankets and the sleeping bags before carrying him down the creek to the bottom of the canyon. When we got to the bottom, his core temperature was ninety-five degrees.

I went to his wedding five years later and his grandmother kept in touch with me until she passed. Thankfully, he gave up hunting.

On that search, my dogs dislodged a rock that tumbled down and broke my finger. I had an abrasion on my eye from a twig and had also banged my knee and it had swelled up. But when you're on a search you continue despite injuries because it's important and time-sensitive work.

For me, the driving force behind doing this work is because of what my family went through after my father went missing. I know what every family is going through: the waiting, the uncertainty, the fear. The search and rescue work is something I can do to give back to the community, to the families, and to the people who worked so hard to try and find my father.

Chapter Twenty-Seven
TRACY

In the spring of 2017, I was on the road for several weeks meeting and interviewing people and dogs for my next book, Magical Dogs 3: On The Road. *Among those I was scheduled to meet were Tracy, Team Hunter, Service Dog Project, and Joy, but for various reasons, we were unable to connect.*

Since I believe every dog, human, and story comes to me for a reason, I decided to interview all of them by phone—starting with Tracy.

The initial plan was for Tracy and me to meet while I was in South Carolina. On the morning of my arrival, Tracy's mother's health took a turn for the worse, and as her mother's caregiver, she did the appropriate and loving thing and stayed with her mother. She is a compassionate, kind woman—traits that have served her human and canine family well over the years and that are clear in her story.

WHEN I WAS TWO, I BROKE MY LEG AND MY GRANDMOTHER brought me a collie puppy to make me feel better. I named the puppy Lady and she became my best friend. My mother fell in love with her too and began breeding and showing collies when I was in middle school.

My mother was diagnosed with breast cancer when I was in eighth grade and spent the following year on chemotherapy. As a result, she stopped showing and breeding dogs. Her partner got the two best show dogs, but the rest of the dogs stayed with us. Honestly, there was never a time that we did not have dogs in our house.

I had a part-time job during high school, and one night I came home from work and found a huge black Doberman lying just inside the front door. I didn't see or hear my parents and was convinced the dog had eaten them. Since this was before cell phones, I had no idea what to do or where to go so I stood there frozen and absolutely terrified. A few minutes later, my parents walked in from the kitchen, saw me, and started laughing.

One of my dad's clients had passed and left his dog, General Lee, to my dad. Of all the dogs we had over the years, General Lee was, without a doubt, the best dog I ever met. He was sweet and a perfect example of how people describe Dobermans: extremely loyal and loving the company of people. General Lee loved everyone in the family equally and instilled in me an absolute and unconditional love for Dobermans.

After my husband and I married, we got a Sheltie named Baloo. In the back of my mind, I knew that one day I wanted a Doberman to honor General Lee's memory, but somewhere along the way, others had instilled concerns in me about the safety of keeping Dobermans around children.

By the time our first son, Nick, was born, Baloo was older and had begun to slow down, so he was great with Nick. After Baloo passed, we had our second son, Daniel.

Several years later, Nick started getting hives and the doctors did allergy testing. While sitting in the doctor's office with needles up and down his back and both arms, Nick looked at me with tears in his eyes and asked, "Do I get a prize for this?" I said yes and asked what he wanted. Without hesitation, Nick said he wanted a golden retriever and he wanted to name it Chipper Jones—which is how Chipper Jones came into our family. He was a great dog and we had him his entire life.

It wasn't until Nick went away to college that I finally got my first Doberman.

I did not know a lot about rescue at the time but began searching online and ultimately found a male Doberman at the local Humane Society. My husband went to see him first, then that weekend my youngest son and I went with him to meet the dog. We were sitting in a large room when they brought the dog in, and he immediately began circling the perimeter of the room. Not knowing much about dog behavior, I thought it was cute. I didn't realize he was circling because he was anxious. I also did not realize the depth of what he had been through or the impact it had on him.

When the dog was seized by animal control, he only weighed thirty-five pounds. The owners said it was because he had Cushing's disease, but after running a full battery of tests, it was determined the only thing wrong with the dog was that he was being starved.

The dog's name was Snoopy, which my son shortened to Snoop. We brought Snoop home in November and he refused to look at anyone. In

Snoop

January, he looked at me for the first time and I will never forget that moment. My heart melted because I realized he was finally beginning to trust me and come out of his shell.

Before we got Snoop, I reached out to several friends since I was unsure if we should adopt him. I wasn't sure what, if any, problems we should expect since he was severely malnourished. Every single one of my friends said Snoop would be different from any dog I ever had because he would understand and appreciate that we had saved him. Those words have come true so many times over the years. Snoop knows and appreciates that we saved him. He also gave me a heart for a rescue dog and sent me on a journey to learn more about rescue.

With Nick away at college and Daniel not far behind, I realized I was going to have time on my hands, so I signed up to foster dogs for Georgia Doberman Rescue (GDR) and was approved. While waiting for my first foster, a woman sent me a message on Facebook about a female Doberman. Since I wasn't really involved in rescue yet, I reached out to my new friends at GDR. After going through all the proper channels to locate the dog's owners, the rescue brought her in and she became my first foster.

She was a sweet, wonderful dog and I could not have asked for a better first foster. After she was adopted, I started fostering one dog after another, joined the board of GDR, and became their foster coordinator.

A call came in one afternoon about Izzy, a female Doberman. Her owner had gotten her as a puppy and was awarded custody of Izzy in her divorce. The woman and Izzy had to move into a new apartment, and Dobermans were one of the breeds apartment management didn't permit. Since Izzy had natural ears, the woman tried to pass her off as another breed. Once management figured out she was a Doberman, they told her Izzy had to go. She initially gave her to a friend of a friend who said Izzy was crazy, but the real problem was that the people were keeping Izzy in a crate all day, every day. Since I did not have a foster at the time, I offered to foster Izzy—and she became my first foster failure.

Izzy
Photo courtesy of Judy Pritash Photography

I have no idea how anyone could ever say Izzy was crazy because nothing could be further from the truth. Izzy is most definitely the perfect dog. She is calm, laid back, loves everyone, and has never done anything wrong.

We now had Snoop and Izzy, and since my husband said two dogs were enough, I just continued fostering. Over time, more and more of my time was devoted to caring for my mom and I found myself with less and less time to foster. I switched to doing transports, home visits, and also remained on the board of GDR.

An unexpected blessing of transporting dogs was that it provided me with opportunities to spend time and create special memories with my mom. The first happened as we left the dentist's office one day. I turned my cell phone back on to find several messages from a woman asking me to please call her back. She explained she was with a bulldog rescue but that someone had dropped off a Doberman puppy and that I needed to get the puppy that day. My mom was still able to do transports with me at that time, so we got in the car and drove to Charlotte.

He was a sweet, young fawn puppy. I have no idea why his owners didn't want him but that was not for me to understand or judge. My son Daniel instantly fell in love with him so he never officially went into res-

Archer

cue. The vet estimated the puppy was around eight weeks old when we got him. Archer is now one year old and still the love of Daniel's life.

My oldest son Nick knew he wanted to get a dog after he graduated college and he began researching breeds. At first, he thought he wanted a Bernese Mountain dog, but after visiting a breeder he realized it wasn't the dog for him so he returned to doing more research.

Next Nick homed in on a Vizsla, and after visiting a breeder, it solidified it was the dog he wanted. I have seen over and over how the right dog finds us, and that is what happened for Nick, because a short while later the Vizsla breeder he met told him about a stray puppy in a kill shelter in North Carolina. The puppy was a mix but appeared to be mostly Vizsla so we all piled in the car, drove to Raleigh, and rescued Brodie. He is now almost three and lives a wonderful life with Nick and his wife, Clare.

When you're in rescue, you see and experience everything under the sun: the good, the not-so-good, and everything in between. Sometimes, after everything is said and done, you think about how everything played out and came together. Many times it can be quite a journey; many times it is nothing short of miraculous and truly magical.

We got an application from a woman in Augusta, Georgia, who wanted a small red Doberman. Her application and her vet check were good but there were two problems: we did not have any small red Dobermans and we did not have anyone in the Augusta area to do a home visit.

In the meantime, we got a call from a lady who wanted to surrender a blue male Doberman in the Augusta area. One of our South Carolina fosters had an opening so my mom and I decided to drive to Augusta, pick up the male dog, and do the woman's home visit while we were in the area.

While Mom stayed in the car with the dog, I did the home visit. The woman was a wonderful person and I instantly connected with her. As I was getting ready to leave, I mentioned that my mom was in the car with a dog and she immediately perked up and said maybe it was her dog. I told her it definitely was not her dog because she wanted a small red dog and this one was a huge blue dog.

Undeterred, she walked out with me, and when she and the dog met it was like something out of a movie. She took one look at him, instantly fell in love, and wanted him.

I reminded her she had been pretty set on what she wanted and he was not at all what she wanted. She was going on vacation, which was perfect because it meant she would have time to really think it over.

Mom and I drove back to South Carolina and brought the dog to his foster. The woman returned from vacation and called saying she wanted to adopt him.

My mom and I planned to meet her halfway between Greenville, South Carolina, and Augusta, Georgia, at a dog park so the rest of her family could meet the dog before they took him home. While we were at the park, I got a call about a male and a female Doberman at a kill shelter in Georgia that had to be out by five o'clock that night or they were going to be euthanized.

Since we were almost in Georgia anyway, Mom and I decided to go get them. I didn't have any real geographical knowledge as to exactly where we were or where we heading but that didn't stop us. Without even checking a map, we hopped back in the car and started driving.

Hours later, realizing we were going to be cutting it close to get to the shelter by five o'clock, I called them. Since I committed to take the dogs, the shelter agreed to move them to a veterinarian's office providing I got there before they closed.

Mom and I pulled into the parking lot of the veterinarian's office five minutes before they closed. They brought the dogs out, we tethered them in the back of my mom's SUV, then we headed back to South Carolina. We were on a busy two-lane road in heavy traffic when suddenly the male got loose and jumped over into the back seat. He was going nuts, and before I could pull over, he pooped everywhere. When I say everywhere, I mean everywhere—it was all over the seat, on the doors, his paws. The only place there wasn't any poop was the front seat, so of course, that's where he headed next.

By the time I was able to safely pull the car over, I had poop in my hair, down my arms, and all over me. We were in the middle of nowhere in the dark without a single napkin, wipe, or towel. I called the volunteer I was supposed to meet in Macon, Georgia, and asked her to bring any supplies she had so I could clean myself up.

We met her in the back of a Waffle House parking lot and I can still remember her face when she saw me. I can laugh about it now, but I was in tears at the time. She took one look at me and said, "Oh my goodness, Tracy, I thought you were exaggerating. I cannot believe how much poop you have on you!" I ended up grabbing a hose behind the Waffle House to hose myself off.

She took the dogs and Mom and I started the drive from Georgia back to South Carolina in a car full of poop. Halfway there, it started to rain so we had to roll up the windows. Then my GPS took us the wrong way and we headed straight into a construction zone. We got home at one o'clock in the morning. When I pulled into our driveway, my husband came out, took one look at me and the car, and said exactly what the volunteer said: that he thought I had been exaggerating.

Back in the beginning, I did transports as a volunteer with the Doberman Assistance Network (DAN). While no longer operational, DAN was a national organization that never actually adopted dogs. Instead, they served as a middle man for moving dogs out of bad situations and into safe, approved rescues.

I was so excited when DAN scheduled me for my first transport to move a dog from Columbia, South Carolina, to Spartanburg, South Carolina, a ninety-minute drive each way. That morning, my car was having issues, so my husband thought it wise for our son Daniel to ride along with me.

Daniel and I arrived at the woman's house in Columbia to pick up the dog, and the instant the dog met me, he was afraid. The woman didn't know me and didn't know why the dog was having such an extreme reaction to me, since according to her, the dog had never been afraid of anyone. Still being new to rescue, I didn't have any idea why the dog was having such a reaction. I promised the woman I was a good person—then she turned and saw my son.

Daniel was only fifteen at the time but was already six foot four. The woman said having a child along was against the rules.

I explained about my car troubles and that my husband thought it wise for our son to come along but, again, she repeated it was against the rules.

With no other option, she finally allowed me to take the dog. I continued to apologize profusely and she continued to tell me to make sure it never happened again. I honestly thought that was the end of my volunteering and transport days.

After tethering the dog in the back of the SUV, we drove almost two hours to a hotel parking lot off the interstate where I was to meet the next driver. Pulling up, I rolled down my window and told her I had never done this before and had no idea how to do a handoff. She asked if the dog was in a crate and I told her it was tethered in the back of my SUV.

She walked over to my car, lifted the back hatch of the SUV, and the dog shot out. I had used a regular nylon leash and, unbeknownst to us, the dog had chewed through it. So here we were in a parking lot right next to the interstate with a loose dog. The woman had snacks and treats and assured me we would get the dog back, but they weren't working. The hotel manager saw the commotion and came out to help. Together, the three of us tried everything but nothing was working—until my son got out of the car. The dog took one look at Nick and instantly ran straight over and sat down next to him.

My son, who had broken one of the cardinal rules of transport by simply being there, had just saved the day—and the dog.

Dobermans are not as brave as people think. I think one of the reasons they get such a bad rap is because people don't understand that when Dobermans are afraid they react in one of two ways: the first, and most typical, is that they shut down. I cannot tell you the number of Dobermans I have seen in the shelter who cannot handle the loud noise and barking and completely shut down or are so afraid they will not even walk.

The other reaction they can have is to lash out. In an attempt to communicate to the person to get away from them, they can react aggressively. A perfect example is what happened once when a man contacted us to surrender his Doberman.

He said she was a great dog but he was moving and couldn't take the dog with him. You hear that a lot. The stories are usually the same: it's either a job, they are moving, or they no longer have time to care for the dog.

One of our volunteers lived about an hour away and went with her husband to pick up the dog. When they got there, the dog went after her husband. Initially it made her nervous, but she took into consideration that transports can be stressful for a dog, that she was on the side of a busy road, and that the dog was going into a car with people it had never met. Thinking the dog was simply afraid, she decided to take her home.

When they got home, the dog refused to get out of the car and kept snapping at them. The volunteer called a board member who, in turn, called a behaviorist in Atlanta. The behaviorist suggested that since it wasn't hot out, they should set a timer and leave the dog alone for fifteen minutes. They did, and when they returned, the dog was even more aggressive. Next, the behaviorist asked if they could get the car in the garage. When they told her it was already in the garage, she told them to shut the garage door, open the car doors, and see if the dog would get out.

By that time, the dog was foaming at the mouth, so the board member called the owner. He picked up the phone and without even saying "hello" simply said, "What's the address? I know I need to get her. She's mean."

When he came to get her, he explained that he had gotten the dog as a puppy but they never left the house. He had never even taken the dog to the vet. Since he lived alone and never had company, the dog had never seen people and was never socialized. No wonder the dog was terrified! He left, and unfortunately, we have no idea what happened to the dog after that.

Many people think owner surrenders are awful, but there are a lot of reasons why people surrender their dog. They can't all be lumped together and labeled "bad." A perfect example is a woman who lived near me and sent us an email saying she had to surrender her dog. Her dog was a beautiful red female Doberman. She also had a new baby. As we talked, it was clear that someone had convinced her that a Doberman and a baby did not go well together and that the dog had to go.

It was also clear that she loved her dog deeply and did not want to give her up. I kept begging her to let me help her keep the dog. She was a wonderful person who loved her dog, but she was being forced to choose between the dog and her child. It was heartbreaking and I felt so bad for her.

We prefer people get preapproved and work with us to find them the right dog rather than coming to us after seeing a picture of a dog and are dead set on getting it simply because of how it looks. This dog was incredibly stunning, but fortunately we never had to put it on the website. One of our volunteers had a red female Doberman who had recently passed and he was looking for another one, so the dog went to him. That woman's dog has a wonderful life with him and his red male Doberman, and while she has since moved away, he keeps in contact with her. Our hope is that it gives her some comfort knowing her dog is happy.

While many of the original owners want to keep in touch with the dog, we need to legally respect the adopter. We give the adopter the prior owner's information but it is up to them whether or not they reach out. I am still in contact with the woman who had Izzy. She doesn't live near me so I send her pictures and videos of Izzy on a regular basis and we both enjoy staying connected.

At the time, my local shelter was a kill shelter, and ironically, it was through them that I learned even more about rescue. Many people automatically think a kill shelter is terrible and end up hating it, but in most cases, they are doing the best they can. I learned that by following the shelter's guidelines, I could develop a relationship with them, which ultimately helped more dogs. The shelter began to contact me any time a Doberman came in so we could rescue the dog and find it a home.

I realized the importance of trying to find the best in a place and in people and not let all the negative get to me. That was a huge lesson for me. However, under the surface, another problem was brewing.

There is an aspect to rescue that is often not recognized, discussed, understood, or addressed: compassion fatigue. I was on the board and saw so much with owner surrenders, the condition of dogs, and dealing with different shelters. As I got into rescue full force, compassion fatigue hit—and it hit hard. Let me tell you, compassion fatigue is real. I am not going to lie; it had a huge impact on me. I grew bitter and began expecting the worst in people.

In addition to that, my mother's dementia has advanced to the point where I am now her full-time caregiver, so my work with the rescue became more limited. Eventually I resigned from the board and stepped away from rescue. There were people who did not understand, but I think a lot of people don't understand dementia and what it does to a person and their family.

Stepping away has given me perspective. It has helped me see that I do not need to look and think so badly of everyone—which, ironically, is the same lesson I learned from my local shelter. Even more, it is the lesson our dogs teach us: to look for and believe the best in people.

Chapter Twenty-Eight
TEAM HUNTER

Our itinerary included a trip to New England to visit Team Hunter and the Service Dog Project, but family commitments kept me in New Jersey so I arranged to speak with them by phone.

As you read the following story of Team Hunter, the main narrator is Kelly, Hunter's mother, but Hunter chimed in throughout the interview as well. I think you'll find that Hunter is an absolute delight, and his family, their story, and their dog are both amazing and magical.

Kelly: Hunter came into the world fourteen weeks early and shortly before his second birthday was diagnosed with cerebral palsy. Although he was walking with a walker by his third birthday, doctors continued to warn us he would probably be unable to walk beyond his fifth birthday.

From the day Hunter came into the world, we always told him he could do anything he wanted to but that it just may look different from the way other people did it. His grandparents made Hunter a walker with skis that allowed him to go out in the snow and ice fishing, and we continued to make adaptations and adjustments to allow Hunter to do everything he wanted.

Living in Maine, we make frequent trips to New Hampshire, and on one of those trips we drove to the top of Mount Washington. Hunter saw a T-shirt in the gift shop that said, "This Body Hiked Mount Washington." He loved it but said he couldn't get it since we rode up and didn't hike up. Later that day, Hunter and my husband, Andy, started making plans to hike up Mount Washington the following year.

The day of the hike, they left early in the morning. Halfway up the mountain, they lost cell service. My daughter and I waited, having absolutely no idea how long it would take them, but we grew increasingly anxious and concerned as time passed. Finally, several hikers coming down saw our expressions and asked if we were waiting for the boy and his dad. When we said we were, they assured us they were doing fine and gave us approximations of how far away they were. It took them a little over seven hours. While Andy carried Hunter on his shoulders for portions of the hike and lifted him up steep spots, Hunter hiked and climbed rocks as much as he could.

Hunter: I did the best I could. There were no major mishaps other than Dad losing a bit of skin from his shin on a rock, so I guess you could say Dad left a piece of himself on the mountain.

Kelly: The doctors had told us repeatedly that Hunter would probably not be walking past his fifth birthday, but here he was having just hiked to the top of Mount Washington at age five! Andy and I bought him the T-shirt.

For years, we drove back and forth to Boston Children's Hospital. Hunter was doing really well but the doctors continued to prepare us for what was to come. They warned us that at around age seven, Hunter would start growing and his muscles would not be strong enough to support his weight. Their prediction was that Hunter would begin to slow down and need a wheelchair. We decided to continue to fight as long, as hard, and as much as we could.

I am a physical therapist, and one day a patient's wife came in with a mobility balance dog. Having never seen one before, Andy and I went online that night to do some research and found the Service Dog Project (SDP), which uses Great Danes as their service dogs. Minutes later, the phone rang. It was Andy's mother calling to tell us she had just seen a television segment about SDP and suggesting we might want to reach out to them.

We emailed SDP that night and spoke with Carlene the next day. She had concerns when she learned Hunter was seven. A child is typically placed with a dog when they are between thirteen and fourteen because they need to be in control of the dog at all times and able to do everything with and for the dog. Parents of able-bodied children still do a lot for them at seven, never mind a child with a disability—so she felt that Hunter was too young. Nonetheless, she suggested we drive to Ipswich, Massachusetts, that Sunday for an open house.

One of the first things Carlene asked Hunter to do was walk while keeping one of his hands in my back pocket. Carlene believes if you can walk like that, you can walk with a Great Dane. We had seen this on the

SDP website and Hunter had been practicing it, so he confidently put one hand in my back pocket and together we walked down a ramp and around the yard.

Carlene said we were welcome to fill out an application but reminded us that it would probably take a while before we got a dog due to Hunter's age. We stressed that we were looking for any and all options that would allow Hunter to keep doing whatever he wanted to do—both now and in the future. Even though he had a walker, Hunter often rode on it, which meant he was not using his legs. We knew walking with a dog would not only help him use his legs but also keep his muscles strong.

In addition to filling out the application, we also needed a medical necessity letter so we contacted Hunter's doctor. She lived in Ipswich but had never heard of Service Dog Project and was fascinated. Since we were going to SDP most weekends to volunteer and play with the dogs, we invited her to join us.

Hunter's doctor came to SDP while we were there the following Sunday. Carlene gave her a tour and she wrote him the letter. We knew we still had a long wait for a dog because at that point, the youngest person to ever get one of their dogs was twelve.

Hunter: Great Danes are big dogs, and at the time, I was only forty-eight pounds!

Kelly: Over the years, there had been ongoing discussions about a major surgery Hunter would eventually need to try to straighten out his bones and lengthen the muscles in his lower legs and hips. Every three to six months we drove to Boston Children's Hospital so the doctors could monitor Hunter. We were waiting for him to reach a plateau where he was no longer improving in his walking or able to maintain the range of motion in his legs in order to schedule the surgery.

We submitted our application with SDP at the end of August, and in early October, Carlene called to tell us she had some dogs she wanted us to meet.

Two days later, we pulled Hunter out of school and drove to Ipswich. While Hunter did all right with the first two dogs, Carlene was not convinced either was the right fit. She asked us to return that weekend to meet some younger dogs who really liked kids, so Hunter and his dad hopped in the car on Saturday and drove back to Ipswich.

The first was a small, sweet dog but the leg braces Hunter was wearing at the time made loud noises when he walked that scared the dog.

Another dog had gotten stung by bees and was out of commission for the day.

Finally, Carlene said they had a slightly bigger dog named Wendy she wanted to try. Wendy was a long, lean, black eleven-month-old Great Dane. Hunter and Wendy had barely walked ten feet together when Carlene

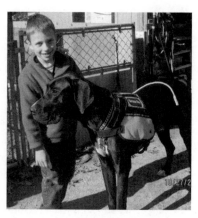

Hunter and Wendy two weeks after being paired
Photo courtesy of Mark Amirault

and a trainer looked at each other and said, "This is the one." While it looked like a match, Carlene explained that the most important thing was to ensure that the dog and human bonded. Without a bond, the dog would not work efficiently or properly with the person. Carlene asked Andy if they could come back the next day for a bonding session.

Andy agreed, and as he and Hunter got ready to leave, Wendy stood behind the truck and refused to move. Carlene had to take Wendy away so Andy and Hunter could leave.

The next day, Andy and Hunter went back to begin the bonding process, which essentially meant having Hunter do everything for Wendy: feed her, take her out, give her treats, everything. No one else was allowed to do anything for the dog. Since Hunter was only seven, Andy had to be with him, but other than helping Wendy up and down the stairs, Hunter did it all. He cuddled with her, fed her, read to her, took her outside. After six hours together, Andy knew it had been a long day for everyone and wanted to get Hunter home, so he asked if they could come back another day.

Hunter: There were other dogs running around so they put them away and had me come downstairs with Wendy. We went through a few more basics and then they handed us food for Wendy and told us to take her home for the night and see how it went.

Kelly: Andy and Hunter called to tell me they were bringing Wendy home. I was shocked. After they arrived, we briefly introduced Wendy to Jasper, our black Lab, and Bailey, our husky–shepherd mix. Then Wendy and Hunter went upstairs to his room and shut the door.

At SDP, the dogs have soft cushy couches and beds with big fluffy blankets to lie down on and sleep. Since we weren't prepared for Wendy to come home, we didn't have a soft spot ready for her and she was having a hard time getting comfortable and settling down.

Hunter: She tried but she couldn't even get comfortable on my bed.

Kelly: Finally we covered Hunter's bed with a king-size comforter and Wendy lay down and went to sleep. A little while later, we heard our Lab go upstairs, which was something he rarely did since he was getting older and stairs were difficult for him. We heard him burst through Hunter's door so we ran upstairs to see what was happening. We saw Jasper standing next to the bed nose to nose with Wendy. Nobody growled or made a noise, they just touched noses, and after a few minutes, Jasper turned and walked back downstairs. He has never gone upstairs on his own again.

It was Columbus Day weekend. Since there was no school on Monday, we went back to the farm to tell them how everything was going and to do more training. Wendy has been with us ever since.

Carlene encouraged us to send Wendy to school with Hunter, so the next day he excitedly announced to everyone at school that he was bringing a service dog to school. The school principal called us, unsure if Hunter was telling the truth, and Andy explained that Hunter had a service dog for mobility. The principal said the school never had a student with a service dog and did not have a policy or procedure for a service dog. This was uncharted territory for the school, the district, and us.

She asked us to please keep Wendy at home until they had something in place. We agreed, because we needed to know that Hunter and Wendy were comfortable and confident working together. Hunter also needed to build up his endurance and control. That entire school year, other than going on several field trips at the end of the year, we kept Wendy home.

Hunter: I needed to relearn how to walk with Wendy because it was so different from using my walker.

Kelly: It was a challenging year. The handler needs to make decisions on the fly and have control of the dog at all times since no service dog is perfect all of the time. Hunter had to be able to walk with Wendy while giving commands, making split-second decisions, anticipating things, and remaining in control.

Hunter and Wendy training at
Service Dog Project
Photo courtesy of Mark Amirault

We faced a lot of responsibility as well as other people's scrutiny because this was outside of the box for some people. We knew we needed to change people's ideas and perceptions about Wendy and what she would be doing for Hunter.

Hunter is very sensitive and extremely observant. He knew there was concern and speculation about what we were doing. It was also a lot on him. He would come home after school, tired and exhausted, but still had to go out and train with Wendy. He walked up and down the road giving her commands. We went to grocery stores, department stores, restaurants, parks, pet stores, and literally any place that might be a challenge for them. At each of these places, they encountered situations that were challenging as a team: from people coming up to ask questions or wanting to pet Wendy to facing the constant barrage of food, dog treats, and toys everywhere.

The more situations they encountered, the more Wendy learned to react to Hunter or sense what Hunter needed. Hunter in turn relearned how to walk with Wendy and learned to give commands and anticipate what they might need to do.

Hunter had been used to using a walker with two hands for support. Now with Wendy he used one hand and arm for support and the other hand and arm for her leash and for commands. Every weekend, we drove to Ipswich to work all day Saturday and Sunday with Carlene and her trainers.

As the next school year rolled around, Hunter and Wendy had done a lot of training and were ready. We knew issues might come up, but the day Hunter and Wendy set off for their first day of third grade, we were extremely excited—and very nervous.

Hunter: Over the summer, we went into the school, especially the few weeks before school started, to get used to everything. We even practiced a fire drill.

Kelly: One of the challenges we faced early on was that it had always been my husband or me (or both of us) along with Hunter whenever we trained or worked together. Wendy learned really quickly, but she also loved routine, so not having all of us together was difficult and confusing for her. She couldn't figure out why we weren't all together and what she was supposed to do.

There was one hallway at the school Wendy did not like going down. It was dark and musty, but the door at the end was used to go in and out for recess. It was important that Wendy got over her nervousness, so SDP sent Megan, their head trainer, to work with Wendy and Hunter at school.

Any time there was a little bump in the road, SDP was there. If something came up with the school or the administration, SDP called or came to answer any questions and concerns. They were also there as Hunter grew and got stronger. As his walking changed, what he needed from Wendy changed, so they went back to the farm for more formal training.

The more Wendy worked with Hunter, the more she anticipated what he needed, including stepping in front of him on the stairs to stop him from falling. Her instincts with Hunter are amazing, and many times she knows his limits before he does. She has blocked or stepped in front of him to stop him from going up or down stairs several times because she sensed that he was tired or knew he just had an injection, which makes his muscles weaker for a period of time.

All the kids loved Wendy but Hunter explained from the start that she was a service dog so they could not talk to or touch her. After the first few days, the kids understood.

Hunter has always been really good about explaining things, whether it is to tell people what he has or how to interact with Wendy. He's equally comfortable talking with a three-year-old child as he is a doctor. We had explained to him from a young age that people would watch him because they did not understand or might wonder what was wrong. If someone made him uncomfortable, Hunter had a practice of simply smiling, waving, and asking if he could answer any of their questions. He has always known people were watching but now he had a hundred-pound dog that brought even more attention to him. SDP had also explained and prepared us for this.

When people are out with us they are shocked at how often we get stopped to answer questions. We don't mind because we think what Wendy and SDP do is extraordinary and are happy to tell people. If we are in a hurry, we simply tell them to check out the Service Dog Project website or Facebook page.

We started a Team Hunter and Wendy Facebook page because the people that support SDP like to know what happens after a dog is matched, and social media makes it much easier to keep everyone updated.

Hunter: We also hand out business cards that we had printed with our Facebook page and SDP's website along with service dog etiquette.

Kelly: Hunter is very charming and people attach to him pretty quickly. A lot of people have known Hunter since he was young and they know how hard he worked over the years, so they were his biggest cheerleaders. Overall the transition went really well and the community was supportive and helpful.

We knew there were people who were still adjusting and questioned what we were doing, but we think some of the other parents spoke up on our behalf because we never had any issues. That was really nice because we knew that we were facing a bigger hurdle: Hunter's surgery.

Hunter's surgery was scheduled for January 2016, so we did a family cross-country road trip in the summer of 2015. We drove from Maine to Colorado and stopped along the way at a lot of different places to create special memories. At Mount Rushmore, Hunter and Wendy hiked almost a mile each way in addition to climbing 422 stairs. Devils Tower was over a mile walk and Hunter and Wendy hiked most of it. We captured it on video and posted it on Facebook for people to see. The day we were hiking at Rocky Mountain National Park, we realized to reach the 12,005-foot summit meant climbing an additional 200 feet, including steps without any railing on either side, but Hunter and Wendy did it. Hunter never would have been able to do without Wendy.

Hunter: At Niagara Falls, people turned away from the falls to watch me and Wendy walk toward the falls.

Kelly: With Wendy, Hunter was walking and hiking, but he was also building muscle and endurance. That, along with all the work he had been doing with Wendy, allowed his surgery to be delayed for two and a half years. It also meant he was going into his surgery the strongest he had ever been.

As word spread about Hunter's surgery, the community stepped up in a way we could never have imagined.

From the time he was a baby, Hunter loved to vacuum. I don't know why vacuuming was his thing but I thought it was wonderful because our Lab was 95 pounds, our husky was 60 pounds, and when Wendy first came home she was 110 pounds. That was over 250 pounds of dog, which is not only a lot of dog but a lot of dog hair!

Knowing the surgery would limit his ability to vacuum, Hunter wanted to get an iRobot Roomba for Christmas to do the vacuuming for him until he was able to do it again. When our friends found out, they started a GoFundMe page to buy Hunter a Roomba.

Someone knew people at iRobot and contacted the company. When iRobot heard Hunter's story, they had Santa give him a Roomba and an iRobot shirt along with an invitation for our family to visit their headquarters in Massachusetts.

At the end of Christmas break, right before his surgery, we drove to Massachusetts, and the people at iRobot were incredible. Hunter is very analytical and loved being able to try out a lot of different robots. He got to check out a bomb-diffusing robot the Department of Defense used and saw their 3-D printers. They gave Hunter an iRobot ID card, a full tour, and told him to come visit anytime.

Since Hunter had received a free Roomba, we used the donated monies in Hunter's GoFundMe account to buy him a telepresence robot. A telepresence robot is essentially a remote-controlled wheeled robot with an iPad that would allow Hunter to remotely attend school while he recovered from surgery.

On January 26, 2016, Hunter went into surgery. The surgeons removed over half an inch from his femur on both sides. To make his hips symmetrical, his left hip was rotated forty degrees and the right hip was rotated twenty degrees. Since Hunter's right foot had always turned out and away from his left foot (which turned in), they cut his right tibia and rotated his right foot to try and even them out. They lengthened a tendon in his inner thighs and inserted four plates and seventeen screws to hold everything in place. Despite all that was done, the surgery was much less invasive than originally planned thanks to Hunter's work with Wendy.

The surgery went well but we were still not sure if Hunter would be able to walk again. After five days in the hospital, we brought Hunter home. With a cast on one leg and a huge foam wedge he had to keep between his knees at all times, it was impossible for him to fit in a normal-sized wheelchair, so he arrived home in an extra-wide wheelchair. It took us over an hour to get him into and out of the car.

For the next four weeks, Hunter was non-weight-bearing. At five weeks, he was able to put weight on both legs and doctors said he could do whatever felt comfortable. All the strength he had gained in the years he was working with Wendy helped accelerate his healing and recovery.

At his first physical therapy session, Hunter had already done everything they asked him to do. The doctor warned him to slow down, but by the end of March, Hunter took his first steps with Wendy. They told us it would take a year, but it had only been eight weeks.

Hunter: I took very small slow steps with Wendy but I was walking with her again—and she was super excited!

Kelly: Hunter was able to keep up with his schoolwork and classmates thanks to the telepresence robot. Controlling the robot from home with his iPad, Hunter could drive it around school and into his classrooms to listen to lectures, see what was written on the board, and even ask questions. He was able to see and talk to his friends for the four and a half months he was home recovering.

In the last month of school, Hunter went back to school for half days. After he returned to school, we donated the robot to the elementary school. Hunter still uses it occasionally if he is out of school for a procedure or for injections but it can now be used by anyone who might be out of school for a period of time.

At the end of June, just six months after his surgery, Hunter was asked to be a representative for Boston Children's Hospital at a family advocacy day in Washington, DC. Hunter would be speaking with and advocating to our senators and representative on behalf of children who need the services of a children's hospital. Hunter was honored to have the opportunity so our whole family, including Wendy, flew to Washington.

It was Wendy's first time on an airplane. We arranged for bulkhead seating since she lies in front of Hunter's feet, and she did great and was a big hit everywhere we went. People were amazed by how beautiful Wendy is and how well she and Hunter work together. We were stopped by CEOs and doctors from children's hospitals around the country who were interested in how Hunter and Wendy worked together. Questions varied from "Where did you get the idea?" to "What changes have you seen in Hunter since he got Wendy?"

They had a dinner and party with music, dancing, games, face painting, and caricatures. Hunter was having fun dancing and closed down the party with some new friends. He also went up the steps of the Lincoln Memorial, which we posted a video of on his Facebook page.

Hunter: Dad and Mom didn't get much to eat on that trip because so many people had questions. As soon as one person was done, someone else had questions. Wendy was at the party, but since it was past her bedtime, she mostly slept. She only lifted her head if she couldn't see me.

Kelly: As Hunter continued to progress, he was doing so well that we decided to plan a family trip. Hunter wanted to go to Disney World.

Since he had already missed a lot of school, we decided to plan it during a school break, knowing that meant seriously pushing the schedule the doctors had originally given us. Hunter was already ahead of the normal healing schedule by three to six months, but we knew the time-frame to take the hardware out was twelve to eighteen months post-op. Because of how well he was doing, Hunter had his hardware removed on December 2, 2016—fewer than twelve months after his surgery. He left the hospital with special rules and conditions since there were holes in his bones, but just like before, Hunter progressed and healed really quickly.

We packed up and headed to Disney World. Since our family enjoys road trips, we drove. We were on the road for two weeks, including eight days at Disney. We invited our extended family to join us in Florida, and at one point there were fifteen people there to celebrate Hunter, including both grandparents, a couple of his aunts, and some cousins.

We planned our days and activities around the heat and sun so Wendy wouldn't get too hot. We also have a cooling coat we used on her. If we were going to be walking, we put the back of our hand on the pavement. If it burnt us in five seconds, we knew it would hurt Wendy's paws so we didn't go out.

Hunter: Wendy even went on some of the rides with us! I used the wheelchair for long distances, but she was very tired because it was so busy and she had to constantly watch out for me. Near the end of the trip, Wendy was so tired that I had to make her get off the bed to eat.

Kelly: We live in the country on twenty acres and Hunter used to need help going in and out of the house. Now he has Wendy to help him and he can go outside whenever he wants. He was able to use his snowshoes this year, so we keep Wendy's nails a little longer in the winter to help her grip the ice. He can navigate curbs and go up and down stairs without a railing now because of Wendy. She allows Hunter to be more independent and do more things for himself.

Hunter used to fall at least a hundred times a day whether he was using his walker or not. The reality is he will always fall, but now he only falls around five times a day, usually when he is outside playing and "running." When he falls, he no longer has to crawl to a place where he can get up because Wendy is like a portable ladder. She stands still and braces herself while Hunter uses her harness to pull himself up.

Hunter: Wendy is my four-wheel drive through the snow and sand. She makes it easier to go anywhere.

Kelly: That's true but we keep the walker as a back-up.

Hunter: If anyone makes me use the walker anymore, I am going to break it into pieces and put it in the dumpster. Every one of my walkers has been bright yellow or bright orange, but whenever we were at the store, people still hit me with their shopping cart. All I could think was,"You goober! You can't see a bright orange walker?"

Kelly: I know you'd love to get rid of it, Hunter, but Wendy has a sensitive stomach. If she gets sick, you certainly don't want a Great Dane with diarrhea at school, so I think it's best if we keep the walker as a back-up.

The school originally thought a walker was easier, but it's a two-story building. In a fire drill or fire, Hunter has to stay on the second floor and wait for a firefighter since the school doesn't want him walking down the stairs. But with Wendy there, Hunter can walk down the stairs with his class.

After having Wendy in school with Hunter for a year, she returned to SDP for additional training and Hunter went back to using his walker. At that point, the school realized how much easier it was for Hunter to have Wendy than the walker.

The only time Hunter and Wendy have been apart was when she went back to SDP for additional training. Typically a service dog looks at a person's feet to pace themselves, but since Hunter's feet go faster than the rest of his body, Wendy had to be trained to look at his hips. As a result, she now slows down to help him pace better.

Hunter: They also taught her hand signals.

Kelly: They put Wendy in a down/stay, gave the signal, and walked away. Before Hunter would try to do that and she would pop up. She needed to be more comfortable with the signals and also more confident that Hunter was all right. Now anytime she is in a down/stay, she stays at attention. If she can't see or hear him, she will stay, but she gets anxious because at the very least, she needs to hear him.

Wendy just wants Hunter to be safe. If she thinks something is a threat, she makes Hunter move, but with Hunter being older, bigger, and stronger now, she is beginning to understand he is in charge and she doesn't need to protect him as much.

Hunter: When we are outside, I let her walk around wherever she wants to go, but if I call her, she is by my side in five seconds.

Kelly: After the surgery, Wendy was more protective. She is very intuitive, and if she feels Hunter couldn't do something, she won't let him. She is still protective of him, is always aware of what is going on, and knows his limitations—even if Hunter doesn't.

Hunter: I was always taught to push through limitations, which I guess doesn't help Wendy because my limitations are always changing.

Kelly: We have always been strict about making Hunter do what he can so he doesn't limit himself. We tell him it may take him longer and he may do it a little differently, but we always encourage him to do things and he always has.

In the fall, he'll be going to middle school where rather than 200 kids, there will be 600 to 700 kids. It's a new building, so the two of them have been going to the school to train. They learn to navigate around the school, practice stairs, and learn where the various classrooms are. That way, when the bell rings and Hunter says it's time to go to math class, Wendy knows where that is. It's a lot of work and they are always learning new things together, but it is definitely worth it.

We also make sure Wendy has down time. When her pack comes off, she is a regular dog. She still keeps an eye on Hunter but she also knows it is time to play.

Hunter: Wendy has "zoomie time" when she just runs. When she does, you need to watch out because she moves fast!

Kelly: Hunter is eleven and Wendy will soon be five. It has truly been an amazing four years they've had together and we are immensely thankful to Service Dog Project for Wendy and for all they do. Wendy has been such a blessing to our family and having her is a miracle.

To our knowledge, Hunter is the youngest person to have been given a dog by SDP, which we think is nothing short of a miracle.

The other miracle was that Carlene's call came during what is normally a very difficult time of the year for us. Our other son passed when

Hunter and Wendy atop the summit in
Rocky Mountain National Park, Colorado.
Photo courtesy of Andy VanBrocklin

he was only seven weeks old and Carlene's call came the day before his birthday, so we believe Hunter's brother helped find him a dog.

Hunter: Wendy used to sleep in my bed, but we didn't want her to accidentally lay on my legs after my surgery, so my dad built her a bed that's even with my bed so we are still next to one another every night.

One of my favorite things is when we go out to restaurants. Everybody sees us coming in with this huge dog. She goes under the table and we make sure the waiters and waitresses know she is there so they don't trip over her.

It usually takes about an hour or longer to eat, so by the time we get up to leave, there is usually a whole new group of people. When Wendy crawls out from under the table, all you hear are forks and spoons dropping as people try to figure out where this huge dog was all this time. I get a kick out of it.

Wendy helps make a lot of things like stairs and hiking easier. I can actually hike now because I have her instead of wheels. It's like bringing your favorite teddy bear and best friend with you everywhere.

Chapter Twenty-Nine
SERVICE DOG PROJECT

Our original travel itinerary was to leave Team Hunter in Maine and head to Massachusetts to visit the Service Dog Project (SDP), its founder Carlene, several volunteers, and the dogs in person, but we were unable to go.

A change in plans isn't easy for me because I love meeting the dogs and the humans in person. The work Service Dog Project does with Great Danes is both important and life-changing and I am grateful that they provided the following information.

SINCE CARLENE FOUNDED THE SERVICE DOG PROJECT (SDP) IN 2003, we have trained and donated 150 fully certified Great Dane service dogs to individuals with severe balance or mobility limitations. While preference is given to veterans, our service dogs have also been placed with children and individuals with multiple sclerosis, Parkinson's disease, cerebral palsy, Friedreich's ataxia, and more.

Great Danes are well suited to both home and office life. They require less exercise than many breeds, making them a good fit for some people with disabilities. Their perfect public persona also makes them extremely conducive to helping with the isolation and depression that often accompany disabilities.

We are located on a twelve-acre property in Massachusetts. SDP dogs are not the tall show dogs but the sturdy working Danes. All of our Great Danes are born, raised, and trained here. Once a dog is fully trained (usually at a year or older) they are matched with a recipient. At that point they receive additional training to meet the individual's exact needs.

Balance support dogs should be at least 45 percent of a person's height and 65 percent of their weight. That means a six-foot-tall man would need a thirty-inch dog in order to put stability at his fingertips.

As a balance (or walker) dog, they must learn to be steady in a harness and match their gait to the handler's speed, which can vary. The dog learns to halt and brace if the handler falls and stands so the person can use the harness to pull themselves up. The dogs learn to turn right and left and ease themselves through doorways, elevators, restaurants, stores, and a variety of other settings while also concentrating amidst distractions and noise.

There are also individualized tasks the dog learns depending upon their recipient's needs, from working around crutches to pulling a wheelchair.

Every working service Dane changes lives for the better, because improved mobility means greater independence for the recipient and less dependence on caretakers, allowing them to live a fuller, richer life in and out of the home.

Chapter Thirty
JOY

Another stop on our journey was in Asheville, North Carolina. Back in the '70s, I graduated from Warren Wilson College just outside of Asheville, so I reached out to a former college friend, Laura, to tell her about the trip and the book. Laura said she didn't have any stories but maybe her friend Gordon did. Gordon said he didn't have any stories either but he knew someone who did: Joy. Joy and her family were going to be out of town when we were there so we made plans to talk when we were both back home.

Gordon was right: Joy definitely had a story to tell about a magical dog named Kali.

I GREW UP IN A LITTLE TOWN ON THE COAST OF MAINE WITH TWO dogs, a beagle and a Scottie, but the first dog I ever fell in love with was Bozo, a golden retriever who belonged to our next-door neighbor. I spent a lot of time with Bozo. We played together in the woods for hours, so his death was extremely difficult for me. I didn't connect with another dog like that again until I met a man named Dave who had a fabulous, incredible golden retriever–Lab mix named Eddy.

Dave and I got married and for years enjoyed bringing Eddy with us on our adventures. Eddy loved hiking and camping and was the ultimate travel and adventure dog, but as Eddy aged, he had to slow down. Eddy's adventures came to an end when he passed six months after his seventeenth birthday.

Dave, I, and our four-year-old son, Zachary, had moved to western North Carolina just before Eddy died. We are both teachers and have the summer off. We alternated where we spent five weeks every summer between Maine (where I was from) and Minnesota (where Dave was from).

Eddy had gotten us hooked on having a dog friend with us on our adventures. While in Minnesota in 2009—two years after Eddy passed— we decided it was time to get another dog. Two days after returning to

North Carolina, we went to the Humane Society where we saw two little puppies. Other than the fact that they were sisters who had been abandoned, very little was known about them, including their breed. One of the puppies sat and leaned up against Dave—and that became our Kali.

Zachary was eight and thrilled to have a puppy. We immediately started taking Kali hiking with us to introduce her to our world of adventure and prepare her for our next summer vacation.

Kali

The next summer, we all packed up and headed to Maine to camp with my sister, Sandy. Kali met Sandy's dog, Jackie, and together they had a wonderful time jumping off the dock, running along the shoreline, and playing in the water.

One day, while we were all hiking and playing at a swimming hole, Kali slipped and went over a small rapid. Even though she scrambled out of the water quickly, she was so freaked out by the experience that she immediately took off into the woods. We caught up with her, but it took us a while to coax her back. Little did we know that a few years later, that experience would play out again in a much more significant way.

The following summer, we went to Minnesota. One of our favorite things to do was to camp, paddle, and portage in the Boundary Waters Canoe Area Wilderness in northern Minnesota. By then, Kali was an incredible adventure dog. While she enjoyed the comforts of life and looked quite princess-like, she also loved being outdoors and was an absolute natural in the woods. We started calling her our Adventure Princess.

We did a lot of Boundary Waters trips with Kali that summer, and she loved being with us in the canoe and out in the wilderness. Even though we took her on walks and hikes when we got back to North Carolina, you could tell she was sad she was no longer in the woods.

The following summer should have been spent in Maine, but we headed back to Minnesota instead. At the end of June, we started out on another Boundary Waters adventure. Five days into our trip, on July 4, we decided to take a side trip to Rebecca Falls, an area Dave was familiar with.

Up until that point, we had been canoeing on calm lakes and walking around larger rapids, but side trips always add interest to our travels. We were all excited to see what Dave described as a beautiful island with a large rapid.

After breaking camp, we paddled about thirty minutes before pulling our canoe onto the island. We put Kali on her leash and walked down one side of the island. We were being extra cautious because there had been a lot of rain, making the rapids very beautiful and impressive but also consequential. My husband and I have been river guides, are experienced kayakers, and know a lot about white water. Dave said he wouldn't have run the rapids because the water level was so high and the rapids were so intense.

There was a funky hole in the rock that afforded a great view of the rapids, so Zachary, Kali, and I sat in the hole while Dave took pictures. We were having a great time but were being extremely careful.

As we continued walking along the bottom part of the island, we came upon another more significant set of rapids. I stopped to look at the lower part of the rapids while Dave and Zachary walked ahead with Kali. Before long, the three of them were out of sight. Suddenly, Zachary came running down the trail shrieking Kali's name. I immediately knew something was terribly wrong. I knew somehow Kali had ended up in the rapids.

I followed Zachary and we stood together at the base of the rapids looking out into the water hoping to see Kali's head pop up. I screamed Kali's name as loudly as possible.

Dave ran to the canoe, got in, and started paddling around in the hopes that Kali would pop up. He paddled to the far shore and back, and as he began to paddle back toward Zachary and me, it slowly sank in that Kali might be gone.

We knew rapids that serious could take you down really fast. Since Kali's head never popped up, we knew she had either taken on water and drowned or she had gone deep and her leg got trapped in the rocks. We couldn't imagine her ever making it out. I'll never forget that moment of realization. It was like a nightmare as we stood there hugging, sobbing, and literally holding each other up. It was a terrible scene filled with unbelievable heartbreak, utter disbelief, and incredible anguish.

We continued staring out at the water for a long time before finally realizing we had to make a decision. The rapids flowed into a part of the river that's in Canada and we did not have a permit to camp there. Knowing it was unlikely we would find Kali's body, we made the heart-wrenching decision to leave to take care of ourselves and help one another through the loss of our dear friend Kali.

Heading east, we portaged past Curtain Falls, where the sight and sound of the rapids made us nauseated. We paddled onto Crooked Lake, where we set camp and went through the motions of making and eating food. There were red squirrels running around and we talked about how much Kali would have loved to be there chasing them. There were moments when we actually imagined Kali was just out of sight chasing squirrels—then it would hit us again. We spent a lot of time that night crying and trying to support one another while moving around the campsite like zombies.

Kali loved being in the tent and we always called her our Den Mother. Crawling into the tent that night without Kali was excruciating. We were a mess. In the middle of the night, there was a thunderstorm, and the three of us talked about how much Kali hated thunder and lightning.

The next morning, we broke camp and kept moving. Calm paddling conditions allowed us to travel far enough that we only had to stay out one more night, but it was difficult because that night we camped at a site we had previously stayed at with Kali.

As the three of us lay in the tent talking, Zachary said he knew what he wanted for his upcoming birthday. He said he wanted us to have another dog by the time he returned from summer camp on July 28. He knew we couldn't replace Kali but he also knew we were a dog family, and he said eventually he wanted to have two dogs.

Once we were out of the wilderness, we began contacting friends and family to tell them what happened. One by one, they helped us grieve the loss of Kali.

In an attempt to distract ourselves, we spent a day walking around the town of Ely. While there, we went into a T-shirt shop and met an amazing guy named Mauricio. He was so kind and loving and made us a T-shirt with Kali's picture on it. We told the outfitter we rented our canoe from what happened and word began to spread about Kali. The people in Ely were wonderful and we were grateful for all the compassion they showered on us.

We knew Zachary would be going back out into Boundary Waters as part of his camp experience, so we contacted them. We wanted them to know what happened in the event being out there was emotional for Zachary.

On July 9, Zachary's fifteenth birthday, we headed out of the woods and drove to the small city of Duluth where we did our best to have fun. Two days later, Dave and I drove Zach to camp then the two of us headed back to North Carolina. We tried to talk about Kali and about Zachary's birthday wish but many hours passed in silence. It was a long, lonely trip.

We dreaded going home knowing Kali's toys, food, and doghouse were there waiting to greet us. Our very good friend Rebecca and her two kids met us at our house and cooked us dinner as we fell apart.

The next day, we went to Brother Wolf Animal Rescue and adopted a black spaniel mix. We name our dogs after rivers that are significant to us in some way. Kali was named after the Kali Gandaki River in Nepal, which Dave and I had been on together. We had even placed a jar of sparkling sand from the river on the altar at our wedding. We decided to name our new dog Baillie after the Baillie River in Canada, which Dave paddled on years before during a two-month canoe trip to the Arctic.

We brought Baillie home on July 18. We had already taken Kali's favorite toys and packed them away, but we let Baillie play with the rest of her toys and did our best to welcome him. Two hours later, our phone rang. A woman from Zachary's camp told me that a dog had been found in Quetico Provincial Park, a large wilderness park in Northwest Ontario along the border north of the Boundary Waters Canoe Area Wilderness and gave me a number to call. I decided not to tell Dave until I could confirm it was Kali because I didn't want to get our hopes up— but in the back of my mind I kept hoping it was Kali.

The photo Sarah sent them of Kali on the floatplane

When I called the Park, they told me Sarah, the woman who knew about the dog, wasn't there but assured me they would have her call us back. While waiting for Sarah's phone call, I decided to tell Dave and Rebecca, who was with us. The three of us sat there staring at the phone, hearts in our throats, anxiously waiting for it to ring.

When Sarah called, she said a dog had been found that looked like a golden retriever–collie mix. Since we never knew exactly what Kali was we decided the best solution was to hang up and exchange pictures.

I texted Sarah a recent photo and she replied with one of the dog sitting in the passenger seat of a floatplane. We looked at it and our hearts soared. It was Kali!

We couldn't believe it! Kali was alive! We were overcome with joy and relief—the complete opposite of every emotion we had been feeling for the last two weeks.

Sarah assured us Kali had become very comfortable being flown around in a floatplane, but we wanted our girl home as soon as possible, so Dave and Sarah figured out the logistics.

Quetico Park floatplanes have a set schedule for border crossing checks, and the next time we could connect with them was Wednesday. That gave Dave only two days to reach the Prairie Portage crossing, so he immediately hopped in the car and began driving back to Minnesota.

On Wednesday, Dave met up with our friend Mary, who was working as a Ranger at Voyageurs National Park. Mary wanted to join Dave for the reunion so together they headed out in a hired motorboat across Moose Lake toward Prairie Portage. As soon as they arrived, they heard a floatplane and began walking across the portage. A couple was portaging in the opposite direction, and as they got closer, the woman recognized Mary. It was her friend Jenny. Mary quickly filled them in on what was happening and Jenny asked if she could come along to take photos and video.

As they rounded the bend, they saw Sarah along with her supervisor, Jason, on the floatplane with Kali. Dave watched Kali get off the plane and started calling to her as she walked down the dock.

Everything from that point on is captured on video. If you Google "Monk and Kali," you can see the video of their amazing and emotional reunion, as filmed by Jenny. If you turn up the sound, in the beginning you can hear a woman saying, "It's not doing anything . . . quick, take a video!" That voice is Mary. Dave had given his phone to Mary to take pictures and video, but in her excitement, she had accidentally turned Dave's phone off. However, Jenny was able to capture the moments as Kali trotted toward Dave and started kissing him. Several seconds into the video, you can see where it must have finally sunk in for Kali that Dave was there and she was going home because Kali went to another level completely of wiggling, waggling, and kissing Dave.

Kali is obviously the only one who knows exactly what happened, but based on what everyone knew and everything we have learned, we were able to piece together what we think happened to Kali.

The day Kali disappeared, she was on her leash and Zachary had a firm hold on it. The trail where Dave and Zachary stopped to look at the rapids went through trees and bushes and was set back from the rapids slightly. Since the trail was rocky in places, Kali went to jump up onto a ledge, but her leash became taut and stopped her mid-jump. Unable to make it to the rock ledge, Kali instead started to fall into a crack in the rock that went down at least ten feet. As Kali was falling, she slipped out of her collar and fell into the swirling water.

Dave, realizing Kali had disappeared, instantly scrambled down the crevice after her yelling her name. He reached out to her, but in her panic, Kali tried to swim as Dave stood by, helplessly watching her disappear into the rapids and out of sight.

Zachary immediately ran down the trail, but by the time he got to the bottom of the rapid, the rushing water must have already pushed her through.

Dave struggled to crawl back out of the crevice, then ran to join Zachary and me at the end of the island, hoping we had spotted Kali and that she was okay.

Since that wasn't the case, the three of us returned to the crevice. Dave had stuffed his camera into a crack in the crevice and we desperately wanted the camera because it contained what we believed were our last pictures of Kali. We belayed him down on a rope to retrieve it, and seeing the

What was believed to be one of the final pictures of Kali with Zachary and Joy

crevice made me feel sick, realizing this had been an awful freak accident.

Although Kali had gotten pulled deep and fast, she never got caught up in the hydraulic or became entrapped. Somehow she survived the rapids. Perhaps she remembered her experience early on with the little rapid—when she panicked and ran off—and did the same thing this time. By the time she reached land, she was likely too far away for us to see her (or her to see us), so she freaked out and took off into the woods. By the time Dave looked along the shore, Kali was long gone.

Based on where people said they had seen and heard a dog, we knew Kali headed east—the same direction we were traveling. We know the furthest east she was seen was Curtain Falls. A couple named Mark and Kathy own Zup's Fishing Resort and Canoe Outfitters on Lac La Croix on the edge of the Canadian part of the park. Mark had clients who reported hearing and catching a glimpse of a dog near Curtain Falls. Other people in that area gave Kali food one night but she was gone the next morning.

From there, we believe Kali headed much further west than we did, in large part because she was on the Canadian side and we had remained on the United States side.

Finally, ten days after going missing in the wilderness, Kali was found.

A guide named Roger was camping on the Canadian side with several fishing clients and heard a lot of extra floatplane activity. Thinking

312 MAGICAL DOGS 2

perhaps there was a missing person, Roger called Mark on his satellite phone.

Mark told Roger about the reports of the missing dog and said to bring it in with him if he found it.

Twenty minutes later, Roger's dog Pippa began to bark. On another point on the island, Roger saw Kali.

He was stunned. They were in an extremely remote area covering hundreds of thousands of acres, yet somehow the dog he had just been told about was standing there. Even more amazing was the fact that they—and the dog—were three islands out from shore!

As quickly as Roger saw her, she ducked back into the woods and disappeared. Roger realized it would take at least fifteen minutes to reach her and was upset, but six minutes later, Pippa barked again. There was Kali standing at the fringes of their campsite.

Kali ducked back into the woods so Roger used some walleye fish and hash browns to slowly coax Kali out. The promise of food eventually won out, and Kali, wet and scared, came in close enough to eat.

As Pippa and Kali played in the campsite, Roger sat down and remained calm. Being a dog person, he knew how to talk to and reassure Kali, eventually getting close enough to check her over and determine that she was in good shape despite all she had been through. He called Mark back on his satellite phone. "You're not going to believe this, Mark. The dog you told me about just walked into my campsite!"

Roger said Kali was one of the smartest dogs he had ever met. His clients, who were from Tennessee, offered to adopt her if her owners weren't found.

Mark sent a boat to pick up Kali then he and Kathy transported Kali by boat to the nearest Quetico Provincial Park station on Lac La Croix, where arrangements were made for Kali's first plane ride. Kali refused to go into the crate they had for her in the plane. Instead, she hopped into the passenger seat and looked at them as if to say, "I'll ride shotgun. Let's go!"

Sarah, a Park Operations Specialist, was on the floatplane and took a picture of Kali. After a few other stops, they eventually delivered Kali to the Park's headquarters in Atikokan, Ontario.

Sarah had reached out to her sister, Laura, to see if Kali could stay with her family. Laura's family recently had a tragedy with their dog and she was concerned her kids would get attached to Kali. She and her husband, Steve, finally decided they would host Kali until other arrangements could be made.

When Kali arrived at Laura's house, she smelled awful and was covered in ticks, so they gave her a bath, removed the ticks, and cut a lot of mats out of her thick fur. She had lost weight, but some animal hair in her poop meant she had eaten something she either killed or found. All things considered, Kali was in pretty good shape and didn't look like she had been on her own for ten days.

Kali was understandably exhausted. In the span of one day, she had gone from being on her own in the wilderness to being found and transported in several boats before finally being placed on a float plane and taken to an unfamiliar home and family.

Since Kali's collar had slipped off, she had no identification. She was microchipped but there wasn't a facility out there to read a chip. The Quetico Park folks checked social media for a missing dog but never saw anything. We had reported Kali's drowning to the Forest Service but that information never made it to Canada. As a last-ditch effort to find Kali's owners, the park headquarters sent an email to all the camps and outfitters in the area about a dog that had been found and that is how Zachary's camp and an outfitter in Ely knew to contact us. The result was that everyone knew about her but no one knew her name.

The people at the park initially called her Lucky, but Laura's kids decided to try and figure out her name. They began searching online for "common female dog names" and read them out loud to see if she reacted to any of them. When they said the name Molly, she reacted, so they started calling her Molly.

When Sarah and I connected by phone, she asked me what her name was and I told her it was Kali, which rhymes with Bali and sounds similar to Molly, so it made sense that she reacted to Molly.

When they started calling her Molly, Kali's demeanor completely changed. After I'd connected with Sarah, she sent me a picture of Kali lying on the green grass, flopping around scratching her back with her feet in the air and wrote: "Here is a photo of your happy girl when we told her last night that she was going home!"

Dave was reunited with Kali on July 20 then returned to Ely to tell the outfitters and everyone we had met the good news. Once again, the news spread. Mauricio was absolutely thrilled and immediately made another T-shirt with Kali's photo. Everyone was thrilled Kali was back.

Dave and Kali stayed at a fancy lodge the first night. When Dave texted me a picture of Kali stretched out on the king-size bed, all I could think was: "Kali, you deserve it!"

In the meantime, I was home with Baillie, eagerly awaiting Kali's return. Dave kept updating me, so shortly before their estimated arrival time, I took Baillie over to our neighbor's house.

It was raining so I was standing in the driveway with an umbrella when they arrived. I dropped the umbrella, ran and jumped into the front seat, and started kissing Kali, saying, over and over, "It's you . . . it's you!" She kissed me and made cute little noises. Kali was home!

We had unpacked all of her special toys and gave her time to roam around the house and get comfortable before bringing Baillie over so they could meet. Kali took one look at Baillie, then gave us a look that said, "I'm gone a few weeks and you replace me?"

On July 28, it was time to bring everything full circle. We loaded Kali and Baillie in the car and headed to the Charlotte airport to pick up Zachary.

We collected Zachary and his gear and headed back to the car. Zachary knew Kali was home, so we let Kali out so they could have their own reunion.

Zachary also knew that we had gotten another dog, but had refused photos of him, saying he wanted to be surprised. Baillie was in a crate in the back of the car and now he and Zachary got to meet for the first time.

Baillie was seven months old and Kali was seven years old, so while initially Baillie annoyed Kali, for the most part she was glad to have a buddy. They liked to chase one another and play tug-of-war, but Kali made sure Baillie knew from the first day that she was top dog.

After Kali put some weight on and her hair grew back, she looked like our beautiful princess once again. She still loved to be in the woods and she showed Baillie the ropes of being an outdoor wilderness dog.

We often think back to that first night Kali went missing. There was a thunderstorm that night. Knowing how much Kali hates thunder and lightning—and that she was out there scared and alone—breaks our hearts. Kali is understandably even more sensitive to thunder and lightning now.

This past summer we went back to northern Minnesota. While Zachary was at camp, Dave and I decided to do the same Boundary Waters route we did the previous year, but this time we skipped Rebecca Falls. We stayed at the same campsite we were at after Kali went missing. To watch the dogs running around chasing red squirrels together was fabulous—and to be out there with Kali again was amazing.

A lot of articles about Kali appeared in the local papers in Ontario and Ely, Minnesota, as well as in Asheville, North Carolina. Kali's story also began to pop up online and, as a result, Dave and Kali were on The Rachael Ray Show via Skype. A woman from Ontario wrote a children's book loosely based on Kali's story that includes key points on how to travel respectfully in the woods. The book is now sold at Quetico Provincial Park locations in Canada and the proceeds from the sale of the book benefit the park.

That Christmas, Sarah and Jason sent us a Christmas card that had a picture of them with Kali. Dave had briefly met them, but Zachary and I hadn't so we planned a reunion for that summer at a restaurant in Atikokan, Ontario. On July 14, exactly one year to the day that Kali found Roger, Zachary and I met Sarah, Jason, and Laura and her family. We had a wonderful meal, took a lot of pictures, and shared a lot of hugs.

Zachary with Baillie and Kali

It was wonderful to get to know them and thank them in person for their help. We treasure the connection we made with them through Kali and are grateful to everyone who helped Kali and us.

When we look back, it is unbelievable how everything magically aligned and came together. What are the chances that out in the wilderness, at the exact moment Dave and Mary were on their way to reconnect with Kali, they would cross paths with Jenny? But they did—and because they did we now have pictures and a video of their reunion.

We love sharing Kali's story because it is a story about so many people coming together and about so much love. It is also a story with a happy ending: Kali is home and Zachary got his birthday wish for two dogs.

Epilogue
CONNECTING THE DOGS

AS AN AUTHOR, I LOVE WRITING THE EPILOGUE BECAUSE IT GIVES me the opportunity to pause and take one final look back at the journey, the dogs, the love, and the lessons. Usually by this point, I can see the Epilogue clearly in my mind and know exactly how to tie everything together in a neat little bow. This time was no different—except it never happened. To understand, we need to go back to the beginning of this journey to the day I met Kristy and Zeke.

As Ava and I prepared to leave that day, Kristy said, "I'm going to text you the name and number of a woman in Texas. Her name is Melodie. You might want to connect with her." Later that afternoon, the text came through along with the message: "This is my gal in Port Lavaca—a force to be reckoned with."

I reached out to Melodie on Facebook and quickly understood what Kristy meant. Melodie was a protector, advocate, and fierce warrior for dogs everywhere—especially those who found their way to the Calhoun County Humane Society where she volunteered.

One afternoon, Melodie posted a photo of a tiny black dog brought in as a stray. The dog, a toy Yorkie mix, was seven pounds of wiry hair and ears that flopped this way and that. While the dog was deemed aggressive, Melodie said she had yet to see any evidence of aggression.

From the moment I saw the dog's picture, I was smitten. The entire time she was on the mandatory three-day stray hold, I stayed glued to my computer to see if anyone would come forward to claim her. When no one did, Melodie took her to their veterinarian, who determined she was approximately a year and a half old, in good health, and pregnant with her first litter.

Of the four volunteers at the Humane Society, Melodie had whelping experience, the necessary supplies, and a direct line to the veterinarian, so the little pregnant mama went home with her.

There was something about this little dog that tugged at my heart in the same deep, intense way Zeke had. Just like with Zeke, I stayed glued to my computer for photos and updates. Once again, Big Dog Rescue Project (BDRP) stepped up to the plate, assuring Melodie that, "Whatever she and her puppies need, we got this."

Every day, Melodie posted photos, videos, and updates of the little black dog, and with every one I felt more and more connected to the dog. I told Mary Jo and Melodie that somehow, somewhere, I wanted to meet her because I knew she was a part of this journey—and this book. Then things got even more interesting.

Melodie has a delightful tradition of giving every litter names based on a theme, and she decided this one would be the Web Litter. She began by naming the pregnant mama Dot-Com, or Dot for short.

No one knew I had written a Prologue about how this journey felt like a wonderful game of connect the dots, nor did they know I had subtitled the book "Connecting the Dots, Connecting the Dogs." As if by magic, here was a little dog I knew was part of this journey—and her name was Dot.

By mid-July, Dot grew increasingly restless and uncomfortable as her due date approached. I selfishly hoped the puppies would be born on my birthday: July 17. Instead, on July 16, Dot went into labor, and at 1:40 p.m., Melodie posted that she had given birth to her first puppy, a tiny black female named Twitter. Twitter was followed by a sister, EBay, a brother, Google, and another little sister, Etsy.

Melodie continued to update all of us, saying that Dot was completely exhausted but that there was one more puppy yet to be born. Knowing she would struggle to birth the last puppy on her own, Melodie took Dot to the vet. We all held our breath and waited.

Shortly after eight o'clock, Melodie posted a photo of Dot's fifth and final puppy: a little girl named Amazon.

The Web Litter was here. The next time Melodie went live on Facebook, we got to see the puppies, who were unbelievably cute and tiny, just like their mother. Each puppy weighed only a few ounces. Every photo and video showed Dot quietly feeding, cleaning, and licking her puppies. She was the personification of a loving, doting mother.

Melodie captioned a photo of Dot-Com and her puppies: "No greater love than a mom for her child." The next day, under another picture, she wrote: "Four days old. Love these Littles." Of all the litters Melodie had birthed over the years, this was her first litter of tiny puppies and she was in love—we all were.

Nine days later, everything changed. Dot stopped eating and drinking and grew disinterested in her pups. Two days later, Melodie posted: "Please keep Dot-Com in your prayers. She has metritis and is scheduled for spay. The Web Litter is going to need some supplies as Dot has no milk and cannot feed them."

Metritis is an infection of the lining of the uterus that can be dangerous to both the mother and nursing puppies. If left untreated, it can turn septic, affect the blood and other organs, and prove fatal, so Dot was rushed in for a hysterectomy and spay surgery. In the interim, Melodie prepared her house so Dot could come home and heal. Since she was no longer able to nurse her puppies, Melodie decided to keep Dot separated from them.

With the rapid turn in Dot's health, things had also changed for the puppies. Melodie began tube- and bottle-feeding them and quickly realized they were allergic to the dairy-based puppy milk and switched them to goat's milk. Every day, amidst the constant feeding and chaos, Melodie posted photos and updates.

On the day the puppies turned three weeks old, she wrote: "The last two weeks have been a roller coaster ride for sure. I've learned so much from these Littles and every day I fall more and more in love with their personalities. They are growing—just on a Little's scale. Twitter is one pound six ounces; EBay is one pound four ounces; Google is one pound seven ounces; Etsy is one pound two ounces; and Amazon is one pound three ounces. Oh, my bitty little Littles. Only six more weeks until your big surprise."

The "big surprise" involved Kristy, Mary Jo, and me. The three of us were going to Texas to bring Dot-Com and her puppies to New Jersey— and to their new homes and families. We had already coordinated our schedules with Melodie and booked our flights.

I was beyond excited. Not only would I meet Melodie and Dot, but this would be my first transport and I was going to do it alongside the two women I had begun this journey and book with. So much about this trip felt sacred, special, and magical. It felt as if everything was coming full circle and would culminate in my wrapping everything up with the proverbial neat little bow I like so much.

As Melodie continued to post updates and we prepared for our trip, a tropical wave emerged off the west coast of Africa. In the days that followed, it merged with an area of low pressure. Now known as Hurricane Harvey, the storm began a westward track. Weather advisories and early predictions warned that Harvey was going to cut across the Caribbean before making landfall somewhere along the Gulf Coast of Texas in the vicinity of Port Lavaca where Melodie and the Web Litter lived.

As Texas prepared for the inevitable arrival of Hurricane Harvey, everyone began evacuating. The puppies, still too little to travel, were transported to a safe haven in Austin. Twenty-four hours before the deadline for the mandatory evacuation, Dot was put on a plane bound for New Jersey.

As we watched early footage coming out of Texas over the next few days, Kristy, Mary Jo, and I quickly realized it would likely be months before Texas returned to any semblance of normalcy. We cancelled our trip and sat back anxiously waiting for updates on Melodie and the puppies.

Several days later, Melodie came back online briefly to let us know they had gotten some water and wind damage and had limited power and internet access but that she and the puppies were fine. In the ensuing weeks, the best of humanity surfaced as people sent supplies to the Calhoun County Humane Society to ensure the ongoing safety and welfare of animals in the shelter and community.

Pictures of Dot happily settled in with her foster family in New Jersey began popping up on the Big Dog Rescue Project Facebook page. Still wanting to meet Dot, I reached out to Christine, her foster mom. Just like Kristy, Christine wrote back and said, "We'd love to meet you. How about Wednesday at 1:00 p.m.?" As Ava and I drove to Christine's house, I felt the same emotions I'd had the day we drove to meet Kristy and Zeke: anticipation, excitement, and immense gratitude.

Christine brought us into her backyard, and as Ava sniffed and explored, Christine and I talked about our dogs, Big Dog Rescue Project, Texas, Hurricane Harvey, and Dot. Then Christine went into the house, coming out a few minutes later with Dot at her side.

I sat down on the steps of Christine's deck. Dot walked over to sniff me, but after spotting Ava, she ran over to greet her. Dot and Ava stood nose to nose sniffing one another, just as Zeke and Ava had done the day they met.

I walked over to Christine, smiling, and gave her a hug. I hoped she understood what this moment meant to me. What I was feeling, seeing and meeting Dot, was completely reminiscent of what I had felt when I met Zeke all those months earlier.

There was a knock at the gate and Christine welcomed Joe, the photographer who had met Kristy and Mary Jo at the veterinarian's office to photograph Zeke. Once again, the dogs had worked their magic and connected the dots to bring everything full circle.

When Christine's two Labs came out to play, Dot was clearly undeterred by the fact that they outweighed and towered over her. She confidently walked over and reminded them who was in charge with a knowing glance.

I laughed, thinking back to a conversation I'd had with Melodie several weeks before. "Early on, Dot-Com was deemed aggressive," she told me, "but she doesn't have an aggressive bone in her body. What she has is confidence. She came into my house where there are six dogs who range from 55 to 150 pounds—and Dot ruled the roost. Her best friend was my 150-pound wolf hybrid. It really became Dot's world and we were just living in it."

Watching Dot looking so happy, carefree, and confident, it was clear that it was still Dot's world—and I, for one, was blessed to be a part of that world, if only for a few hours.

As Ava and Dot played, I walked over and sat down in the grass. Together, they walked over and sat down next to me. The only sound was the shutter of Joe's camera. Looking into their eyes, I realized *this* was the perfect ending and culmination to the journey and book.

I had thought the perfect ending would be about my trip to Texas and doing my first transport, but the truth is none of this was ever about *me*. Everything was, is, and would always be about the dogs and their magic.

The magic had begun with Zeke, who connected me with Kristy, who connected me with Mary Jo. From there, the dogs continued to connect the dots between me and the stories they wanted on the pages of this book. Now here was Dot, the final dog, the final story, and the final bit of magic.

Sitting in the grass watching Ava and Dot play, I recalled Kristy saying that Zeke wasn't lying there thinking about how he ended up in the puddle but was "probably thinking about when I am going to feed him." Watching Dot run around Christine's backyard, the same was true for her. She wasn't holding onto the fact that somewhere along the way someone had wrongly deemed her aggressive. She wasn't constantly replaying scenes from her past life as a stray, the hours spent in labor, her subsequent illness and surgery, or ultimately being separated from her puppies. She wasn't wondering, over and over, what had gone wrong or what she could have done differently. She wasn't concerned about whether Joe was taking photographs from her most flattering angle. Dot wasn't worried about any of it. Instead, she was running around Christine's back yard unencumbered, unconcerned, and fully embracing the moment.

If I were able to have Dot, or any of the dogs, sit at my computer and write their own stories, I believe it would be a book of very short stories. Every story would consist of only a few short, sweet sentences: "They chose me!" or "They take me for walks and hikes and you wouldn't believe all the smells!" or "I go to school with my boy every single day and on weekends we play in the backyard!" or "Can you believe how lucky I am? I get to lay on the couch, watch TV, and get belly rubs!" or "I really love these people—and I really, really love the food!"

Despite where or how any dog's life begins, or where it takes them, they choose to forgive, forget, move on, and embrace life fully. A dog views the world through a lens of incredible hope and unending possibility. For a dog, the true meaning of life really can be summed up by one word: love.

And that, my friends, is the magic of a dog.

Dot
Photo courtesy of Joseph Frazz

Acknowledgments

Back at the very beginning, there was one person and one dog: Kristy Stracuzzi Linney and Zeke. Before long, a tribe of kind, incredible, magical dogs, people, rescues, and organizations joined me on this journey and the result is this book. I would like to thank everyone who came forward with courage, honesty, and openness to share their story, experience, and knowledge: Yvonne Adkins; Michele and Jeff Allen (Monkey's House); Mark Barone and Marina Dervan (An Act of Dog); Carla L. Boyd, Colleen Little; Deborah Marsh, Barbara Pickering (Blind Dog Rescue Alliance); Christopher Boyer (National Association for Search and Rescue); Mindi Callison (Bailing Out Benji); Mary Jo Conley, Alicia Harck, Lisa Garrison (Big Dog Rescue Project); Joe Dwyer (Daniel's Dream); Patricia Ebel; Tracy Estes; Edna Gorby; Nancy Hachmeister (Utah Search Dogs, Inc.); Kristian Hammermueller; Sharyn Hankins; Bonnie Harlan (Preventing Pet Suffocation); Amy Good, Heather Hatt, Cindy Morgan, John Plummer, JoJo Puhalsky, Sam Thorburn (Delaware Valley Golden Retriever Rescue); Kimberly Johnson, PhD, LMHC, DAAETS, CCFP (Rescuer Therapy); Jackie Keeney (United Against Puppy Mills); Roger Keyser (Eleventh Hour Rescue); Carol Lang; Cari Meyers (The Puppy Mill Project); Christine Maihle; Judy Morgan DVM, CVA, CVCP, CVFT; Joy Neily and Dave and Zachary Kareken; Walter John O'Brien; Kerry O'Connell; Beth Park; Karen Rudolph (Schnauzer Savers Rescue); Wallace Sife, PhD (Association for Pet Loss and Bereavement); Patricia Smith (Compassion Fatigue Awareness Project); The Van Brocklin Family; Carlene White (Service Dog Project).

I am grateful to my Creative Dream Team: my editor, Raquel Pidal; my graphic designer, James Lebbad of Lebbad Design; my layout person, Susie Kenyon of Sans Serif; and photographer extraordinaire, Joseph Frazz. Thank you for blessing me, the dogs, and this book with your brilliance and creative genius.

My unending love and gratitude to the people who are my inspiration and biggest blessings: my family. Thank you for your love and support on this journey—and always.

And finally to the dogs, thank you from the bottom of my heart! Without you, and the love and magic you so easily and effortlessly bring into the world, this book would not exist. Thank you for choosing me once again to be the one to share your stories with the world. I am incredibly honored, humbled, and grateful.

Notes

Prologue

1. Kerr, Patti. *Magical Dogs: Love and Lessons from Our Canine Companions.* Along the Way Press, 2017. www.magical-dogs.com
2. Virtue, Doreen. *Daily Guidance from Your Angels: 365 Angelic Messages to Soothe, Heal, and Open Your Heart.* Hay House, Inc., 2009

Chapter 2: Big Dog Rescue Project

1. Big Dog Rescue Project: www.bigdogrescueproject.org

Chapter 3: Let's Paws: Compassion Fatigue

1. Compassion Fatigue Awareness Project: www.compassionfatigue.org
2. The Professional Quality of Life Self-Test: www.proqol.org
3. Healthy Caregiving, LLC: www.healthycaregiving.com
4. Rescuer Therapy: www.rescuertherapy.com
5. Figley, Charles R. and Roop, Robert G. *Compassion Fatigue in the Animal Care Community.* Humane Society Press, 2006

Chapter 4: Delaware Valley Golden Retriever Rescue

1. Delaware Valley Golden Retriever Rescue: www.dvgrr.org

Chapter 7: Let's Paws: Puppy Mills

1. United Against Puppy Mills: www.unitedagainstpuppymills.org
2. The Puppy Mill Project: www.thepuppymillproject.org
3. Bailing Out Benji: www.bailingoutbenji.com

Chapter 8: Monkey's House

1. Monkey's House: www.monkeyshouse.org

Chapter 9: Judy Morgan, DVM

1. Dr. Judy Morgan: www.drjudymorgan.com

Chapter 10: Kristian

1. It's A Miracle Training: www.miracledog.com

Chapter 11: Let's Paws: Prevent Pet Suffocation

1. Prevent Pet Suffocation: www.preventpetsuffocation.com

Chapter 12: Trisha

1. The Seeing Eye: www.seeingeye.org

Chapter 13: Blind Dog Rescue Alliance
1. Blind Dog Rescue Alliance: www.blinddogrescue.org

Chapter 15: Joe
1. Daniel's Dream: www.danielsdream.org
2. The Association for Pet Loss and Bereavement: www.aplb.org

Chapter 16: Karen and Joe
1. Schnauzer Savers Rescue, visit: www.schnauzersavers.org
2. Eleventh Hour Rescue: www.ehrdog.org

Chapter 17: An Act of Dog
1. An Act of Dog: www.anactofdog.org

Chapter 18: Carol
1. Ballston Spa Witch Walk: www.facebook.com/ballstonspawitchwalk

Chapter 20: Let's Paws: Pet Loss and Bereavement
1. The Association of Pet Loss and Bereavement: www.aplb.org
2. Sife, PhD, Wallace, *The Loss of a Pet: A Guide to Coping with the Grieving Process When a Pet Dies* (Fourth Edition). Howell Book House, 2014

Chapter 26: Let's Paws: Search and Rescue
1. National Association for Search and Rescue: www.nasar.org
2. Utah Service Dogs, Inc.: www.utahsearchdogs.org

Chapter 29: Service Dog Project
1. Service Dog Project: www.servicedogproject.org

green press
INITIATIVE